A GUIDE FOR CURRICULUM WRITERS

Delbert Mueller
Concordia University
River Forest, Illinois

UNIVERSITY
PRESS OF
AMERICA

Lanham • New York • London

Copyright © 1991 by
University Press of America®, Inc.
4720 Boston Way
Lanham, Maryland 20706

3 Henrietta Street
London WC2E 8LU England

Library of Congress Cataloging-in-Publication Data
Mueller, Delbert.
A Guide for Curriculum Writers / Delbert Mueller.
        p.   cm.
    1. Curriculum planning—United States.
    2. Teacher participation in curriculum
    planning—United States.   I. Title.
        LB2806.15.M84   1992
    375' .001' 0973—dc20   91-27675 CIP

    ISBN 0-8191-8398-9 (cloth, alk. paper)
    ISBN 0-8191-8399-7 (pbk., alk. paper)

The paper used in this publication meets the minimum requirements of
American National Standard for Information Sciences—Permanence
of Paper for Printed Library Materials, ANSI Z39.48–1984.

dedicated
to my wife, Dorleen
our children, Christine, Paul, Lois, Susan
our special family, Lee, Joy, Debra, Mark
our grandchildren, Brandon, Emily, Rachel, Michael, Luke, Mitchell
with praise to God

Special thanks to Dr. Patricia Kranzow for her helpful counsel. Grateful acknowledgement for the many suggestions and corrections by students who used this volume over the several years from its initial writing to its present form, and especially Diane Wasman, who volunteered the final editing.

A significant goal for educators is improved teaching that results in optimal student learning. To that end, teachers and administrators need to be concerned about and proficient in selecting learning outcomes, designing instruction, and measuring achievement toward outcomes. This book is dedicated to help attain that end.

Part One: Curriculum -- What It Is and How to Write It

A Word to Those Who Teach

If you are or plan to be a teacher, you will write curricula. Writing responsibilities are part of the job. You may write:

> lesson plans, unit plans, early childhood, grade school or high school level course guides, and school/district-wide instructional programs.

Your writing efforts may result in state or national curriculum guides. More frequently, however, your writing will be directed at district and building concerns.

> If your writing is directed to the overall district or building mission, you will be challenged to form educational philosophy statements and school goals.

> If you write at an instructional program level such as the K-8 Language Arts Program or the English Department Program, you will, after examining the philosophy and goals, begin with program/department rationale and goals.

> When your work brings you to an early childhood, grade school/high school course level, a rationale may be written and objectives, course content, methods, and evaluations must be included.

> Finally, when planning at a unit or lesson level, you will detail objectives, content, methods, and evaluations. This book will teach you how to write each of the curriculum components listed above.

Many teachers, when given a curriculum writing task, find they have little formal training or previous experience as curriculum constructors. Undergraduate experience is usually limited to writing lesson plans and perhaps one or two unit plans. An assignment to write goals and objectives or to plan the scope and sequence for a portion of the school's program is a task for which teachers have had little training.

This book can become your best friend when asked to write curriculum. **It is not, however, a recipe book**, for there is no single prescription that assures successful writing. It is rather a book designed to help you think about how to plan and write curriculum appropriate to your local setting.

A Word to Those Who Teach

If you are or plan to be a teacher, you will write curricula. Writing responsibilities are part of the job. You may write:

> lesson plans, unit plans, grade school or high school level course guides, and school/district-wide instructional programs.

Your writing efforts may result in state or national curriculum guides. More frequently, however, your writing will be directed at district and building concerns.

> If your writing is directed to the overall district or building mission, you will be challenged to form educational philosophy statements and school goals.

> If you write at an instructional program level such as the **K-8 Language Arts Program** or the **English Department Program**, you will, after examining the philosophy and goals, begin with program/department rationale and goals.

> When your work brings you to a grade school/high school course level, objectives must be written and course content, methods, and evaluations considered.

> Finally, when planning at a unit or lesson level, you will detail objectives, content, methods, and evaluations. This book will teach you how to write each of the curriculum components listed above.

Many teachers, when given a curriculum writing task, find they have little formal training or previous experience as curriculum constructors. Undergraduate experience is usually limited to writing lesson plans and perhaps one or two unit plans. An assignment to write goals and objectives or to plan the scope and sequence for a portion of the school's program is a task for which teachers have had little training.

This book can become your best friend when asked to write curriculum. **It is not, however, a recipe book**, for there is no single prescription that assures successful writing. It is rather a book designed to help you think about how to plan and write curriculum appropriate to your local setting.

Part One

Curriculum

+ + +

What It Is

and

How to Write It

Chapter One

What is Curriculum?

Inquisitive Visitor

Imagine the mythical little green man from Mars coming to earth and inviting himself into your home. After the initial shock of meeting him wears off, you agree to acquaint the man from Mars with life on earth. You will be his guide.

You begin by discussing the many facets of human culture and enterprise, such as government, economics, family, history, and religion. You then decide to drive the visitor about the community and show him points of interest. You drive past the post office, a bank, a store, factory, churches -- discussing each as to place and function in society. Finally, you drive up to a school building and exclaim,

"That building is where I work. It's called a school."

* *The man from Mars inquires, "What's a school for? What's it supposed to do?" You think for a moment and reply.*

* *The man from Mars follows your reply by asking, "How does your school do what it's supposed to do?" Once again you provide explanation.*

* *An answer to a final question, "How do you earthlings decide if your school is doing a good job of what it's supposed to do?" is also attempted.*

The three questions asked by the man from Mars represent the major issues faced by educators since the conception of formal schooling. Early Jewish fathers of Bible times, Plato, Luther, Frobel, Eliot, Dewey, Babbitt, and an host of other educators wrestled with similar concerns.

Ralph Tyler, in his little volume, *Basic Principles of Curriculum And Construction*, (1949) posited these same issues using similar questions.

1. What educational purposes should the school seek to attain?

2. What educational experiences can be provided that are likely to attain these purposes? and How can these educational experiences be effectively organized?

3. How can we determine if these purposes are being attained?

These questions will be our primary concern as we explore what curriculum is and how curriculum is written.

* In Part One we will examine the parts that make up a curriculum, and suggest strategies for writing them.

* Part Two will provide examples of a variety of written curricula.

What Does Curriculum Mean?

Before we launch into plans for writing curriculum we need to agree on what curriculum is. Some have defined curriculum by its Latin root -- **racecourse**; a racecourse of subjects to be mastered to reach the finish line.

"When I finish this last course I will get my diploma," sighs the high school student.

Historically and currently, a dominant concept of curriculum is a **program of studies**.

"The curriculum should emphasize reading, writing, and arithmetic," says a back-to-the-basics advocate.

"American history should be an important part of every curriculum," asserts the patriot.

Curriculum is sometimes described as the **content** included within the various subject areas.

"What is the proper scope and sequence for a K-12 social science curriculum?" asks the superintendent.

Today's literature frequently regards curriculum as **all the learning experiences offered by a school.**

"Our athletic program is a critical part of the total curriculum," insists the coach.

A broader definition of curriculum refers to the totality of **all encounters experienced by students while under the authority of schools.**

"Even the pictures on the wall, the way we organize our classrooms, and the rules of conduct are part of our curriculum," proclaims the professor.

Educators may also disagree when distinguishing between curriculum and instruction. Some will contend that the (written) **plan for action** is curriculum, while the action between teacher and student is instruction. Others contend that to separate the plan from the implementation of the plan is unreasonable.

"How can the curriculum be evaluated separately from implementation," they ask, "for the two are combined when offered to the learner."

Since this book is concerned with how to write curriculum, we will define curriculum as a written plan for instructing students.

Defining Curriculum According to Function

Glatthorn (p. 1-7) describes how the written plan, the curriculum, can be examined in greater detail by dividing it into four categories, based on the kind of intended learning. Curricula may be:

* mastery
* organic
* team planned, or
* student determined.

To help you understand these four categories, you should use a subject you know well and work through the following steps:

1. First, divide that subject in terms of the necessity of the intended learning as either

     *   basic or
     *   enrichment.

The basic learnings are those the district thinks all students, except for approximately the bottom 10 percent, should learn.

The enrichment learnings are what's left. They consist of those learnings that may be considered desirable to possess, but remain an option.

2. Now divide all intended learning associated with the subject in terms of structure as either

        *   structured learning or
        *   non-structured learning.

Structured learnings are best understood when they are carefully planned, specifically taught, and carefully measured. Behavioral objectives, such as:

Should be able to: compute, write, read, distinguish, demonstrate, etc.,

define intended learning of a structured curriculum.

Non-structured learnings are those that do not require such specific teaching and careful planning and measuring. Humanistic objectives, such as:

Will: enjoy poetry, show kindness, be a good citizen, feel empathy, listen attentively, etc.,

describe intended learning of a non-structured curriculum.

When the categories, structured and non-structured are mapped with the categories, basic and enrichment, a matrix results showing four cells.

The mastery curriculum is **essential** for all students and requires careful structuring. It will have objectives, texts, and tests. It may be considered the "hard core" of the curriculum. It is that part of the curriculum the school district selects as essential and for which it **holds itself accountable**.

The organic curriculum is also **essential** for all students, but it is not easily adapted to highly structured organization, focused teaching, and careful measuring. It may be seen as the "soft core" of the curriculum. It contains essential elements that do not require the systematic approaches of the mastery curriculum. It is that part of the curriculum the school district espouses as essential, but for which it usually does not accept systematic accountability.[1]

The Four Curricula

	Basic	Enrichment
Structured	MASTERY	TEAM PLANNED
Non-Structured	ORGANIC	STUDENT DETERMINED

The team-planned curriculum has high structure but includes only enrichment content. It is that part of the curriculum **teachers** select and for which they hold students accountable.

The student-determined curriculum has low structure and includes only enrichment content. It is that part of the curriculum **students** select and for which there is only self accountability.

To illustrate three of the four curriculums, think about three social studies objectives for a single grade 5 classroom.

At the completion of this unit students should be able to:

1. Retell the Pilgrim odyssey.

---

[1] Schools in which Cooperative Learning is an essential part of the planned curriculum will require systematic approaches to those objectives that are the organic curriculum and define attitudes and behaviors such as: positive interdependence, individual accountability, shared leadership and responsibility, supporting social skills, positive self image.

    2. Appreciate the impact of religious conviction on human decision making.

    3. Understand how the Horn Book was used to shape children's values.

Most teachers would probably consider the first objective a mastery objective. The second would be organic, and the third an enrichment objective.

The first objective would be considered a learning outcome for all students in the district and would be tested. The second objective would also be an expectation for all students, but may not be formally assessed. The third objective would be a learning outcome for all students in this one classroom, but would not necessarily be an objective for students who learn fifth grade social studies in other classrooms or buildings.

We will concentrate on writing mastery, organic, and team planned curricula.

The Curriculum Design

When designing an instructional program you will wrestle with issues related to learning outcomes, scope and sequence of instructional content, instructional strategies, and evaluation of student mastery of intended learning outcomes.

Specifically, you will deal with selection of:

* goals and objectives,
* content,
* methods of implementation, and
* evaluation plans.

When you are finished you will have produced a written document. If your writing begins at the building level, a **comprehensive** design document will contain:[2]

---

[2] The example that follows begins with the educational philosophy of the school, reducing each part through to unit objectives, content, methods, and evaluation. However, many building level guides that begin at the educational philosophy level end with listings of grade level/course level objectives.

1. For the educational unit (building/district)

    a. a statement of the mission or philosophy of the school
    b. a statement of the educational goals of the school

2. For each curriculum field offered by the school/district (subject/instructional program)

    a. rationale showing linkage of the curriculum field to the statement of mission or philosophy and to the other curriculum fields
    b. listing of curriculum field goals
    c. theoretical[3], organizational[4] information
    d. listing of grade level/course objectives[5]
    e. listing of unit objectives,[6] [7]
    f. content for instructing toward mastery of goals and objectives
    g. methods for teaching content
    h. evaluation of student progress toward learning outcomes[8]

Summary

Curricula are usually regarded as products written for use by teachers. They may be divided into four categories, mastery, organic, team planned, and student determined. Most writing is for the mastery curriculum. The major components of curriculum design are educational philosophies and rationale, goals and objectives, instructional content and methods, and evaluations.

---

[3] A statement describing the theoretical basis upon which curriculum field components are built should be included when necessary for understanding how to implement the design.

[4] A statement describing the organizational structure of the curriculum field's content should be included when necessary for understanding.

[5] Rationales frequently cap course offerings.

[6] Rationales frequently cap unit offerings.

[7] Many curriculum guides do not detail to a unit level. Some guides provide objectives and content below the unit level.

[8] While items e, f, and g may not be included in some curriculum guides, they must necessarily be determined before the curriculum can be implemented.

Bibliography

Glatthorn, A. A. (1987). Curriculum renewal. Alexandria, VA: Association of Supervision and Curriculum Development. 1-7.

Tyler, R. (1949). Basic principles of curriculum and instruction. Chicago: University of Chicago.

Chapter Two
Curriculum Design

Before we get into the "nitty-gritty" of curriculum writing, let's examine what are considered appropriate subject matter and instructional methods, for these, finally, will determine what you write. We will do this by considering three popular curriculum designs in American schools during the past half century.

Your beliefs about what is appropriate subject matter and about how best to teach it will influence what you believe is the best way to structure curriculum. Yet, every **best** way has it weaknesses. The brief essay that follows will help illustrate this dilemma.

*American educators are accused of joining education **band wagons**. It is said that they, as do pendulums, swing back and forth between education fads. The 1950's is remembered as a time when conservative voices dominated education journals. With the 1960's a swing toward liberal thought brought new methods, contents, and organizations, each heralded as improvement. The eighties brought the back-to-the-basics call. Today we are encouraged to teach critical thinking and problem solving skills, and use revived strategies such as cooperative learning and heterogeneous groupings. The layman asks:*

* *Why the vacillating?*
* *Why can't educators take a position and stay with it?*
* *Isn't there a **best way** to organize for effective teaching?*

*One could argue that there is a **best way** to design curricula. A **best way** may be defined as:*

Those curriculum designs that make it possible at all times for each student to be engaged in learning that is most appropriate for that individual.

Traditionally, educators have looked to subject matter when planning instructional programs. Bodies of organized knowledge were divided as separate subjects and sequenced by grade level.

However, when confronted with an understanding that students are different with regard to ability, interest, learning style, and more, educators strove to design and implement curriculum programs which addressed these concerns.

The search for better programs produced a variety of formats. Some employed team teaching models. Others stressed individualized instruction with non-graded-continuous progress advancement. Variations of open-space use were tried.

*Many attempted a mix of the above. It was hoped these formats would make it possible at all times for all students to be engaged in learnings that were appropriate for each of them, regardless of the many individual differences these students brought to the classroom. Subject matter would no longer dictate instruction. Instruction would use as its organizer, student interest, ability, learning style, and a variety of other student information. Thus the **student** would become the focus of interest as subject matter was selected to fit individual student needs.*

Over time it became evident that the implementation demands of student centered designs exceeded reasonable expectations of what teachers could accomplish. Good intentions seemed to produce less than satisfactory results and the designs were cast aside for something more manageable.

Instruction which used as its organizer, subject matter, appeared to be more easily managed. These bodies of knowledge required coverage. Subject matter could easily be divided into segments and be offered to students piecemeal. It then would be the determiner of daily study activities. Such organization was understandable by teacher, student, and parent.

However, when subject matter dictated design, individual student needs could not readily be accommodated. These designs required students to fit the demands of organized knowledge. Group instruction, grade level placement, and norm referenced assessment again dominated the classrooms of America.

Today's subject matter focus once more forces the question of student need: If subject matter is to control selection of curriculum offerings, how will educators respond effectively to the individual student? Is a design that highlights subject

*matter rather than the individual student when choosing
instructional content pedagogically defensible? Can cooperative
learning resolve some of the problems a subject matter focus
brings?*

*Ultimately, the problem of curriculum design selection becomes
one of priority. The choices appear to be:*

   *a. Design curricula around student needs and know
       that in past times they have proven less than
       successful.*
   *b. Design curricula around subject matter and know
       that student individuality will be compromised.*

Classifying Curricula

Two important concerns that curriculum designers address are
summarized below:

   *   Should design emphasis be placed on the subject matter or
       upon the learner?
   *   Should the content be offered as distinctly separate entities
       or as broad fields of inquiry?

We will address these questions by examining three basic curriculum
designs:
   *   Subject-centered,
   *   Theme-centered, and
   *   Student-centered curriculum designs.

Subject-Centered Curricula

The most commonly used set of curricular designs, subject-centered
curricula, looks to organized knowledge for its definition and
structure. Pages 12 and 13 provide diagrams modeling a subject-
centered curriculum in a traditional elementary school setting. The
design begins with a statement in which the school defines its
educational philosophy or mission. Growing out of the school's
philosophic statement are rationales that defend each instructional
program as a necessary contributor toward meeting the requirements
of the school's mission.

The model identifies school goals. These goals are defined and elaborated through various instructional programs, each capped with program goals. Each program is broken at grade levels in which objectives are set and content is chosen to meet the objectives. Instructional content for a particular program is sorted and organized vertically and horizontally. It is classified according to level of difficulty and assigned to the appropriate grade. Portions of the instructional content appropriate to a particular grade are selected -- enough to cover the school year -- and sequenced according to a

SUBJECT-CENTERED CURRICULUM
DESIGN
ELEMENTARY SCHOOL

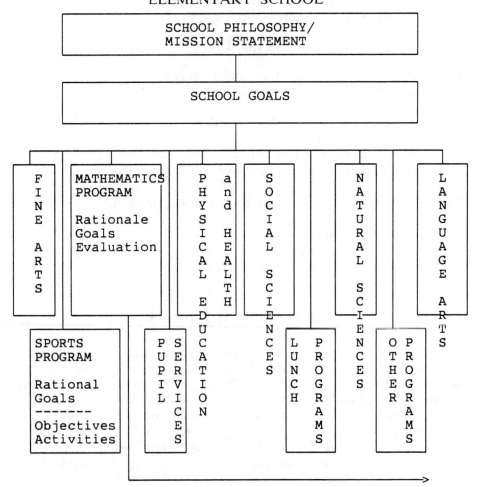

For elaboration of individual courses see next page

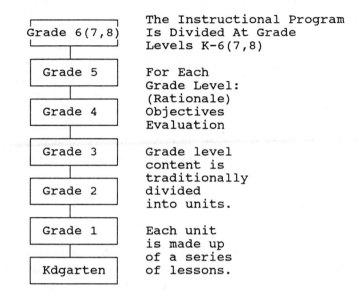

Grade 6(7,8)	The Instructional Program Is Divided At Grade Levels K-6(7,8)
Grade 5	For Each Grade Level: (Rationale) Objectives Evaluation
Grade 4	
Grade 3	Grade level content is traditionally divided into units.
Grade 2	
Grade 1	Each unit is made up of a series of lessons.
Kdgarten	

Diagram Showing Individual Lessons within A Set of Ordered Units
(Lesson within units show a variety of ordering options)
Unit Level: (Rationale), Objectives, Evaluation

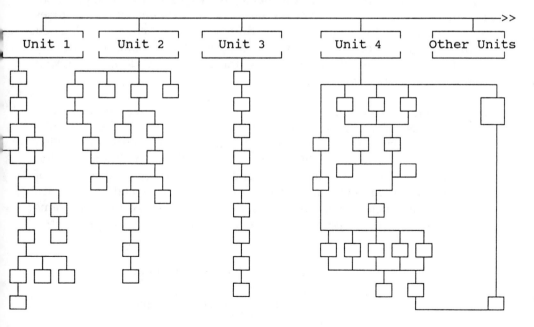

Lesson Level: Objectives, **Content, Methods**, Evaluation

preferred formula. Methods appropriate to both students and content are selected. Integral to the design is well defined evaluation procedure.

Many schools will consider non-academic programs as part of the overall curricular design. A school may require **co-curricular** programs such as inter-school sports, counseling services, referral services, lunch program, and bus program as vital to attainment of the school goals, and therefore a needed part of the curriculum. Methods appropriate to both students and content are selected. The model suggest that the totality of individual programs is the curriculum offered students.

On pages 16 and 17 are diagrams modeling a subject-centered curriculum in a traditional high school setting. The design begins by stating what the school defines as its educational philosophy or mission. Growing out of the school's position statement are department philosophies that state beliefs regarding the contribution each makes to the overall school mission. Each of the several department course offerings is defended through a course rationale.

The model identifies school goals. These goals are defined and elaborated through the several department goals. Each department identifies courses appropriate to meeting department goals. Courses are categorized for sequence and difficulty. Each course is headed with objectives. Content for courses is sorted and organized vertically and horizontally to satisfy objectives. Integral to the design is a well defined evaluation mechanism.

As with elementary school, many high schools consider non-academic programs as part of the overall curricular design. A school may require **co-curricular** programs such as inter-school sports, counseling services, referral services, lunch program, and bus program as vital to attainment of the school goals and, therefore, a needed part of the curriculum. Methods appropriate to both students and content are selected. The model suggests that the totality of individual programs is the curriculum offered students. Variations of subject-centered curricula include:

> *   the Separate Subject Curriculum,
> *   the Disciplines Curriculum,
> *   the Correlated Curriculum, and
> *   the Integrated Curriculum.

Separate Subject Curriculum

The oldest of all curriculum designs is the separate subject curriculum. It organizes the instructional content as totally separate bodies of knowledge and teaches it in isolation from other bodies of knowledge. It allocates instructional time by dividing the school day into time segments, each segment intended as time to transmit a selected portion of the body of knowledge to the students.

The separate subject curriculum is supported with a philosophic viewpoint that defines the role of schools as transmitter of the instructional content -- that heritage of understanding passed on from former generations. Mastery of content and associated skills is its major goal. The textbook and the informed teacher are the significant transmission vehicles. This design has traditionally assumed that the best way to transmit knowledge to students is through direct exposition from teacher or textbook to the learner. Action is centered on the teacher. The learner tends to be a passive recipient of information rather than an active seeker of information.

Elementary school subjects traditionally considered part of a separate subject curriculum include reading, English, grammar, spelling, penmanship, arithmetic, health, physical education, music, and art. Secondary subjects may include such diverse interests as typing, bookkeeping, woodworking, animal husbandry, choir, speech, band, literature, and **remedial** arithmetic or reading.

Disciplines Curriculum

Some elementary and secondary school offerings classified as subjects are better categorized as disciplines. Among them are algebra, trigonometry, history, economics, geography, sociology, anthropology, psychology, meteorology, physics, and chemistry. During the fifties and sixties extensive curriculum development resulted in a great many new programs to improve instruction. Emphasis centered on the content areas: mathematics, science, foreign language, and social science.

From these efforts grew many new curriculum programs in which a subject matter classification, the **discipline**, became the fundamental unit for design. An idea was promoted that certain bodies of knowledge had an inherent organization which was its cognitive framework. It had its own integrity. It was the body of knowledge that its scholars, the subject matter specialists, came to know and

SUBJECT CENTERED CURRICULUM DESIGN -- HIGH SCHOOL

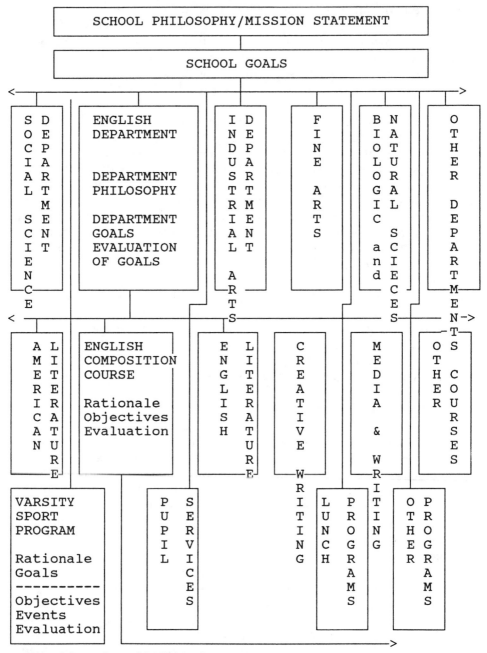

For elaboration of individual courses see next page

For Each High School English Course:
Rationale
Objectives
Evaluation

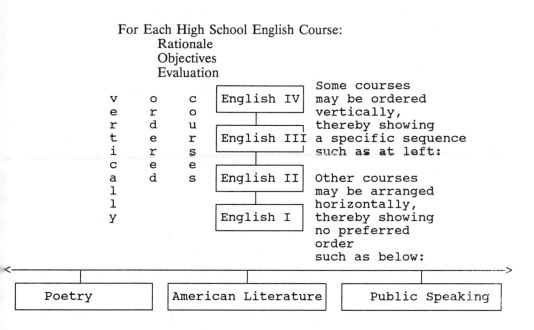

```
v    o    c   ┌──────────────┐   Some courses
e    r    o   │  English IV  │   may be ordered
r    d    u   └──────┬───────┘   vertically,
t    e    r   ┌──────┴───────┐   thereby showing
i    r    s   │ English III  │   a specific sequence
c    e    e   └──────┬───────┘   such as at left:
a    d    s   ┌──────┴───────┐
l            │  English II  │   Other courses
l            └──────┬───────┘   may be arranged
y            ┌──────┴───────┐   horizontally,
             │  English I   │   thereby showing
             └──────────────┘   no preferred
                                order
                                such as below:
```

```
<─────────────┬──────────────────────┬─────────────────────>
┌──────────────┐   ┌──────────────────────┐   ┌────────────────────┐
│   Poetry     │   │ American Literature  │   │  Public Speaking   │
└──────────────┘   └──────────────────────┘   └────────────────────┘
```

Diagram Showing Individual Lessons within An Ordered Set of Units
(Lessons within units show a variety of ordering options)
Unit Level: (Rationale), Objectives, Evaluation

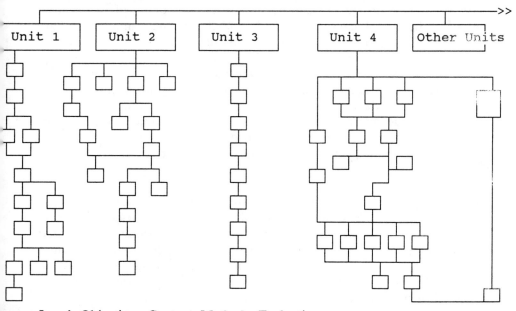

esson Level: Objectives, **Content, Methods**, Evaluation

believe as truth, and the process of inquiry by which this truth was discovered.

Even today, scholars maintain that each discipline has its own mode of inquiry, the special ways of gathering information, processing it into data, and inferring truth. The product of this inquiry is information organized in a framework which identifies its conceptual structure. The structure of a discipline is described as those concepts, rules, and principles that define and limit a body of knowledge and control its methods of research and inquiry. Structure unifies and organizes a discipline. It dictates appropriate ways of thinking about knowledge.

A discipline is not considered to be a fixed or permanent body of truth. It continues to change through discovery of new truth. Knowledge of the discipline's structure and an ability to use the modes of inquiry appropriate for that discipline are seen as basic to learning new truths and refining the old truths.

Concept, principle, and generalization building are an important organizing construct. A discipline, it was argued, is by its very nature an organization of knowledge in which significant concepts, principles, generalizations, conceptual schemes, laws, and theories can be identified. The curriculum maker's task is to convert the more powerful ideas of the discipline into optimal units of instruction which a beginner can learn and which at the same time are meaningful units in terms of the discipline.

The disciplines curriculum is considered an acceptable design by many educators. It lends itself to systematic organization and is easily changed and evaluated. It is familiar to parents and the general public. It allows teachers to specialize using the same taxonomy for dividing the instructional content used by colleges. It is understandable and manageable by both the **typical** teacher and student in the **typical** classroom.

Critics of the disciplines curriculum argue that it is deficient as an organizational construct since it compartmentalizes knowledge in ways unrelated to reality. When selection of learning experiences is dictated by structures of bodies of knowledge, these experiences have little relevance to students' present needs or interests. What is learned in isolation from practical life considerations does not transfer readily to **real life** happenings.

Since the content selected for instruction and the methodology used to instruct reflect the knowledge of the specialists' perspectives on the what and the how teaching should happen, technological implications and practical applications of the discipline tend to be ignored. The disciplines curriculum is characterized as a training appropriate for the college bound -- those who will ultimately become specialists in the discipline -- but as inappropriate for the average student's needs.

Obviously the problem of curriculum design was not resolved for all educators by either the separate subject design or by introduction of the disciplines approach. Educators continue to search for organizations which more satisfactorily address a concern to relate subject matter with student needs and interest.

The two subject-centered designs considered next are an attempt to bridge that gap.

Correlated Curriculum

The correlated curriculum, as an extension of subject-centered curricula, attempts to bring subjects together when there is evidence of a common denominator. Subjects remain as separate entities, but points of contact are sought between related contents from each subject.

One common expression of correlation is relating other subject matter with social studies. Consider the following: The English teacher agrees to match literature assignments so they correlate with the instruction in American history. While students are studying the Colonial Period, literature topics will include American classics such as The Scarlet Letter, Rip Van Winkle, The Courtship of Miles Standish, and The Legend of Sleepy Hollow.

Further correlation results when the art teacher agrees to teach about Indian and Colonial Art, and school music focuses on the Puritan hymns, folk songs, and the Virginia reel and other colonial dance forms.

Appropriate literature to match a study of the War Between the States includes O Captain My Captain, Gone with the Wind, and Uncle Tom's Cabin. Art topics include architecture and American-African art. Music appropriate to this period may be those songs called Negro spirituals, "The Battle Hymn of the Republic", and "Dixie."

It is important to note that what each teacher selects for instructional subject matter is normally considered to be part of the curriculum even if no correlation is practiced. Content is not changed, but time of teaching and emphasis on relation to history become important. Correlated curricula aid transfer of learning and help students see relationships between subject matters. It is a design that is understandable and manageable by teachers and students within **typical** classroom settings.

Integrated Curriculum

Separate subjects or disciplines are sometimes combined to form an integration of subjects. Examples of integration include:

* Reading, writing, spelling, speaking and listening to form language arts; or currently, whole language.
* Botany, zoology, anatomy, and bacteriology to form biology.
* Geology, meteorology, and astronomy to form earth science.
* Algebra, arithmetic, geometry, and trigonometry to form mathematics.
* Sociology, geography, history, political science, anthropology, economics, and psychology to form social studies.
* Physics, chemistry, geology, meteorology, astronomy to form general science.

Simply including several separate content titles under one heading does not assure integration. While arithmetic and geometry might be included in a single course offering they might be taught in isolation from each other. Integration assumes that content from each of the several components is offered as parallel instruction. When a social studies class studies England, it is studying about England's history, government, economics, geography, and social form.

Integration of subject matter helps students merge separate contents in an effort to develop concepts, principles, and generalization over a broad range of interest. It shows relationships between related knowledge and helps students see the **big picture**.

Commonalities across subject matter are emphasized. Learning is not fractured as in the separate subject and disciplines curriculum. Textbooks are able to package integrated subject matter as palatable content for student consumption. The integrated curriculum meets requirements necessary for general acceptance by educators and the public. It is understandable and manageable by teachers and students in typical classroom settings.

Theme-Centered Curricula[1]

Some schools have attempted to broaden the scope of interest in a single set of classroom investigations by breaking subject-matter barriers. They unify separate subject matter when they select as the focus of study a broad topic or theme, thus organizing instruction across traditional divisions. Theme-centered curricula, then, focus on problems, issues, or interests, and develop units or projects from them.

Topics or themes tend to emphasize a social role of the school. Selection may begin by asking the question: What are common and appropriate problems which students need to solve? Topics chosen include:

* Energy for America
* Going to the Circus
* My Changing Body
* Ecology and Technology
* A World without War
* Our Community: Then, Now, Tomorrow
* Central School's Fifth Grade Manufacturing Company

As students seek to build an understanding of the theme, they also gain in a variety of other learning. The theme becomes an agent to teach inquiry skills, library skills, improve the language arts communication skills (reading, writing, speaking, listening), and build proper values.

As an example: The theme -- America's Need for Energy -- will cause students to research topics, such as fossils and fossil fuel formation, mining and processing of fuels, pollution concerns, R-factors, fuel efficiency, the home building industry, transportation, oil producing nations, energy national policy, and more.

---

[1] The structure, theme centered curricula, may be known by other titles. Models employing a similar structure include The Interdisciplinary Concept Model described by Heidi Hayes Jacobs, <u>Interdisciplinary Curriculum: Design and Implementation</u>, Alexandria, VA: Association for Supervision and Curriculum Development, p.53-66.

Oral and written presentations are expected. Handwriting, grammar, and spelling receive attention. Tables, graphs, and mathematics computation related to energy studies follow. Opportunities are included for art and music instruction.

Thematic curricula can be classified as following either a **topic driven theme approach** or a **discipline/subject field driven theme approach**. Examples of the topic driven approach include British thematic teaching, pages 22-25, the themestorming whole language strategy, pages 25-26, and the units described on pages 152-154. Examples of the discipline/subject field approach to unit construction are found on pages 154-163.

The British Approach to Thematic Teaching

For years British Primary Schools have used a theme-centered approach when identifying and developing appropriate subject matter for study. They call it Thematic Teaching. The staff of the school may select several broad topics to serve as the focus for study over the school year.

Names such as,
* Light and Color,
* Buildings and Structures,
* Canals and Rivers, or
* Our Church at Barwell
* Electricity
* Our visit to France

become the **social studies-science** units to be studied. Theme development is the school's method for integrating the communication skills, the humanities, and the social and physical sciences in a meaningful study.

Two themes are shown on the following pages. From these **science oriented** themes emerge a multitude of topics for examination. Students are expected to complete assignments on selected topics. One such theme is entitled, Space. The flow chart, Space, guides development of the theme. Following initial observation and vocabulary work, students may be led to explore the solar system and other planets, and/or stars, constellations, or galaxies. Another group might engage in a study of space travel, while others investigate the multitude of interests related to the earth.

An examination of interests associated with the theme, Heat, is shown next. Following a brief introduction of heat, questions about its source, effect, motion, confinement, and use may be explored by different groups or individuals.

SPACE

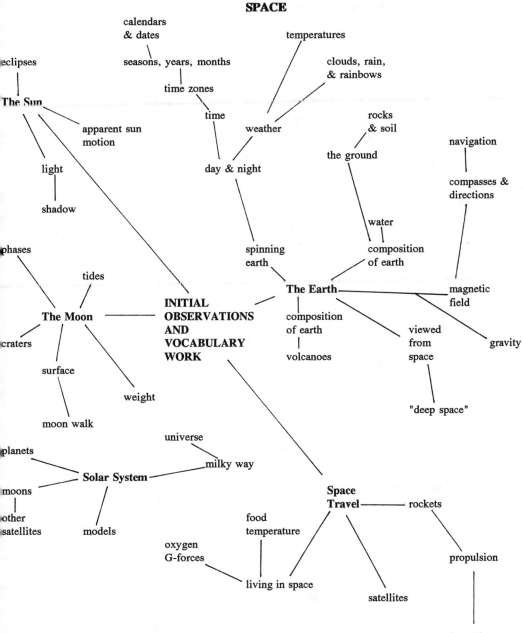

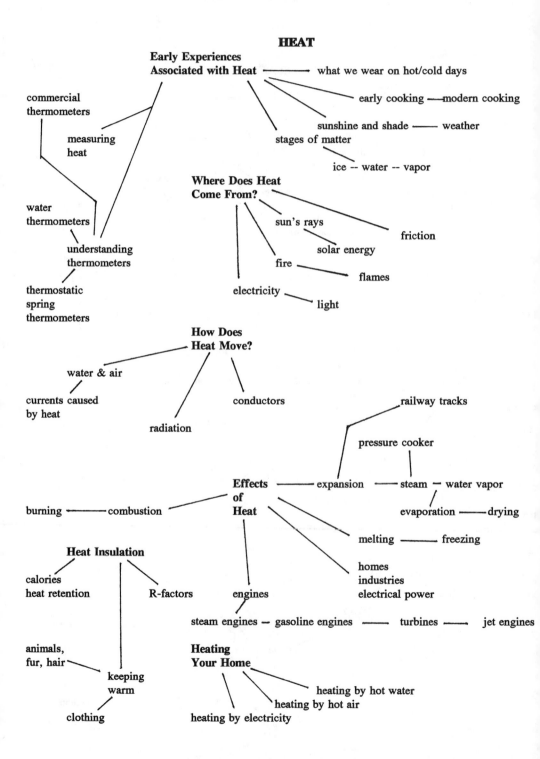

Some thematic topics require students to read while others direct them to hands-on manipulation. Bulletin boards are covered with compositions, drawings, and displays. Booklets are constructed. Materials find their way from home to school as students show-and-tell about a chosen topic. Field trips help explain and clarify. Sewing, cooking, experimenting, building, singing, dancing, and dramatizing are included.

In many buildings all age levels work to develop the single school theme. In some cases each age level chooses a different set of topics to explore, while in other cases the same topic is chosen by several age levels, but each age level develops the theme at a different stage of sophistication. A single theme may be kept as the integrated study for as long as three months.

Themestorming: A Whole Language Strategy[2]

As part of a whole language approach to teaching reading, teachers may engage in a planning process called themestorming which enables them to determine the potential of a particular theme, as well and provide them with a planning structure that offers a flexible organization. A theme rich in literature, with obvious potential in science, social studies, mathematics serves well. The theme, Take Flight, (Baskwill, 1988, p. 80-82) shown below enables teachers to organize material in such a way as to make the most of children's natural ability to find connections between what they already know and the experiences with which they are involved.

Most whole language themes need about six to eight weeks to complete. Organization may begin with a "twenty-day plan" sufficiently flexible so it can grow over the several weeks as more literature is discovered. The plan provides *routines*, activities or short bits of teaching that grow out of the literature. The teacher's concern is to support rather than control children's natural learning capabilities Theme-centered curricula encourage cooperative planning between teachers and students. Provision for special needs and interests of students is incorporated into the planning. Traditional subject matter, as it relates to the topic for study, does find a role.

---

[2] Reprinted with permission of the publisher, Early Years, Inc., Norwalk, Connecticut 06854, From the September, 1988, issue of *Teaching/K-8*.

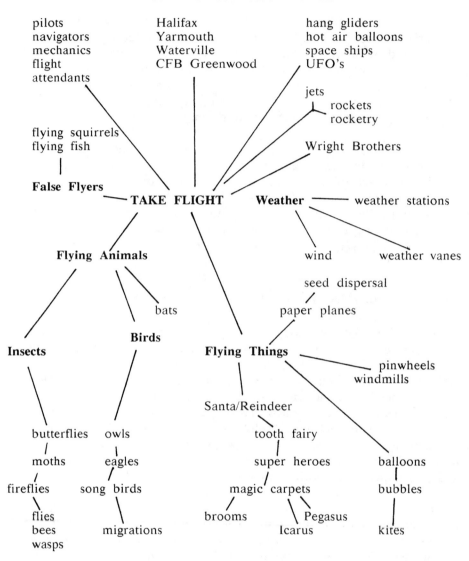

Vestiges of the subject matter curricula can be found in the theme-centered design. But it is more closely related to a student-centered approach. Theme centered curricula are less well defined than those curricula previously discussed. They present challenges to both teachers and students not easily resolved by "tradition bound" teachers. Re-education of both teachers and student in theory and practice of theme-centered curricula is a necessary step towards its successful implementation.

Student-Centered Curricula

Student-centered curricula look to the learner for selection and organization of content and activity. The curriculum-maker is concerned with students' needs and interests, rather than the dictates of subject matter, when making curriculum decisions. Human growth and development of youth are considered.

Learning must have a social or personal meaning. Instruction focuses on topics or problems which have a present relevance and interest to the learner. Students are directly involved in the planning and implementing of study. Learning tasks tend to be experiential and process-oriented. Motivation may be high since students are usually emotionally involved in the learning task.

The late 60s and early 70s saw numerous attempts at student-centered curriculum building. The open classroom, open schools, and free schools were examples. Howes lists characteristics essential to a student-centered approach as he discusses informal teaching in the open classroom[3].

1. The curriculum moves away from being an independent variable to being a dependent variable. It becomes children centered. It is relevant to children's needs, interests, curiosities, and purposes. The concept of essential knowledge takes on personal meaning rather than sameness for all.

2. Pupils have freedom to make legitimate choices. Self-selection is recognized as a crucial form of human development. Children make learning decisions and significant choices, and they accept responsibility for the outcomes.

3. How children learn, the questions they ask, the way they solve problems, and their thinking development are of prime importance. The process of learning is at least as important, if not more so, than the knowledge that is gained.

4. Teachers actively participate with children as they engage in experiences of personal relevance. The hierarchical roles of teacher-director and learner-recipient are gone. Teachers support, facilitate, guide, question, connect, and bring to a conscious level learning and insights of the children.

---

[3] Reprinted by permission of Macmillan Publishing Company from pages 7-8 of *Informal Teaching in the Open Classroom* by Virgil M. Howes.

5. There is an atmosphere, human relationships, and conditions that allow children to change, to reconsider perceptions, and to integrate new insights freely. There is no fear of losing face if one admits error or holds varying values and beliefs. Children are not defenseless. They are free, they are accepted, they can "bare their souls" without repressions, guilt, or loss of ego.

6. Skill learning grows out of children's own work. Skills follow rather than precede experiences and activities that provide a base for understanding and concept development. Skills taught as programs divorced from children's own learning not only result in rote learning, but more importantly, may block indepth understandings.

7. Children are free to explore an individual interest deeply. The work and flow of a child's day is viewed as individual. Balance in terms of learning is viewed over the long range. The focus is on intellectual growth rather than the specific knowledge acquired.

8. Children collaborate with each other when interests are similar, when there are activities that demand group endeavors, when combining individual talents and learning helps in the accomplishment of goals beyond the capabilities of an individual, or when working together yields meaningful results, joys, developments to the individuals concerned.

9. There is creative work. A wide range of resource materials is available for children to use. Teachers help children explore new techniques, learn new ways of expressing themselves. There is discussion, personal talk with children about their explorations and work. Questions that help to bring out conscious understanding of learning or that may foster further exploration are asked.

Those who support children-centered designs believe they are solidly rooted in good educational philosophy, supportive of the accepted learning theories, and most importantly, contribute more fully to children's best interests emotionally and psychologically -- to self actualization and the development of the **whole** person.

Student centered curricula call on students to an extent greater than in any other approach to select their own learning activities. Students are assisted to become engaged in fruitful study, exercise self-discipline, and in general, behave responsively (Charles, 1988, p. 131,132). They give students a greater stake in their own education.

However, since student-centered curricula require students to accept a major responsibility for managing their own education, it is a legitimate concern to ask, What do students select as desirable learning? Society expects schools to show student progress in specific learning, e.g., reading, writing, mathematics, history, etc. The 1960-70 experiment showed that students rarely selected academic work as preferred activities.

Student-centered curricula can improve student attitude and morale, but it often takes away from learning the instructional content usually recommended for the curriculum. If used under optimal conditions -- by serious students working with skilled teachers -- student-centered curricula might produce the sort of learning envisioned by Carl Rogers and other **romantics** who would have school programs consist of students delving diligently into matters of central importance to their lives, assisted by able teachers working skillfully to facilitate the students' progress (Charles).

In the extreme, open classroom, open schools, and free schools offered a less than desirable student learning environment. During the late 1960s and early 1970s free schools sprang up throughout the country. These schools interpreted their responsibility as a maxim to let the child alone. Little guidance was given to students when selecting goals or learning experiences. It was thought that the most desirable learning would happen when students were left to choose how to utilize school time. These disciples of student-centering maintained that students' immediate interests and urges generated the most valuable educational outcomes.

Success with student-centered curricula has been limited. Primary reasons seem to be related to lack of a clearly understood definition for such curricula and the implicit difficulty of its implementation. A program built on student needs and interests, while having a **gut-level** appeal, requires, when implemented in a classroom of twenty to thirty quite unique individuals, extra-ordinary ability and effort on the part of teachers.

Each child must be guided to select and persist on worthy tasks which appeal to that child's needs and interests. Most teachers find the task beyond their ability to manage. There are no workable strategies that can be easily applied to classroom use. There are no clearly defined guidelines to help correlate student- centeredness with appropriate and well defined content. Those who promote student-centered curricula must formulate guidelines which can be readily implemented as teacher and student classroom behaviors. They must show that these guidelines can work successfully with **typical** teachers and students in **typical** classroom settings. Only then will efforts to encourage general use of student-centered curricula in American schools find a broad acceptance.

Summary

Educators are involved in a constant search for improved curricular designs. The search is an attempt to find ways to make it possible at all times for all students to be engaged in learning that are most appropriate for each of them.

Three curriculum designs may be used to illustrate education's attempts at providing a **best way** to organize for instruction. They are subject-centered designs, theme-centered designs, and student-centered designs.

Subject-centered curricula look to organized knowledge for design definition and structure. Variations of subject-centered design are the separate subject curriculum, the disciplines curriculum, the correlated curriculum, and the integrated curriculum.

Theme-centered curricula break down subject matter barriers and unify separate subject matter by forming studies on broad topics or themes. Theme-centered curricula may focus on problems or issues of current interest. British primary schools, when using a thematic teaching approach, identify broadly defined topics to serve as the focus of **integrated-unit** study during the year.

Student-centered curricula look to the learner for selection and organization of content. Student interests and needs, rather than subject matter, become the basis for design decisions. Student- centered curricula give students a major responsibility in their own education. Students may be asked to select their own learning goals and plan and manage their own learning experiences. If used by serious students working with skilled teachers, student-centered curricula may produce highly desirable holistic educational results.

BIBLIOGRAPHY

Baskwill, J. (1988). "Themestorming," Teaching K-8. August/September. Norwalk, CN: Early Years, Inc.

Charles, C. M. (1983). Elementary classroom management. New York: Longman, Inc.

Howes, V. (1974). Informal teaching in the open classroom. New York: Macmillan Publishing Co., Inc.

Chapter Three

Writing Rationale and Learning Outcomes

If you are a typical teacher, you most readily identify with those parts of the curriculum design called content and methods. You have probably asked questions like:

"What should I teach?
What materials should I use?
How should I teach it?"

But, how often have you inquired:

"What **should** be the student learning from my teaching? How will I decide if this learning happened?"

You may argue:

"Why waste time and energy on identifying and measuring goals and objectives. Valuable time is better spent in planning effective lessons. Good classroom teaching is what really counts, not lists of goals and objectives written on paper. The lists are looked at once and then forgotten."

As you consider the comments above, reflect on a definition of teaching as highlighted in the following scenario:

*Professor Lee was speaking to a group of education majors just prior to their placement as student teachers. He concluded his **pep talk** with this comment.*

"Tomorrow you begin the task called student teaching. You will, for the first time, be a real teacher. Your job will be to teach. But before you begin the task called teaching, let me ask this question, 'What is teaching?'"

After some hesitation, they responded with definitions such as:

*"Teaching is helping the learner.
Teaching is guiding the learner.
Teaching is stimulating the learner."*

Professor Lee then asked,

> *"But why do you wish to help, guide, and stimulate the learner? What is your purpose for doing these things?"*

After surveying a number of questioning faces staring back at him, he offered this answer.

> *"You will attempt to help, guide, and stimulate the learner to effect a **change** in that person. Teaching is **affecting change**. Education is the process of **affecting change**. When Mr. and Mrs. Parent bring their child to your school and place the child in your care, they are in essence, saying to you and the school,*
>
> > *'Change my child. Change my child according to the ways in which the school determines children should be changed. Report to me regularly how well the change is being affected.'"*

Professor Lee added a concluding remark.

> *"When you were high school seniors many of you said,*
>
> > *'I want to be a teacher. But I do not, as a high school senior, have the competencies to be an effective classroom teacher. I must be changed. I will become a student in a college. It will change me so I become a competent teacher.'*
>
> *You see, that's what teaching is. It is **changing people**. You then, as educator, must answer the important question,*
>
> > *'What changes should my teaching affect?'"*

Basic Curriculum Components Related to Purpose and Outcome

Since education can be defined as a process intended to bring about **change** in the learner, identification of intended **change** is a logical pre-requisite to selecting content and methods. A statement describing the **changed** student is called a goal or an objective. You may have wondered: "Education professors talk about goals and objectives. But how are they different? How should we use them? How can they help our teaching?"

You may also have questioned the need for statements labeled educational philosophies or rationales. You may have you wondered: "Why should we spend valuable time writing philosophies and rationales? How will they make us into better teachers?"

In this chapter we will try to answer these questions by examining some basic curriculum components related to purpose and outcome. We will also learn how these elements may be written. We will consider:

* The Educational Philosophy of the School,
* School Goals,
* Program/Department Rationale,
* Program/Department Goals,
* Grade Level/Course Rationale,
* Grade Level/Course Objectives,
* Unit Rationale,
* Unit Objectives, and
* Lesson Objectives.

Since examples are a useful way to demonstrate what to include in curriculum documents, a variety will be offered.

Writing An Educational Philosophy

A school's written curriculum should be headed with a student focused statement of the school's basic educational beliefs and values. This declaration is usually called The Educational Philosophy or The Mission Statement. It may describe a learning environment designed to enhance development of the individual -- morally, socially, and academically.

It may exclaim the point of view of the traditionalist or the progressivist. It may describe a vision of the school's planned future. It may be the school's **quest for excellence**; that level of quality education the school hopes to attain through concerted effort of professionals and community. The statement of educational philosophy or mission may include:

a. A declaration of those values from which the school derives its purpose.
b. An articulation of what the school believes about the education for its students.
c. A vision of what the school sees as its mission.

School Philosophy Documents

Below are examples of educational philosophy and mission statements representing a variety of beliefs about schooling. We will begin with two progressive philosophic statements and follow with more traditional points of view.

CENTERVILLE PROGRESSIVE SCHOOL

The Philosophy Of The Faculty of Centerville Progressive School Can Be Inferred From An Examination Of The Following -- We Believe -- statements.

Schooling is a collegial, supporting enterprise where educators assist learners grow to their physical, emotional, and intellectual potential, according to what learners and educators determine this potential to be; and according to how learners and educators deem the potential can best be attained.

Therefore, we, the faculty and administration, offer as our consensus, these -- WE BELIEVE -- statements:

1. The school should be organized into teams. Each team should include students, teachers, aids, and a team leader.

2. Teachers who work as a team should be responsible for teaching in all subject areas; however, each team member should accept responsibility for leadership in at least one instructional program.

3. Teachers who work together should serve students whose ages, in September, span at least three years.

4. Each student's learning program should be based on specific learning objectives appropriate for that student.

5. Learning programs should be tailored for each student and include:

   a. A variety of learning modes as appropriate for the student's learning style.
   b. A variety of learning activities.
   c. Use of a variety of media.
   d. A range of study group sizes from individual to large group.

6. Students should be taught to increasingly accept responsibility for their learning program.

   ...

The School of Student Centered Learning expressed its philosophy by considering the question:

What, above all else, should be the concern of education?

THE SCHOOL OF STUDENT CENTERED LEARNING

When asking the question, What above all else, should be the concern of education? many considerations come to mind.

A school might focus on learning reading, writing, addition, or multiplication.

It might center on use of communication skills to solve problems and gather information.

It could dwell on the integrated day, open school, self-contained classrooms, team teaching, vertical groupings, and the like.

While all of the above are important considerations, it is our belief at the Affective/Cognitive School that the proper focus of the education enterprise should be on **student -- as person -- as human**.

The concern of education must center on two aspect of humanness. Each is related to the other.

The first speaks to the humanness of individuals while the second considers persons as part of a larger universe in which each is but one of the many participants.

The first concern of education should be that of assisting students to become individuals who, when viewing their image in a mirror, can truthfully state:

> "I like myself,
> I like the person I was yesterday,
> I like who I am today,
> I like the individual I will actively
> seek to become tomorrow;"

and who, when interacting with a neighbor, demonstrates a behavior which proclaims:

> "I love you, also!"

The implications of this declaration are many. It assumes certain cognitive attainment on the part of the individual as prerequisite to "I like myself." It assumes certain interpersonal relationships as prerequisite to "I love you, also."

The children described above will most probably read well, be able to work with number and space, express themselves well in written and oral language forms, possess a knowledge of literature, the arts, and be literate in both the natural and social sciences.

But the learning of this knowledge and skill is complementary to the first goal of education -- to help children become persons who correctly feel they have the right to, and can, like themselves and others.

Therefore, the teaching of reading must strengthen, not weaken achievement toward this central goal. Mathematics, as experienced by children, must lend support to a condition which raises self image and encourages cooperation. All school activities should focus on this major purpose of education.

———

Our home, earth, is a system made up of many interdependent factors -- animals, plants, and the numerous non-living components, such as air, water, and minerals.

Humans are a part of this ecosystem -- not apart from it.

Therefore, the second major concern of education should be that of assisting all students to become contributing members of this global, social, and ecological community.

The school environment must provide a setting which leads students to an acceptance of world citizenship in which social justice becomes the hallmark. The school curriculum should encourage attitudes and instruct in knowledge which support a concept of earth as a closed biological system with limited resource. All school activities should relate to this second purpose of education.

Against these two criteria, schools can measure their work. They can determine if their efforts are supportive, neutral, or actually detract from the ultimate goals.

———

Magnet schools express educational foci by describing their unique mission. Below is the Statement of Mission adopted by the Sayre Language Academy.[1]

Sayre Language Academy is a public elementary school (kindergarten through grade 8), deriving its student body from the rich diversity of the city of Chicago. As a foreign language magnet school, Sayre is in a unique position to enrich the outlook of its students by early exposure to the languages, cultures, and peoples of the world, including their own city and community. ...

Sayre's mission is to cooperatively create quality learning environments where all students experience enthusiasm for learning, an appreciation of their individual abilities, and an awareness of the unique abilities and potential of others. The development of self-esteem in Sayre students is linked to the development of appreciation and respect for others. Critical thinking and cooperative learning, with an emphasis on language arts, serve as the cornerstone of Sayre's instructional program. ...

Many mainline schools define their educational philosophy as related to teaching subject matter. The two educational philosophies that follow represent a traditional point of view.

MAINLINE SCHOOL

Schools are obligated to prepare all students to live socially useful and individually meaningful lives. Primary and secondary education are considered the introductory steps in a continuous process of preparation and growth for whatever life goal an individual may seek.

The school has, as its primary responsibility, the efficient transmission of knowledge, the passage of tradition and values, and the development of individual potential for each student. Certain subjects are seen to possess the generative power necessary to accomplish the educational task.

These basic and generative subjects are the most effective ones for the transmission of knowledge and are the basis for future learning. They are the subjects, once mastered, which enable learners to master new subjects. Subjects which possess the generative power are language arts, mathematics, social sciences, natural sciences, and aesthetics.

---

[1] Based on the Statement of Mission, Sayre Language Academy - LSC 1850 North Newland Avenue, Chicago, Illinois 60635.

Subject matter which is not highly generative or is self-terminating has no place in the curriculum. . . .

It is therefore the intention of the Mainline Community School to restrict its curriculum offerings to basic and generative subject matter.

Lyons Township High School clarified its philosophy as a mission statement.[2]

LYONS TOWNSHIP HIGH SCHOOL MISSION STATEMENT

Drawing from its long tradition and reputation for excellence, Lyons Township High School commits itself to making dedicated teaching and meaningful learning its highest priority and to creating an atmosphere of encouragement, trust, and mutual respect.

Within this environment, Lyons Township High School pledges to provide a comprehensive curriculum and extra-curricular options that foster the **full** intellectual, physical, moral, and aesthetic growth of each student.

To be successful, teachers and students need to empower one another. Each assumes the responsibility for mastery of the subject matter, development of critical thinking and problem solving methods, and recognition of personal growth through this interchange.

Through this mission, Lyons Township High School is reinterpreting our century-old motto, *Vita Plena*, the quest for the fulfilling life. This becomes possible as the entire high school community, in cooperation with family and the larger community, continues to encourage and assist each student towards a lifetime process of learning and an attitude of self respect.

Church or Temple related schools may describe their philosophy in terms of the Bible or other holy books and the Congregation's mission. One Christian school expressed its Credo by answering the question, why Christian education?

---

[2] Based on Lyons Township High School, Illinois School District 204, Mission Statement.

IMMANUEL LUTHERAN SCHOOL

Why Christian Education?

Immanuel Lutheran School is an integral part of the preaching/ teaching ministry of Immanuel Congregation as it responds to the Lord's command that children be nurtured and instructed in worship of the Triune God: Father, Son, and Holy Spirit.

> "Bring them (your children) up in the discipline and instruction of the Lord."(Ephesians 6:4), and

> "These words which I command you this day shall be upon your heart and you shall teach them diligently to your children."(Deuteronomy 6:6,7)

Christian education is the process of directing human development toward God's objective: knowledge of salvation in Christ Jesus, and a life of godliness in character and action. All instruction should be nested in the Word of God. It should be directed and guided by Scripture throughout the total school day.

Immanuel holds that the concept, Christian community, should permeate every facet of the students education. ...

Some teachers see their schools as mainstream, establishment enterprises and therefore believe it redundant to define a statement of philosophy or mission statement, since it is part of the community culture. It will, however, be worth your time and effort to examine carefully what are the dominant values of the community and ask if they are the same values desired by the school's faculty and Board of Education.

Writing School Goals

What learning outcomes should your school set for students under its care?

When should your school say, "No," that is not our primary responsibility.

Your response to these questions will be stated as district/school goals. They will be a definition of your school's responsibility to its constituency. It will define the overall purpose of the educational endeavor.

PDK Goal Assessment

Phi Delta Kappan offers a process to help educators and community work toward consensus in goal selection and emphasis. The "Educational Goals and Objectives Model"[3] provides an efficient method to analyze and prioritize selected educational goals. A list of the eighteen goals used in the goals selection model follows:

1. *Learn to respect and get along with people with whom we work and live.*
2. *Develop pride in work and a feeling of self-worth.*
3. *Gain information needed to make job selections.*
4. *Understand and practice the skills of family living.*
5. *Gain a general education.*
6. *Appreciate culture and beauty in the world.*
7. *Understand and practice democratic ideas and ideals.*
8. *Develop skills to enter a specific field of work.*
9. *Practice and understand the ideas of health and safety.*
10. *Learn how to examine and use information.*
11. *Develop good character and self-respect.*
12. *Learn to be a good citizen.*
13. *Develop a desire for learning now and in the future.*
14. *Develop skills in reading, writing, speaking, and listening.*
15. *Learn how to respect and get along with people who think, dress, and act differently.*
16. *Learn about and try to understand the changes that take place in the world.*
17. *Learn how to use leisure time.*
18. *Learn how to be a good manager of money, property, and resources.*

Those who use the kit are encouraged to supplement the list with goals of their own. Each of the eighteen goals in the kit is explained more thoroughly by addition of subheading descriptors.

The kit can be used with a community and/or faculty and/or student participant group. A forced choice rating procedure, together with a small group consensus forming activity, results in a ranking of the eighteen goals on the criteria: Which goals should receive priority in your school.

---

[3] Taken from Phi Delta Kappa, Inc., Eighth and Union, PO Box 789, Bloomington, IN 47402.

School Goal Documents

A school goal document should be the product of administration, faculty, and community consensus. It should:

a. Give direction to the overall instructional program of the school.
b. Establish the parameters of the school's responsibilities to the community it serves; explain what the school perceives as its job, its primary task.

The school goal statements are:

a. Broadly stated, general, and abstract.
b. Representative of educational ideals.
c. Relatively timeless and not concerned with specific achievement with a specific time period.

School goals do, however, suggest what the population of students at the time of graduation from the school will be like.

A natural outgrowth of an educational philosophy or mission statement is the educational goal statement. Below are examples of goal statements representing differing educational philosophies.

CENTERVILLE PROGRESSIVE SCHOOL

As a result of their schooling, Centerville Progressive School students will grow into individuals who:

1. *Are self motivated learners.*
2. *Have developed the knowledge, skills, and attitudes necessary to select appropriate learning goals and plan supportive programs leading to fulfillment of these goals.*
3. *Have the ability and desire for life-long learning.*
4. *Understand and practice democratic ideas and ideals.*
5. *Work cooperatively with peers and elders to improve themselves and their environment.*
6. *Seek to build a world of understanding, peace, and unity; a world in which all persons work together as global citizens.*

    ...

One school district established goals for all of its early childhood through high school buildings. It limited interest to six subject matter fields.

DELL SCHOOL DISTRICT

As a result of their schooling, K-12, students should possess:

Goal 1.Skills and knowledge of the language arts, including reading, writing, speaking, and listening, applicable to a range of futures.

Goal 2.Mathematics problem-solving skills applicable to a range of scientific disciplines, businesses, and everyday situations.

Goal 3.An understanding and appreciation of citizenship and its responsibility in a democracy and a world community.

Goal 4.Scientific literacy, social responsibility, and an understanding of cause and effect of natural phenomena.

Goal 5.An understanding and appreciation of the fine arts as creative expression and a record of human experience.

Goal 6.Knowledge and attitudes that lead to healthful living and physical fitness, coordination, and leisure skills.

One high school[4] declared its educational goal as **Providing A General Education for All Students**. General education was defined as:

Learnings in common deemed essential for all students to function with competence, discernment, responsibility, and creative imagination in our ever-widening world.

---

[4] Based on goal statements prepared by the River Forest-Oak Park High School, River Forest, Illinois.

Rather than state school goals as a list of learning outcomes, this high school chose to list nineteen learning experiences considered essential for achieving a general education.

Oak Park/River Forest High School

Seven learning experiences are essential for development of skills for life-long learning.

Those that:

1. *Provide opportunities for competence in symbolical language, including written, oral, visual, and mathematical;*
2. *Teach how to locate, assimilate, synthesize, and process information;*
3. *Teach how to conceptualize and utilize ideas;*
4. *Develop an understanding of methods of problem solving and of critical thinking;*
5. *Prepare for understanding, influencing, and adjusting to change;*
6. *Teach varied and alternate ways to learn;*
7. *Encourage the ability to create images, forms, and ideas.*

Five learning experiences are essential to foster a sense of global consciousness.

Those that:

8. *Provide an understanding and appreciation of the heritage of our country, including the literary, artistic, political, economic, historical, philosophical, and scientific;*
9. *Provide an understanding and appreciation of the contributions made to world civilization by non-western and other western cultures, including the literary, artistic, political, economic, historical, philosophical, and scientific;*
10. *Provide opportunities to develop an awareness of the interdependencies which exist among individuals and nations;*
11. *Show how the past has affected the present, and how the past and the present help determine the future;*
12. *Develop in students a sense of responsibility as citizens of the world, the nation, and the community.*

Seven learning experiences are essential to gain a sense of selfworth.

Those that:

13. *Encourage the establishing of personal goals, the making of decisions leading toward those goals, and the accepting of consequences of those decisions;*
14. *Enable the building upon personal strength and the recognizing of personal weakness;*
15. *Encourage growth in relationship with others, both competitively and cooperatively;*
16. *Encourage the recognition and acquisition of good health in all of its aspects;*
17. *Create experiences which will enable students to know and to value success;*
18. *Encourage aspirations to do the very best;*
19. *Develop attitudes and habits needed in the world of work and play.*

The Immanuel Lutheran School stated its school goals in terms of its primary interest.

IMMANUEL LUTHERAN SCHOOL

Immanuel Lutheran School is Owned and Maintained by the Parish for the purpose of guiding youth to:

1. *Know, believe, and worship the Triune God: Father, Son, and Holy Spirit as Creator, Preserver, Redeemer, and Sanctifier.*
2. *Grow into persons of good moral character.*
3. *Develop basic academic knowledge and skills which lead to productive citizenship.*
4. *Become persons who act caringly for the spiritual and physical welfare of others both locally and across the globe.*

    ...

A school may wish to combine both philosophy and goals into a single, concise declaration. The example below illustrates this point.

THE COMMUNITY SCHOOL FOR ENCULTURATION

Philosophy and Goals Statement

Each society is confronted with the responsibility of inducting its immature members into its culture. Education is the social process by which such individuals are led to acquire the ways, beliefs, and standards of the society.

To this end, The Community School for Enculturation has structured a set of learning experiences, the curriculum. Primary to all learning are four values related to living in a democratic society. These values are:

* recognition of the importance of every individual human being as a human regardless of racial, national, social, or economic status;
* opportunity for wide participation in all phases of activities in the social groups in the society;
* encouragement of variability rather than demanding a single type of personality or response;
* faith in intelligence as a method of dealing with important problems rather than depending upon the authority of an autocratic or aristocratic group.

Education at the Community School of Enculturation, as experienced through its curriculum, serves to help students grow into individuals who:

* *can demonstrate proficiency in basic language arts and communication skills: reading, writing, speaking, and listening; mathematics skills; natural, biological, and social sciences; understanding and appreciation of the fine arts; and understanding of physical development and health.*
* *can demonstrate proficiency in a second language.*
* *accept and appreciate persons of other races, colors, religions, and cultures.*
* *love their country and work to improve its laws and values.*
* *will work to improve the economic, social, and physical condition of the world's people.*

    ...

As you examine goals of different kinds of schools in our pluralistic society, you will find a wide range of educational priorities. Perhaps your school is representative of one of the examples above. Perhaps it borrows from several or is different from all. It is important that you know your school's philosophy and goals. You should be able to respond with specifics when asked,

"What does your school see as its mission?"
"How are students under your care being changed?"

Only then can you evaluate how effective your educational program is.

Writing Program Rationale/Department Philosophy[5]

Program rationales and department philosophies are important parts of well written curriculum designs. They show why the programs or department offerings should be included in the school curriculum. They tell how the components fit together with the other components to support the school's philosophy.

Art Program Scenario, Part 1

Imagine that you are the principal of a K-8 Elementary School that places an unusually great emphasis on art education. You, your faculty, and the Board of Education have determined that art education should hold a central focus in education. On each day, five days a week, for the full school year, thirty-five minutes is allocated to art teaching.

A father and mother are interested to enroll their child in your school. They examine a description of the weekly schedule and discover the apparent disproportionate amount of time given to art education. They appear concerned and ask,

"Why do you devote so much school time to teaching art?"

Anticipating their concern, you respond by welcoming their

---

[2] To avoid unnecessary repetition of terms, the word **program** will be used to identify major curriculum divisions, such as The Mathematics Program, N-12; The Science Program K-12; The Early Childhood Program, N-K; The Music Program K-6; The Reading Program, 1-8; The Fine Arts Program, 7-9; The Social Science Program, 9-12; The Intramural Program; The Inter-school Competitive Athletics Program.

Most high schools are organized as **departments**. Departments often write philosophies to state beliefs about the subject matter specialty housed in the department and its relationship to the total school curriculum. Program Rationale and Department Philosophy will be treated under this single heading.

question and suggest they read the document you have, entitled: "Rationale for the K-8 Art Program."

You suggest that the document will explain the school's position on the centrality of art in the school's curriculum. You further suggest that the rationale will show them:

1. the unique contribution art makes to a quality education,
2. how art articulates with the other programs in the curriculum, and
3. how art is related to the school's mission.

The Illinois State Department of Education Guides[6]

The state of Illinois has written a series of curriculum guides to assist in developing instructional programs. Each guide includes:

    a. Program Rationale,
    b. Program Goals,
    c. Clarification of each Program Goal, and
    d. Grade Level Objectives.

We will highlight the Language Arts guide to model these four elements.

A portion of the rationale from the Language Arts Curriculum Guide is shown below.

ILLINOIS STATE LANGUAGE ARTS PROGRAM

Rationale:

The skills and knowledge of the language arts are essential for student success in virtually all areas of the curriculum. They are also central requirements for the development of clear expression and critical thinking. The language arts include the study of literature and the development of skills in reading, writing, speaking, and listening. ...

---

6 Taken from the curriculum guides for grades 3, 6, 8, 10, prepared by the Illinois State Board of Education, Department of School Improvement Services, Springfield, Illinois, 1985. A more description is found in the remainder of the chapter and in Chapter 8.

The document below represents one district's understanding of how a program rationale can be used to defend and define the role of the physical education program as part of the regular curriculum.

MAPLEWOOD SCHOOL: PHYSICAL EDUCATION DEPARTMENT

Department Philosophy

The educational philosophy of Maplewood Community School District declares that the focus of all curricular development shall be the physical, intellectual, ethical, and emotional growth of its youth. Emphasis shall be given to helping all students know and accept themselves, work cooperatively and creatively with others, and become responsible persons. The program of the physical education department is designed as a linkage, bringing together through activity, those characteristics that build the well-rounded, contributing adult. ...

Physical activity is an essential part of healthy living. Regular vigorous activity appropriate to age, sex, and health status is beneficial to all but a medically-excepted few. Research continues to show that adequate exercise and sports activity contribute significantly to good health. ...

The development of emotional maturity can be aided through sports. Sports competition fills students' need for adventure, trains them to meet and accept challenges, and teaches them to accept limitation, while increasing self-esteem. ...

Physical education constitutes an essential part of the total educational program. It is education through, as well as of, the physical.

Writing Program/Department Goals

Goals statements at the program and department level are often more specific than at the school or district level. Program and department goals define specific paths along which learning will progress. These paths become the several content strands students will seek to master as they work within the program or department offerings.

When goals define learning paths for major curricular components such as a language arts program, K-8, science program, 9-12, or physical education program, K-12, the term, **Program Goal** is used. When goals define high school department learning paths the term, **Department Goal**, is used.

Program and department goals while general, do clearly set focus for learning. They are not, however, concerned with specific student achievement at a specified time period. Goals guide the selection of content to be used by identifying the content strands that instruction will follow.

Once goals have been established, a curriculum writer may construct learning objectives that direct and mark progress along these goals. Goals, then, are the vertical content strands upon which the series of more specific outcome statements, learning objectives, are ordered (see pages 114 115, 191-193).[7]

Art Program Scenario, Part 2

Let us resume our observation of yourself and the parents as they inquire further about your school's art program. Imagine the parents responding to their reading of the Art Program Rationale by saying,

"You presented a strong case for emphasizing art education in this building. We like what we read, but need more information. Tell us, what will our child learn in your art program?"

Again you are pleased. You tell the parents that their best source of information for expected learning from this art program is the statement of program goals.

You explain that the program goals describe, in a general way, what the school has chosen as the emphasized learning in its art program. The goals, you tell them, identify the paths along which their child's learning will progress over grades K-8.

Program and department goal statements identify those learning paths students will follow as they experience instruction. Thus, goals define the parameters of the education unit. For example:

Goals for an early childhood language arts program list the major learning focuses of the language arts program.

Goals for a K-8 music program list broadly defined paths upon

----

[7] If elementary school goals are perceived as bundles of reeds set vertically on a philosophic foundation, program goals are the individual reeds that make up each bundle, and learning objectives are a series of regularly spaced horizontal lines to mark points that indicate progress upward on each reed.

which student learning will progress as students complete the music program.

Goal statements for a high school science department describe the specific focuses of science learning within the department's offerings. These may be made operational as department courses.

The guidelines that follow offer criteria for selecting program/department goals.

1. Program/department goals should identify the paths of learning within a program/department.
2. There should be an obvious connection between program/department goals and school goals.
3. The total number of goals should be limited to a number which can be easily remembered.
4. Program/department goals should be capable of division into grade/course level objectives.

The Illinois Department of Education identified six State Goals for Learning for the Language Arts program.

ILLINOIS STATE LANGUAGE ARTS PROGRAM

Program Goals:

As a result of their schooling, K-12, students will be able to:
1. *Read, comprehend, interpret, evaluate and use written material;*
2. *Listen critically and analytically;*
3. *Write standard English in a grammatical, well-organized and coherent manner for a variety of purposes;*
4. *Use spoken language effectively in formal and informal situations to communicate ideas and information and to ask and answer questions;*
5. *Understand the various forms of significant literature representative of different cultures, eras, and ideas;*
6. *Understand how and why language functions and evolves.*

Clarifying Program Goals

A goal statement, because it is a single sentence may need clarification. Each of the six language arts goals is clarified by listing specific knowledge and skills related to the goal.

The Illinois State Language Arts goal #5 reads --

As a result of their schooling, students will be able:

To understand the various forms of significant literature representative of different cultures, eras, and ideas.

The goal is clarified in the following manner:

As a result of instruction in literature, students will read a variety of literary works.

General Knowledge/Skills Related to Goal 5

The following knowledge and skills are related to this State Goal for Learning:

A   Differences among poetry, drama, fiction, and nonfiction.
B   Differences among the types of factual literature.
C   American, English, and non-English literary works.
D   Selected literary works from various historical periods.
E   Selected literary works that manifest different value systems and philosophies.
F   Elements of fiction and nonfiction.
G   Figurative language.
H   Literary themes and their implications.
I   Symbolism, allegory, and myth.
J   Evaluation of selected literary works supported with evidence.

Elaboration of goal statements may be provided through other means. Below is a set of goal statements for a high school social science department in a multicultural community. Each of the goal statements is augmented with explanatory commentary.

SOCIAL SCIENCE DEPARTMENT GOALS OF FORESTVILLE HIGH SCHOOL

The primary goal of social science education is instruction toward good citizenship. Its focus is on persons, persons as they interact with each other and with their environment.

The social sciences help students understand themselves and the society and world in which they live, so that they may act intelligently and responsibly as individuals and citizens.

The subgoals listed below are considered necessary to attainment of the primary social studies goal, good citizenship.

Students who have completed the requirements of the Forestville High School Social Science Program will:

1. *Possess a knowledge of basic information from the social sciences which encourage competence as responsible citizens.*

   Explanation: For purposes of socialization(including national loyalty and pride) students should acquire and be able to share a body of knowledge (knowledge assumed common to the educated American public) which contributes to their civic competence.

   Students will learn this body of select content from each of the seven social science disciplines; with lesser emphasis on Anthropology, Sociology, Economics, and Psychology, and greater emphasis on History, Geography, and Political Science.

2. *Be able to apply inquiry skills used by social scientists.*

   Explanation: Skills include --

   Inquiry steps used to acquire new knowledge:

   a. *stating the problem*
   b. *selecting data sources (data sources used are primary sources)*
   c. *collecting data (techniques include direct and indirect observation)*
   d. *processing data (use of charts, graphs, tables)*
   e. *making inferences from processed data.*

   Inquiry steps used with secondary sources:
   a. *data collecting (students use textbooks, encyclopedias, and other secondary sources)*
   b. *data organizing (emphasis on development of communication skills: reading, writing, constructing graphs, charts, tables)*

c. *presentation of organized data (emphasis on development of communication skills: reading, writing, oral presentation)*

3. *Be able to demonstrate positive intra- and inter-personal behaviors.*

    Explanation: As a result of participation in activities which develop and strengthen social interaction skills and encourage selection of personally held and cherished values, students will be able to compare, clarify, critique, and evaluate their own behaviors on the basis of democratic principles, other people's needs, empathy, and their own self-concept.

4. *Have grown in their appreciation and understanding of other cultures and ethnic groups.*

    Explanation: Students will acquire a knowledge of the world's people and an understanding of the United States as a member of a global community. They will realize cultural linkages between other parts of the world and the United States, and between American policies and practices and other parts of the world. Empathy with all members of the world community is the ultimate goal.

To help you better understand the power of goal statements when planning department course offerings, let us consider the expectations embodied in the four goal statements. Goal #1 assumes development of a minimal body of knowledge for all students to master. Suppose you asked a young adult:

"Who was the first president of the United States? or, Name the capital of our country? or, What ocean borders California? or, What was a major issue in the War Between the States? or, Was Japan a friend or foe during World War II? or ... ; "

and the person could answer none of these questions? What would you think about that person's education? You would not expect such a response from the typical young American who experienced the typical American schooling. Most social science educators believe there is a minimal body of common knowledge that all citizens should possess, and that this body of knowledge of a common history and culture serves to bond individual members of the society into a united people; a people who because they possess so much in common, their heritage, feel that they belong together.

Goals #2,3,4 provide an area of special interest. Their accomplishment will require teachers and students to adopt classroom behaviors different from the traditional. Goal #2 requires development and application of inquiry skills. Therefore, students will become researchers, seeking to generate new knowledge by solving socially related problems or answering socially related questions of interest to students, problems such as:

Use photographs as a visual response to the assignment,
-- Women's clothing styles from 1920 to the present; --

or questions such as,
-- What are the national origins of students in our school? --

will be part of the expected behavior.

Students will also be asked to respond to problems by processing data gathered from secondary sources and reporting these findings to the class. A direction, such as

-- "Peter, Manuel, and Roberta: Your assignment is to learn about life among Aztec Indians before the arrival of Europeans. Organize your information into a ten minute report and present your report to the class;" --

encourages students to utilize a wide range of communication skills.

The emphasis, as expressed in goal #3 on values, will require students to participate in activities which develop and strengthen social interaction skills. Values clarification strategies, such as role playing, sensitivity models, values continua, values voting, consensus forming strategies, and moral reasoning through solving dilemmas, will be used.

Finally, goal #4 directs that content be identified and taught which focuses on global understanding. Interdependence and acceptance among nations and peoples will be highlighted, and the United States will be pictured as but one of many nations in a global community.

Selected content and teaching strategies will encourage children to internalize the generalization: all persons are equally human; all persons have the right to adequate diet, clothing, shelter, and a happy life. Truly, the department goal statements for Forestville High School, if taken seriously, should direct construction of a quality social science program.

Writing Course Rationale[7]

You may choose to write a rationale/department philosophy to introduce courses/department offerings that are part of the instructional program. Therefore, courses, such as:

eighth grade industrial arts, kindergarten language arts, grade six computer literacy;

or a single year or semester offering of a high school department, such as:

Freshman English, Typing II, Latin IV, Bach to Rock, and Consumer Education

may be headed with a statement entitled, the course rationale. A course rationale may be used to defend inclusion of the course in the program, and/or show how the course articulates with other courses in the program/department, and/or how it supports the program rationale/department philosophy.

Art Program Scenario, Part 3

Again your parents ask about the art program offered in your school. They announce,

"You know, our child will be in third grade this year. We are especially interested to learn more about the third grade art program."

---

[7] Henceforth, the term, course, will be used to identify all instructional levels; that is -- age level/grade level/high school course level, instructional and co-curricular offerings.

Commonly agreed to levels are age levels for N-K programs (mathematics for pre-kindergarten); grade levels for K-8 curriculum programs (seventh grade physical education and health, grade three social studies, grade six music, grade one reading); high school department curriculum programs (American History, Kapelle, Physics II, Journalism I, Freshman Art, Woodworking, Advance Typing).

You respond,

"Let me begin by directing your attention to the rationale written by our art curriculum committee for the third grade course of study. You will note that it shows you how the third grade course fits into the total K-8 program. It speaks to learning achieved so far and learning that will follow. It will help you to understand the role of grade three art within the total art curriculum. Each of our grade level courses of study is headed with a rationale."

The following is a statement of rationale that discusses the role of a Freshman English course for low level achievers.

ENGLISH I -- OPPORTUNITY LEVEL --

Department Rationale:

In our district, the shift from a small elementary, K-8 school to a large high school proves, for most students, to be a major and sometimes, traumatic adjustment. New problems are confronted for which students have little experience. The move from a neighborhood environment with immediate friends under the tutelage of an individual classroom teacher for each grade to the high school with its confusing array of unfamiliar problems is a critical period in young peoples' lives. Establishing a sense of security, forming worthwhile friendships among fellow students, and building a rapport between pupils and teachers are aspects of an orientation that require more time and effort than usually afforded in freshman courses.

The language arts curriculum at Concordia High School is tracked on four levels, denoted Alpha, Beta, Gamma, and Opportunity. The curriculum for each level is specifically tailored to aid students assigned to that level. Concordia ninth grade students are assigned to Opportunity English if their Classification Index on the Otis Lennen I.Q. score is below 88 combined with a reading score on the Davis scale below the 20th percentile. ...

Opportunity Class students come to Concordia High School with student folders that read much the same -- poor self-image, discipline problem, emotionally maladjusted, socially maladjusted. Opportunity class size is usually limited to eighteen students. ...

If there is a dominant characteristic of this group, it is a defeatist attitude toward accomplishment in school. However, language arts offerings can make possible a fuller measure of development helping these students. A dominant characteristic of Opportunity Classes is the belief each student can succeed in meaningful activities within their intellectual levels.

In Opportunity Class groups **nothing succeeds like success**. Activities and procedures employed in an Opportunities Class plan that each student succeeds. Therefore, the task of each opportunity class teacher is to:

a. Determine the abilities of each student in all language arts areas.
b. Promote each student's optimum growth in the language skills.
c. Provide continuing experience in reading, writing, spelling, and basic grammatical skills throughout the year.
d. Provide at least three different activities per period.
e. Identify those students who will profit by eventual transfer to Gamma classes and provide background for such transfer.
f. Provide opportunities for success in all areas of the English curriculum.

Writing Course Objectives[8]

Course objectives are written as definitions of expected student learning resulting from instruction. They describe the course related competencies students should possess when they have completed the course.

Art Program Scenario, Part 4

The parents are delighted with the careful thought put into formation of your art program. They ask for more information.

"We are impressed with your thoroughness. We can see how grade three fits into the total art education program in your school, but tell us," they continue, "what specifically will our child learn about art while in third grade? Can you specify any knowledge or skills our child will get?"
You are flattered with their interest and appreciation.

---

[8] The term, **course objective**, will be used to identify early childhood/elementary school grade level and high school course objectives. Therefore, objectives for high school course titles, such as Chemistry I, Dramatic Arts II, Advanced Foods, French IV, Accounting, Journalism, and for (N)K-8 grade level subjects, such as Grade Three Reading, Grade Six Music, Grade Eight Girls' Physical Education, Early Childhood Mathematics, will be identified as course objectives.

"Certainly," you respond. "We have a set of objectives written for each grade level. These objectives specify what competencies we believe our typical third grader will possess when ending the school year. You should become familiar with these objectives so you know what learning outcomes to expect. We hope you will help us as we teach toward them."

Illinois State Language Arts Program

Objectives are written to define **grade level** learning outcomes for each of the language arts learning goals. Since there are six Learning Goals, there are, in a completed curriculum guide, six sets of objectives written for each grade level.

The objectives for Learning Goal #5 at grade level 3 are listed below.

Each objective is keyed to one of the General Knowledge/Skills Related to Learning Goals #5, A-H listed on page 53.

Language Arts, Grade Three

State Goals for Learning 5

As a result of their schooling, students will be able to understand the various forms of significant literature representative of different cultures, era, and ideas.

Sample Learning Objectives for Goal 5

By the end of <u>GRADE 3</u> students should be able to:

A1.   Recognize a given literary work as a poem.
A2.   Recognize that not all poetry rhymes.
A3.   Identify various types of poetry: riddles, chants, tongue twisters, nonsense verse, jump-rope rhymes.
A4.   Recognize nursery and Mother Goose rhymes.
A5.   Recognize a given literary work as prose.
A6.   Recognize a given literary work as a play.

B1.   *Recognize the factual nature of biography and autobiography.*

C1.   *Compare English, American, and non-English versions of the same folktale.*

D1.   *Identify words, phrases, descriptions and events which indicate whether a given work takes place in the past or in the present.*

D2.   *Compare similar stories from two different time settings.*

E1.   *Recognize cultural differences shown in a given work: holidays, clothing, dances, language.*

F1.   *Recognize the plot sequence and actions of the major characters in a given literary work.*

F2.   *Identify the setting of a given literary work.*

F3.   *Identify important traits of the main characters in a given literary work.*

F4.   *Explain causes for character behavior.*

F5.   *Identify ways in which characters change throughout a story.*

G1.   *Recognize simple similes in a given work.*

G2.   *Identify personification and onomatopoeia in given literary works.*

H1.   *Recognize the main idea of a given literary work.*

———————

Note that objectives A1 through A6 are keyed to **Knowledge/Skills** associated with

    A. Learning Differences Among Poetry, Drama, Fiction, and Nonfiction.

Also, objective B1 is keyed to **Knowledge/Skills** associated with

    B. Learning Differences Among the Types of Factual Literature.   etc.

Below are objectives for a grade eight course in a K-12 music program.

OTTO HAASCH SCHOOL DISTRICT

MUSIC PROGRAM -- K-12

The instructional content of the District Music Program is organized as a three strand spiral curriculum. The strands **General Music, Instrumental Music, and Choral Music** provide the focus for planning each year's instruction.

The objectives for the eighth grade music program are listed below:

General Music Strand -- Grade Eight

By the end of grade eight, students will be able to:

1. *Describe selected major concepts and events associated with popular music.*
2. *Sing selected popular music compositions.*
3. *Compose a "popular song."*
   ...

Instrumental Music Strand -- Grade Eight

By the end of grade eight, students will be able to:

1. *Play all major scales at eighth note = 120, and all harmonic minor scales at quarter note = 120.*
2. *Describe the structure of a harmonic minor scale.*
3. *Tune instruments correctly 50% of the time.*
   ...

Choral Music Strand -- Grade Eight

By the end of grade eight, students will be able to:

1. *Maintain the proper posture for singing.*
2. *Sight-read selected two part songs.*
3. *Sing selected three and four part songs.*
   ...

Writing Unit Rationale

The term, unit, is loosely defined as a select set of learning experiences bonded with a common purpose. A unit may be a learning or interest center, a learning activity package, and independent study selection, a major project, a theme, a topic study, a resource unit, a teaching unit, or other long term teaching/learning sequences.

Units are often prefixed with a statement entitled: Rationale or Significance. A unit rationale is a statement that defends the inclusion of the unit in the course, shows how the unit articulates with other units in the course, and shows how it supports the course rationale.

Art Program Scenario, Part 5

Since your parents have shown such a keen interest in the art program, you offer to share an overview of the grade three course of study with them. You say,

"Our grade three course is made-up of nine study units. Each unit is prefaced with a rationale that helps the teacher see the reason for including that unit in the grade level course of study. It also tells the teacher how the unit relates to the other units at that grade level. You may wish to examine our units and read some of the rationales."

Below is a rationale for an alcohol abuse unit. The unit is part of the Hillside Junior High School science course.

HILLSIDE JUNIOR HIGH SCHOOL

SCIENCE UNIT -- FREE TO CHOOSE

Rationale -- Alcohol Abuse Unit

This unit is included as part of the health education component of the science program. It relates to that part of health education identified as defense against chemical abuse. It provides a basis for students to make responsible physical and mental health decisions. Need for this unit is demonstrated by the following statistics:

* 2/3 of 7th grade boys and 1/2 of 7th grade girls have already had one drink.
* As many as one in five seventh grade boys drinks beer at least once a week.
* 1/4 of all seventh graders report having been drunk one or more times in the past year.
* Before high school most students will have experienced peer pressure to drink.

Writing Unit Objectives[6]

Art Program Scenario, Part 6

Your parents examine the several unit plans. They note that each unit begins with a rationale and follows with a set of unit objectives. They tell you,

"We know now what these objectives are. They tell us what our child should be able to learn from each unit. It's reassuring to know that these learning outcomes are so clearly and understandably stated. We feel confident our child will find this to be an excellent school."

The writer of the Alcohol Education unit included the following unit objectives:

By the end of this unit, students will be able to:

*   *identify the psychological effects of alcohol.*
*   *identify the effects alcohol has on their lives socially and on the lives of others.*

Writing Lesson Objectives[7]

The most specific form of objectives you will write is lesson objectives. They identify intended student learning outcomes resulting from a single learning experience. These are the statements which are a part of every lesson plan. Some of the lesson objectives for the unit, Alcohol Education, are listed below.

---

[6] The term, objective, will also be used to designate unit and lesson learning outcomes. At the unit level, the term used will be unit objective, and at the lesson level, lesson objective. Therefore, we will use the terms course/grade level objective, unit objective, and lesson objective.

[7] A more comprehensive discussion of grade level, course, unit and lesson objectives is found in chapter four.

By the end of this lesson, students should be able to:

* *identify the amount of alcohol contained in beer, wine, and whiskey.*
* *identify the amount of alcohol necessary for intoxication.*
* *examine their own values regarding drinking.*

A Hierarchy of Outcome Statements

You will get a clearer understanding of how school goals, program goals, course objectives, unit objectives, and lesson objectives may be incorporated within the curricular structure by examining an array of learning outcome statements that range from school goals to individual lesson plan objectives.

Below is a school goal from the Wagner High School and one department goal statement. At the next lower level a course objective is listed as part of the focus for a course, Consumer Mathematics. One unit of the Consumer Mathematics course is singled out -- Mathematics for Banking -- and a unit objective is listed. Supporting the unit objective are three of the several lesson objectives.

As a result of their schooling, Wagner High School students should be able to:

* *Apply those basic and fundamental processes necessary for productive membership in the community.*
    ...

As a result of their learning experiences within the Mathematics Department, students should be able to:

* *Apply those basic and fundamental mathematics processes necessary for productive membership in the community.*
    ...

By the end of the course, Consumer Mathematics, students should be able to:

* *Demonstrate mastery of mathematics processes as measured in the District's <u>Basic Mathematics Competency Test</u>.*
    ...

By the end of the unit, Mathematics for Banking, students should be able to:

* *Correctly maintain a checking account -- writing checks and other forms, showing deposits, withdrawals, and account balances.*

   ...

By the end of this lesson, students should be able to:

* *Correctly write information on the face of a check.*

   ...

By the end of this lesson, students should be able to:

* *Correctly show deposits and check drafts in a sample set of ten transactions.*

   ...

By the end of this lesson, students should be able to:

* *Use a monthly balance statement to verify check transactions.*

   ...

Summary

Schooling is the process of affecting change in students. Goals and objectives are statements which describe the changed students.

The variety of instructional programs offered by a school should be orchestrated as a single set of integrated learning experiences, where each instructional program is related to all other instructional programs, and where each component in an instructional program is related to all other components in that program/department. The educational philosophy, or mission statement, and the program/department course and unit rationale describe linkages within and among the various parts of the curriculum. Each broader statement holds within it the values from which each narrower statement is generated.

School goals describe the overall purpose of schooling. Program/department goals are learning outcome statements, usually general in nature, which define curricula. Objectives define learning outcomes for course, units, and lessons.

The school goals, program/department goals, course objectives, unit objectives, and lesson objectives should show an obvious relationship to each other. Each narrower purpose statement establishes its validity from the broader purpose statement.

Rationale and purpose statements form the curriculum skeleton to which instructional content, methodologies, and evaluation strategies are set.

Chapter Four

Writing Objectives

Several years ago my daughter-in-law, a bright, energetic, beginning teacher, telephoned from Minnesota to ask for assistance. She was teaching third grade children. She asked,
  "Pop, do you have any material on Eskimos? I'm going to teach a unit on Eskimos and I need some ideas?"

Rather than answer her question immediately, I did what curriculum instructors are apt to do. I asked,
  "Why do you want to teach about Eskimos?"

After some hesitation, she replied,
  "Because I'm supposed to."

I probed,
  "Why are you supposed to? What good will it do?"
  "They should know about them," she answered.
  "Why?"
  "We always teach Eskimos in third grade."
  "Why"
  "It's in the book."
  "Aha!" I mused smugly. "It's in the book."

Then I suggested,
  "Think with me. What good is instructional content? Why does a teacher decide to teach something to children? Isn't it because the teacher wants to change them?

A faltering,
  "I guess so," struggled across the wires.

I concluded with the following admonition:
  "Content is used to teach learning objectives. These objectives are descriptions of how students will be when changed. A primary instructional concern is: How does the teacher intend to change the pupils? These intended changes are the instructional objectives."

Because we were discussing a social studies unit, I suggested that she identify objectives related to social studies knowledge, skills, and attitudes.

    "Ask yourself these questions," I added, "When the unit is finished,

        What do I want the children to know?
        What do I want them to be able to do?
        And how do I want them to feel about certain things?

If you find the answers to these questions you have generated worthwhile objective statements when considering Eskimos; then I urge that you pursue development of the unit and I will help you find materials. If, however, you find nothing more than trivial changes resulting from the study, select something else to teach."

In this chapter we will examine objectives with respect to their:

* structure,
* specificity, and
* function.

We will look at the essential parts of objectives.

We will rank objectives with regard to how specifically they define learning outcomes.

We will consider a sampling of ways in which you may use objectives to construct curriculum.

Finally, we will examine how objectives can be used to target the kind and level of knowledge you wish students to achieve.

Learning Outcomes as Learning Objectives

Learning objectives state student behaviors expected as a result of instruction. They describe the changed students after the learning experience has ended.

+ Instruction is the process of changing students.
+ Learning objectives describe students after the change is complete.

Learning objectives do not describe how the change will be effected. They do not identify the condition of learners before the change process begins. They simply state:

At the end of this learning experience, the students will ... .

Focus on Learner

Learning objectives focus on the student. Compare the two statements below.

1. *Students should understand how a bill becomes a law.*

2. *Teachers should increase the students' understanding of how a bill becomes a law.*

The first statement describes an expected student outcome from instruction. The students will possess some knowledge. The second statement is not an appropriate learning objective because it focuses on the teachers. It suggests that teacher competence is the primary concern.

Focus on Outcomes

Learning objectives should focus on learning outcomes. On what do the following statements focus?

1. *Students should gain knowledge of the basic cycles that occur in an ecosystem.*

2. *Students should understand the basic cycles that occur in an ecosystem.*

Both statements express student behavior. The second one is preferred because it indicates what students will know at the **end** of instruction. The first statement is not appropriate because it emphasizes the learning process, rather than a learning outcome.

As you write objectives guard that your statements do not become descriptions of, or directions for, class time activities. Which of the following statements suggest class time activities?

1. *Students will read pages 16-20 in the text.*

2. Students will view the filmstrip, "Perception in Drawing."

3. Students will be able to correctly write answers to the assessment questions on page 17.

4. Students will be able to demonstrate an understanding of perspective through pencil drawing.

Statements 1 and 2 speak to the instructing process rather than the product of that process. They are directives toward reaching an objective. The statements tell the teacher what activities to include in the lesson. Statements 3 and 4 define competencies students should possess following instruction.

Describing instructional intent in terms of outcomes provides greater direction for planning, carrying out, and evaluating learning than does stating suggestions for class time activities.

Essential Parts of Learning Objectives

A learning objective should have at least three parts:

1. Standard preface
2. Verb
3. Description of the behavior

Standard Preface

Each set of objectives should begin with the same preface. Examples of acceptable prefaces are:

1. By the end of this lesson, students should be able to ...
2. By the end of this unit, students should be able to ...
3. By the end of this chapter, students should be able to ...
4. By the end of this course, students should be able to ...
5. By the end of this grade, students should be able to ...

This style preface places the focus of the objective on the students and tailors the objective to the students' learning situation.

Verb

The second part of an objective is the verb which assigns the behavior or activity the learner should perform. The verb is highlighted in each of the learning objectives below.

+ *By the end of this course, students should **know** the history of the Plymouth Colony.*

+ *By the end of this grade, students will be able to **recognize** ways that a music theme is varied in a recorded example.*

+ *By the end of this chapter, students should be able to **construct** right, acute, and obtuse triangles.*

+ *By the end of this lesson, students will be able to, when given samples of ten substances, **identify** each substance as a gas, a liquid, or a solid with 90% accuracy.*

Description of the Behavior

The third essential part of a learning objective describes the competency that students should demonstrate. The description is highlighted in each learning objective below.

+ *By the end of this course, students should understand **how classical and baroque architecture differ**.*

+ *By the end of this grade, students should be able to **follow a theme in an oral presentation from its introduction to its conclusion**.*

+ *By the end of this unit, students should be able to **write statments that summarize the intended message of the newspaper cartoonist**.*

+ *By the end of this lesson, students should be able to **select from a list of statments the one that best summarizes the opinion of the editorial**.*

Level of Specificity

All learning objectives use verbs to identify a changed behavior. The change may be

* non-observable;
* observable and measurable, but not referenced to a criterion;
* observed, measured, and referenced to a criterion.

Objectives That Are Not Observable

An objective may use a verb that describes a non-observable behavioral change. Examples of frequently used non-observed behaviors include:

appreciate	grasp	discern	master
ascertain	feel	remember	believe
perceive	regard	comprehend	fathom

The following verbs describe non-observable behaviors:

+ *By the end of this course, students should understand the carbon, oxygen, and nitrogen cycles.*

+ *By the end of this course, students should know the history of the Plymouth Colony.*

+ *By the end of this course, students should realize the differences between classical and baroque architecture.*

While these verbs indicate a behavioral change resulting from instruction, they offer no clear indicator to determine if a change has taken place.

Objectives That Are Observable and Measurable, but Not Referenced to A Criterion

An objective that describes an observed behavior uses an **action** verb to indicate evidence of the change. Action verbs describe a behavior or activity learners should be able to perform as a result of learning. With some verbs the action is difficult to observe. Other verbs display a more obvious action. The product of readily observed actions are easier to measure. Examples of somewhat irresolute action verbs include:

relate	evaluate	contrast	show	organize
merge	critique	define	assist	assess

observe   diagnose   demonstrate   synthesize   facilitate

The level of observation and measurement of an objective is also influenced by that part of the objective called the description of the behavior. Consider the following objectives:

a. *By the end of this lesson, students should be able to recognize how political party platforms influence the voting practices of those elected officials running on those platforms.*

b. *By the end of this lesson, students should be able to recognize the difference between transitive and intransitive verbs when used in sentences.*

Observation and measurement of objective (a) is demanding, for recognition of degree of influence is obscure, making judgment of mastery difficult. In objective (b), judgment of whether students recognize transitive verbs as "carrying" action from subject to direct object, and intransitive verbs as linking a redundancy between subject and predicate nominative or linking the predicate adjective as modifier of the subject is obvious.

The following statements demonstrate use of not easily observed and measured objectives:

+ *By the end of this grade, students should be able to follow the development of a plot in a selected novel from its introduction to its conclusion.*

+ *By the end of this grade, students should be able to analyze how body line, shape, space, time and energy interact in a dance.*

+ *By the end of this grade, students should be able to show ways that a music theme is varied in a recorded example.*

While the above objectives specify actions as evidence of achievement, it is not easy to observe and measure how well the actions were performed. Measurement of student competence is aided when actions are simple to assess, when the behavior is sufficiently obvious so an observer can judge degree of mastery. Examples of more observable and measurable actions include:

trace	write	identify	find	name
tell	read	assemble	list	state
draw	select	define	build	choose

The following objectives suggest behaviors that are easier to observe and measure:

+ *By the end of this chapter, students should be able to list differences between classical and baroque architecture.*

+ *By the end of this chapter, students should be able to construct right, acute, and obtuse triangles.*

+ *By the end of this lesson, students should be able to write statements that summarize the intended message of a newspaper cartoonist.*

+ *By the end of this chapter, students should be able to demonstrate the proper way to display the United States flag.*

+ *By the end of this chapter, students should be able to distinguish between renewable and nonrenewable resources.*

+ *By the end of this grade, students should be able to perform a variety of physical activities that require cooperation, direct physical assistance, and partner relationships.*

+ *By the end of this grade, students should be able to predict how the United States would be different if settlement and colonization began on the West Coast and move eastward.*

+ *By the end of this chapter, students should be able to compose a four page theme describing the history of Plymouth Colony. The theme will include one structurally correct paragraph each on the topics:*

    (1) leaving England,
    (2) the stay in Holland,
    (3) the trip in the Mayflower,
    (4) the arrival to Plymouth,

(5) the first winter,
(6) the first growing season,
(7) the first Thanksgiving.

Objectives That Are Observed, Measured, and Referenced to A Criterion

When the design of the curriculum requires objectives in which the behavior is observed, measured, and referenced to a specific level of competence, criterion referenced objectives are the appropriate choice. Criterion referenced objectives state a minimum acceptable level of satisfactory task performance. The following are examples of criterion referenced objectives:

By the end of this lesson, students will be able to:

+ *locate, on an outline map, 48 of the 50 United States.*

+ *write a poem with Haiku characteristics, that the teacher judges acceptable.*

By the end of this unit, students should be able to:

+ *select from a list of 21 sentences, those which state facts and those that state inferences, with 70% accuracy.*

+ *classify vowels in 20 single syllable words as either long or short with 90 percent accuracy.*

+ *match, with 80% accuracy, the names of the elements listed on a periodic chart of the atoms with their respective symbols.*

By the end of this chapter, students should be able to:

+ *complete the chapter examination with 90% accuracy.*

+ *correctly answer 90% of the chapter test items correctly.*

A form of criterion referenced objective that defines a specific environment in which the task is to completed may be desirable for some curriculum models. This form of the criterion referenced objective adds as a first stipulation, the condition under which students must function. The example below illustrates the rule:

+ *By the end of this unit, students should be able,* **without use of a textbook,** *to hand compute with 80% accuracy, 10 problems involving division of whole numbers less than 5 by the fraction 3/4.*

The required criteria are identified as:

1. Condition -- without the use of a textbook.
2. Specific task -- hand compute 10 problems involving division of whole numbers less than 5 by the fraction 3/4.
3. Minimum acceptable level -- 80% accuracy.

The following are observed, measured, reference learning objectives that state the condition under which students must function:

By the end of this lesson, students will be able to:

+ *when given representative samples of ten substances, identify each substance as a gas, a liquid, or a solid with 90% accuracy.*

+ *when given copies of two different national school news publications written for 10 - 12 year old students cite an example of at least one content and one format difference among them, that the teacher judges acceptable.*

+ *when given a blank standard size paper, standard electric typewriter, and a 420 word script, type the script at a minimum speed of 60 words per minute with no more than 3 errors, during a four minute timed typing test.*

Selecting Level of Specificity

There is no single, best level of specificity to use when writing good learning objectives. There are times when they should be written so the expected behavior is clearly observed, readily measured, and easily referenced to a set criterion. However, the use of criterion reference objectives is usually limited to situations where success of a subsequent objective is dependent on mastery of the previous objective, and evidence of mastery is necessary for monitoring student progress. Many computer assisted instructional programs employ a "built-in" criterion reference objective structure.

Other times the behavior required to show mastery of objectives need not be referenced. Your lesson plan objectives will usually be written so they are observable and measurable, but without a specified mastery criterion stated. Absence of written mastery criteria in the objective does not suggest that no standard exists. When you evaluate students' work, you provide the criteria. It may be assignment of grades based on number wrong, or quality of writing, or level of thinking displayed. Whenever you evaluate students' work, you compare the work to a standard. The question, when writing objectives is, do you wish to write the standard into the objective, or do you prefer that decision be left to a later time.

Sometimes the behavior need not be readily observed. If you decide that a criterion should not be part of the objective, you also may prefer to deliberately allow for a variety of ways to observe and measure objectives. Such decisions are often made when writing objectives for elementary school grade levels or high school courses. Consider the following:

a. *By the end of this course, students should be able to diagram and label the stages in the carbon, oxygen, and nitrogen cycles.*

b. *By the end of this course, students should understand the carbon, oxygen, and nitrogen cycles.*

c. *By the end of this unit, students should be able to list the steps necessary for a bill to become a law.*

d. *By the end of this unit, students should know how a bill becomes a law.*

You may not wish to limit evaluation of student competence through use of a diagraming or listing assignment, but rather allow teachers to choose evaluation methods. Some teachers may use an objective test format, others a written or oral report, or perhaps use of an interview. Objectives (b) and (d) give teachers the freedom to select their own evaluation strategies.

A guiding principle when writing good instructional objectives is that instructional objectives should be written so they best serve the needs of good instruction. They should guide learning as they relate to

a. form of the instructional content, (cognitive, psychomotor, affective domain);

b. kind of teaching strategies, (expository, inquiry, reflective thinking, values analysis, creative expression); and

c. desired evaluation methods (criterion, norm, self-referenced).

Enabling Objectives and Terminal Objectives

Enabling objectives, as the term suggests, assist attainment toward an end. Terminal objectives define the state of that end. Enabling objectives may be lesson objectives which lead to mastery of the terminal objective, the unit objectives. Unit objectives are considered enabling objectives when they lead to fulfillment of course objectives. Enabling objectives are sub-competencies to be mastered as the learner moves toward mastery of the terminal objective, the target competency.

In a skill oriented subject such as mathematics, and when mastering selected skills in physical education, music, reading, geography, --- in fact any subject where a defined sequence is desired, --- enabling objectives may be ordered as a hierarchical sequence of prerequisite learning. When organizing non-sequential learning, a composite of the several enabling objectives may result in mastery of the terminal objective.

Since learning objectives describe student competency after a learning experience is completed, you will use learning objectives to identify the terminal behaviors to be mastered at the end of a series of lessons, as well as use learning objectives to identify the enabling behaviors expected following teaching of each individual lesson. Thus, both terminal and enabling objectives (in this case unit and lesson objectives) will be written using the learning objectives structure, standard preface, verb, and description of behavior.

A unit objective (terminal objective) might read:

At the end of this unit:

*   *Given selected story introductory data, the learner will be able to supply additional relevant and complementary data, and to develop and complete a plausible story line.*

Five lesson objectives (enabling objectives) might read:

At the end of this lesson:

a.   *Given a story that describes a specific incident, the learner will identify the sentence that best implies a logical result from the incident.*

b.   *Given an incomplete paragraph, the learner will write a concluding sentence that the teacher judges acceptable.*

c.   *Given an incomplete story, the learner will write a one paragraph ending that the teacher judges acceptable.*

d.   *Given the beginning of a story, the learner will write a developmental paragraph and an ending paragraph that the teacher judges acceptable.*

e.   *Given a set of circumstances surrounding a story character, the learner will write a one to two page story about the character that the teacher judges acceptable.*

Teacher Directed Statements

Some teachers find it helpful to include teacher goals as part of a unit or lesson. These statements direct teacher action during instruction. They assist by sharpening the focus of instruction and by setting boundaries which redirect instruction back to main purposes. They speak directly to the teacher role rather than to student outcome, and therefore may provide additional clarification of intent for instruction. Below is a sample of one teacher's attempt to provide both teacher goals and student objectives.

BANKING UNIT

Teacher Goals

1. *To develop in students an awareness of banking as an occupational interest.*

2. *To increase student knowledge of the process of banking.*

3. *To provide students opportunities for problem solving using critical thinking.*

4. *To broaden student experience by introducing cross-subject matter concepts and skills into an activity-centered learning situation.*

5. *To stimulate student respect for individuals, regardless of their occupation.*

Student Objectives

At the end of this unit, students will be able to:

1. *Define the term, bank.*

2. *Identify a minimum of four different types of banks.*

3. *Identify a minimum of ten workers in the bank and describe briefly the duties of each.*

4. *Utilize multiplication skills when solving simple money/interest problems relating to banking. ...*

Taxonomy of Educational Objectives

Many years ago Herbert Spencer asked,
"What knowledge is of most worth?"

He asked the question as a guide for identifying major school goals. Our concern is writing objectives that lead to attainment of school goals. An appropriate question for us to ask might be:

"What kinds of learning outcomes are of most worth?

If you teach toward mastery of objectives, the worthiness of the objective is a primary concern. If instructional objectives are limited to remembering facts, no problem solving skills will be learned. If value education is an important process, then instruction toward affective objectives must be included.

In order to discuss the various levels of objectives, several taxonomies have been developed. Some educators simply separate objectives as low level and high level -- where low level objectives solicit behaviors such as recall and understanding, and high level objectives require students to reason as part of problem solving by sorting, comparing, analyzing, and evaluating.

For example, consider the two objective statements below:

   a. *After reading the chapter, "Curriculum Designs," students will be able to name the three major curriculum design groups.*

   b. *After reading the poem, "O Captain," students will be able to infer who Walt Whitman is eulogizing.*

   c. *After listening to a lecture on playground rules, students will be able to explain why throwing snowballs is forbidden.*

   d. *After reading the book, The History of 20th Century Education in America, students will be able to predict an emphasis in education in the year 2000.*

Objectives a and c suggest low level student behaviors such as simple recall and evidence that the content of a lecture was understood. Objectives b and d require students to infer and predict, both high level expectations.

Benjamin Bloom and others developed a system for organizing educational objectives into three major classes -- cognitive, affective, and psychomotor domains, and each class into levels. The cognitive domain includes those objectives which deal with recall or recognition of knowledge and of intellectual abilities and skills.

The affective domain includes objectives which describe changes in interest, attitudes, and values, and the development of appreciations and adequate adjustments. The psychomotor domain is directed toward physically oriented competencies. Our interests will be limited to the cognitive and affective domains.

The Cognitive Domain

The Bloom taxonomy (Bloom, 1965) has six levels of cognition:

1. knowledge,
2. comprehension,
3. application,
4. analysis,
5. synthesis, and
6. evaluation.

Following a definition of each level of cognition, behavioral (action) verbs, general instructional objectives, and specific examples of objectives are provided.

Knowledge

Knowledge is defined as the remembering of previously learned material. This may involve the recall of a wide range of material, from specific facts to complete theories. Included are methods and processes, patterns, structures, and settings.

All that is required is the bringing to mind of the appropriate information. If one thinks of the mind as a file, the process is that of finding in the problem or task the appropriate signals, cues, and clues that most effectively retrieve whatever information is filed or stored.

Knowledge represents the lowest level of learning outcome in the cognitive domain.

Illustrative Behavioral (action) Terms

Defines, describes, identifies, labels, lists, matches, names, outlines, reproduces, selects, states, ...

Illustrative General Instructional Objectives

* *Students*   *label common terms.*
*   *name specific facts.*
*   *know methods and procedures.*
*   *list basic concepts.*
*   *select principles.*

Specific examples

At the end of instruction,

* *Students will identify the four components that make up curriculum development.*

* *Students will list the major parts in a unit plan.*

* *Students will name the six levels in Bloom's taxonomy of cognitive knowledge.*

Comprehension

Comprehension is defined as the ability to grasp the meaning of material. The individual knows what is being communicated and can use the material of information without necessarily relating it to other material or seeing its fullest implications.

Students are expected to give reasons for things; to show they understand the information -- not merely possess information. Understanding may be shown by translating material from one form to another (words to numbers), by interpreting material (explaining or summarizing), and by estimating future trends (predicting consequences or effects).

These learning outcomes go one step beyond the simple remembering of material, and represent the lowest level of understanding. Objectives require convergence of thought.

Illustrative Behavioral (action) Terms

Converts, defines, distinguishes, estimates, explains, extends, generalizes, gives examples, infers, paraphrases, predicts, rewrites, summarizes, ...

Illustrative General Instructional Objectives

* *Students* *understand facts and principles.*
* *interpret verbal material.*
* *explain charts and graphs.*
* *translate verbal material to mathematical formulas.*
* *estimate future consequences implied in data.*
* *justify methods and procedures.*

Specific Examples

At the end of instruction,

* *Students will describe what is meant by the term, instructional objective.*

* *Students will explain the steps in constructing a curriculum using the perspective -- Instructional Content First: Then Goals.*

* *Students will define each of the six levels in Bloom's taxonomy of cognitive knowledge.*

Application

Application requires students to use learned material in new and concrete situations. This may include the application of such things as rules, methods, concepts, principles, laws, and theories. Since the cognition taxonomy is arranged as a hierarchy, each higher classification holds within it the lower levels.

Application requires both knowledge and comprehension.
Therefore students must know an abstraction well enough so they can correctly demonstrate its use when the use and mode of solution is specified. Students suggest actual uses of ideas.

They identify novel situations in which an event, thing, or idea occurs.

Illustrative Behavioral (action) Terms

Changes, computes, demonstrates, discovers, manipulates, modifies, operates, predicts, prepares, produces, relates, shows, solves, uses, ...

Illustrative General Instructional Objectives

*	*Students*	*relate concepts and principles to new situations.*
*		*apply laws and theories to practical situations.*
*		*solve mathematical problems.*
*		*construct charts and graphs.*
*		*demonstrate correct usage of a method or procedure.*

Specific Examples

At the end of instruction,

* *Students will select a subject matter and write one objective statement at each of the six levels of Bloom's cognitive taxonomy.*

* *Students will select a subject matter and construct a criterion referenced objective.*

* *Students will select a subject matter and prepare a lesson plan in which the three basic components: introduction, body, and conclusion are a part.*

Analysis

Analysis requires students to perceive relationships. It refers to the ability to break down material into its component parts so that its organizational structure may be understood. This may include the identification of the parts, analysis of the relationships between parts, and recognition of the organizational principles involved.

Students are expected to differentiate, determine structures, and identify patterns. An understanding of both the content and the organizational form is required. Divergence of thought is tolerated.

Illustrative Behavioral (action) Terms

Breaks down, diagrams, differentiates, discriminates, distinguishes, identifies, illustrates, infers, outlines, points out, relates, selects, separates, subdivides, ...

Illustrative General Instructional Objectives

* *Students*   *recognize non-stated assumptions.*
* *identify logical fallacies in reasoning.*
* *distinguish between facts and inferences.*
* *evaluate the relevancy of data.*
* *analyze the organizational structure of a work (art, music, writing).*

Specific Examples

At the end of instruction,

* *Students will distinguish between a teaching unit and a resource unit.*

* *Students will differentiate between uses of instructional time in Christian and public schools.*

* *Students will show relationships among the several levels of goal statements, educational task through lesson objective.*

Synthesis

Synthesis requires students to put parts together to form a new whole. Components are arranged and combined to constitute a pattern and structure not clearly there before.

Students construct novel solutions to problems, create new systems. These may involve the production of a unique communication (theme or speech), a plan of operations (research proposal), or set of abstract relations (scheme for classifying information).

Learning outcomes in the area stress creative behaviors, with major emphasis on the formulation of new patterns or structures.

Illustrative Behavioral (action) Terms

Categorizes, combines, compiles, composes, creates, devises, designs, explains, generates, modifies, organizes, plans, rearranges, reconstructs, relates, reorganizes, revises, rewrites, summarizes, tells, writes, ...

Illustrative General Instructional Objectives

* *Students*   *compose a well organized theme.*
*   *give a well organized speech.*
*   *write a creative short story (or poem, or music).*
*   *propose a plan for an experiment.*
*   *integrate learning from different areas into a plan for solving a problem.*
*   *formulate a new scheme for classifying objects (or events, or ideas).*

Specific Examples

At the end of instruction,

* *Students will create a workable student centered curriculum design for an elementary school building.*

* *Students will construct a unit entitled: Our Community.*

* *Students will design the school they believe would exist if teachers had the exclusive right to determine curricula.*

Evaluation

Evaluation is concerned with the ability to judge the value of material (statement, novel, poem, research report) for a given purpose. Judgments may be quantitative or qualitative. Students make appraisals, state opinions, express feelings.

The judgments are based on definite criteria. These may be internal (organizational) or external (relevant to the purpose) criteria, and the student or the teacher may be the determiner of the criteria.
Learning outcomes at this level are highest in the cognitive hierarchy because they contain elements of all of the other categories, plus conscious value judgments based on clearly defined criteria.

Illustrative Behavioral (action) Terms

Appraises, compares, concludes, contrasts, criticizes, describes, discriminates, explains, justifies, interprets, relates, summarizes, supports, ...

Illustrative Instructional Objectives

*   *Students*   *critique written material for logical consistency.*
*   *critique the adequacy with which conclusions are supported by data.*
*   *appraise the value of a work (art, music, writing) by use of internal criteria.*
*   *judge the value of a work (art, music, writing) by use of external standards of excellence.*

Specific Examples

At the end of instruction,

* *Students will judge if values clarification strategies are appropriate for use in public schools.*

* *Students will justify use of the discovery approach as a major emphasis when teaching science.*

* *Students will declare and defend their educational philosophies.*

The Affective Domain

Bloom (Krathwohl) defines five levels of affective objectives. They are:
1. receiving,
2. responding,
3. valuing,
4. organizing, and
5. characterizing.

In the cognitive domain we were concerned that students be able to do a task when suggested. In the affective domain we are more concerned that they **do it** when it is appropriate, after they have learned that they **can do it**. Even though the school system rewards students more on a **can do** than on a **does do** basis, it is the latter that teachers usually seek.

Receiving

Receiving refers to the student's willingness to attend to particular phenomena or stimuli (classroom activities, textbooks, music, games, assignments). From a teaching standpoint it is concerned with getting, holding, and directing the student's attention.

Learning outcomes at this level range from the simple awareness that a thing exists to selective attention on the part of the learner.

Receiving represents the lowest level of learning outcome in the affective domain.

Illustrative Behavioral (action) Terms

Asks, chooses, describes, follows, gives, holds, identifies, locates, names, points to, selects, sits erect, relies, uses ...

Illustrative Instructional Objectives

* *Students*   *listen attentively to directions.*
*   *describe the importance of learning.*
*   *demonstrate sensitivity to human needs and social problems.*
*   *accept differences of race and culture.*
*   *perform classroom activities.*

Responding

Responding refers to active participation on the part of the students. At this level they not only attend to a particular phenomenon, but also react to it in some way.

Learning outcomes at this level may emphasize acquiescence in responding (read assigned material), willingness to respond (voluntarily read beyond assignment), or satisfaction in responding (read for pleasure or enjoyment).

The higher ranges of this category include those instructional objectives that are commonly classified under **interests**; that is, those that stress the seeking out and enjoyment of particular activities.

Illustrative Behavioral (action) Terms

Answers, assists, compiles, conforms, discusses, greets, helps, labels, performs, practices. presents, reads, recites, reports, selects, tells, writes, ...

Illustrative Instructional Objectives

*	*Students*	*finish assigned homework.*
*		*obey school rules.*
*		*participate in class discussion.*
*		*complete laboratory work.*
*		*volunteer for special tasks.*
*		*express interest in subject.*
*		*request opportunity to help others.*

Valuing

Valuing is concerned with the worth or value students attach to a particular object, phenomenon, or behavior. This ranges in degree from the more simple acceptance of a value (desire to improve group skills) to the more complex level of commitment (assume responsibility for the effective functioning of the group).

Valuing is based on the internalization of a set of specified values, but clues to these values are expressed in the student's overt behavior. Learning outcomes at this level are concerned with behavior that is consistent and stable enough to make the value clearly identifiable.

Instructional objectives that are commonly classified under **attitudes** and **appreciation** would fall into this category.

Illustrative Behavioral (action) Terms

Completes, describes, differentiates, explains, follows, forms, initiates, invites, joins, justifies, proposes, reads, reports, selects, shares, studies, works, ...

Illustrative Instructional Objectives

*	*Students*	*recognize the need for balance between freedom and responsibility in a democracy.*

*	*recognize the role of systematic planning in solving problems.*
*	*accept responsibility for their own behaviors.*
*	*understand and accept their own strengths and limitations.*
*	*formulate a life plan in harmony with their abilities, interests, and beliefs.*

Organizing

Organizing is concerned with bringing together different values, resolving conflicts between them, and beginning the building of an internally consistent value system. Thus the emphasis is on comparing, relating, and synthesizing values.

Learning outcomes that may be concerned with the conceptualization of a value (recognize the responsibility of each individual for improving human relations) or with the organizing of a value system (develop a vocational plan that satisfies each student's need for development of a philosophy of life) would fall into this category.

Illustrative Behavioral (action) Terms

Adheres, alters, arranges, combines, compares, completes, defends, explains, generalizes, identifies, integrates, modifies, orders, organizes, prepares, relates, synthesizes, ...

Illustrative Instructional Objectives

*	*Students*	*demonstrate belief in the democratic process.*
*		*defend reading of good literature (art or music).*
*		*appreciate the role of science (or other subjects) in everyday life.*
*		*show concern for the welfare of others.*
*		*demonstrate problem-solving attitudes.*
*		*show commitment to social improvement.*

Characterizing by A Value or Value Complex

At this level of the affective domain, individuals have value systems that have controlled their behaviors for a sufficiently long time for them to have developed characteristic **life styles**. Thus the behaviors are pervasive, consistent, and predictable.

Learning outcomes at this level cover a broad range of activities, but the major emphasis is on the fact that the behavior is typical or characteristic of students.

Instructional objectives that are concerned with students' general patterns of adjustment (personal, social, emotional) would be appropriate here.

Illustrative Behavioral (action) Terms

Acts, discriminates, displays, influences, listens, modifies, performs, practices, proposes, qualifies, questions, revises, serves, solves, uses, verifies, ...

Illustrative Instructional Objectives

* *Students* *demonstrate safety consciousness.*
* *display an attitude of self-reliance when working independently.*
* *practice empathetic behaviors when working with others.*
* *use objective approaches in problem solving.*
* *act with industry, punctuality, and self-discipline.*
* *maintain good health habits.*

Summary

Schooling is the process of affecting change in students. Objectives are purpose statements that describe intended learning outcomes. Their essential parts are a standard preface, a verb, and a description of the behavior. Objectives should be written as descriptions of student behavior following instruction. Objectives may be non-observable, observable and measurable, but not referenced to a criterion, or observable and measurable and referenced to a criterion. Some instructional strategies require use of criterion referenced instructional objectives that the specific task to be performed, the condition under which the task is to be performed, and the minimal acceptable level of performance required. Objectives may function as enabling or terminal purpose statements.

Bloom classifies objectives as cognitive, affective, and psychomotor.

The six levels in the cognitive domain are knowledge, comprehension, application, analysis, synthesis, and evaluation. The five levels in the affective domain are receiving, responding, valuing, generalizing, and characterizing.

BIBLIOGRAPHY

Bloom, B. S. (1976). Human characteristics and school learning. New York: McGraw Hill Company.

Bloom, B. S., and others (1965). Taxonomy of educational objectives, Handbook I: Cognitive domain. New York: David McKay Company,Inc.

Krathwohl, D. R., Bloom, B. S., and Masia, B. B. (1964). Taxonomy of educational objectives, Handbook II: Affective domain. New York: David McKay Company, Inc.

Chapter Five

Planning the Design

The curriculum design directs selection and sequence of instruction. It is the blueprint from which day-to-day lesson planning proceeds. As stated in chapter one, curriculum design is concerned with goals and objectives, content, methods of implementation, and evaluation plans. One important design consideration is sequencing of instructional content.

Ordering Instructional Content

When planning the curriculum you may determine that the order in which the instructional content is sequenced is not important, or you may find that a specific ordering is necessary. In either case, you will need to decide which objectives and related content are to be placed first, second, third, ...

Non-Sequenced Designs

Some instructional content does not require implicit ordering. Consider a unit constructed to examine the states called the North Central States. If the study is to be sequenced, state-by-state, selecting states to be studied first, second, and last becomes a matter of choice. If a topical approach is used, it matters little if one begins with agriculture, industry, or transportation. The topic, agriculture, may begin with dairy farming, grain farming, meat production, or another kind of farming.

Mastery of unit objectives is not dependent on a particular sequence. All topics must be learned, but there is no single best order for learning them. Figure One illustrates one way to diagram a non-sequenced set of learning experiences that support a unit's terminal objective.

Figure One

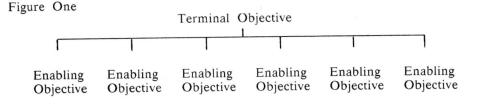

Linear Sequenced Designs

While a decision to sequence, and the determination of an order for sequence, may sometimes be a matter of teacher preference, these decisions are at other times not open to choice. Such is the case when mastery of a specific objective is dependent on mastery of one or more prerequisite objectives. For instance, one cannot successfully diagram sentences until the parts of speech are learned and relationships of parts of speech to each other is understood.

The simplest form of instructional ordering uses a linear progression. A series of objectives leading to a terminal objective is identified and ordered from prerequisite to prerequisite, beginning at the lowest useful level. Below is a list of objectives for sequencing an instructional unit. The sequence directs students through a series of ordered learning activities to find the area of triangular and certain four sided polygons.

The unit (terminal) objective reads:

At the end of this unit, students will be able to --

* *Explain their reason for selecting the appropriate formula and compute to find the areas of triangles and the areas of quadrilaterals with at least two parallel sides.*

The eight lesson (enabling) objectives read:

* *At the end of the lesson, students will be able to explain the rationale for the formula and be able to compute the area of:*

8. *A trapezoid with no right angles*
7. *A trapezoid with one right angle*
6. *An obtuse angle*
5. *An acute angle*
4. *A right angle*
3. *A parallelogram that has no right angles*
2. *A rectangle that is not a square*
1. *A square*

The eight lesson objectives could be illustrated with a drawing.

Figure Two   *At the end of the lesson students will be able to explain the*
                  rationale for the formula and be able to compute the area of:

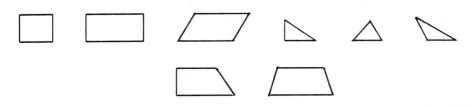

Note that each objective assumes understanding of previous objectives. For
instance, an understanding of why the formula for a triangle, $1/2bh = A$, is
reasonable cannot be readily achieved until students understand the
rationale of the formula for finding the area of a parallelogram, $bh = A$. An
understanding of the logic for finding the areas of triangles and parallelograms is a prerequisite knowledge to an understanding of the formula for
finding the area of a trapezoid, $1/2(b1 + b2)h = A$.

Figure Three shows a further expansion of the linear hierarchial model that

Figure Three

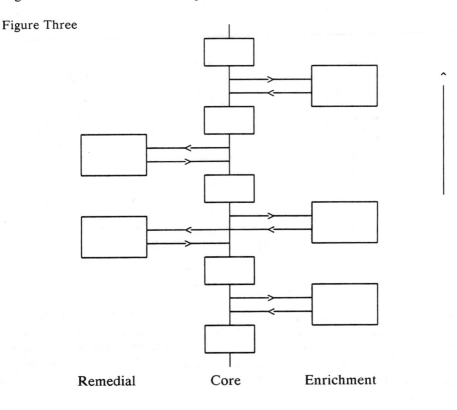

Remedial   Core   Enrichment

offers quests as optional side trips for enrichment or remedial work. All students are expected to follow the basic linear sequence of core activities, while selected students are directed toward remedial or enrichment lessons at appropriate times. Following instruction from a quest experience, students are reinstated into the linear core.

Figure Four shows a variation of the linear hierarchical model that offers tracking options. Alternate sets of enabling objectives lead to a common

Figure Four

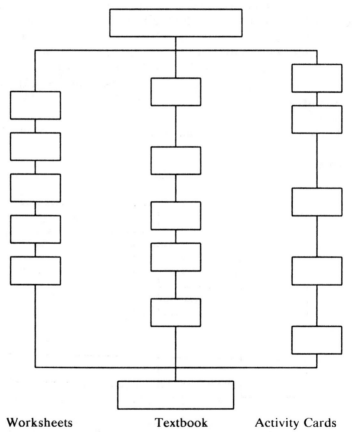

Worksheets   Textbook   Activity Cards

terminal objective. Parallel routes are useful to accommodate differences in student learning styles. For instance, an arithmetic terminal objective rmight be met by following any of three learning modes -- paper and pencil work sheets (abstract), textbook with narrative and pictorial representations (semi-concrete), and activity cards that direct students to use manipulatives (concrete).

Alternate routes allow the teacher to select the approach most appropriate for a particular student. A class could be divided according to learning preference and each subgroup directed to complete the linear sequence of the preference. Alternate modes can also be useful when it becomes evident that a student will fail to meet the terminal objective after working through the initially selected sequence of instruction.

> George's learning objective for the week required that he be able to add two fractions not having common denominators, and with values less than one. The class normally used the textbook as the learning mode. After completing most of the assigned pages, George and his teacher agreed that he needed more work at the concrete level. His teacher advised that he work through a series of activity cards which paralleled the textbook pages. The activity cards directed George to use fraction disks to demonstrate addition of common fractions with unlike denominators. A student was assigned to assist George as he completed the first two activities with the disks. George then felt confident that he understood the process and was now able to complete the remaining task card assignments independently, thus satisfying the terminal objective.

Branching Designs

Sometimes the hierarchial structure of objectives allows branching. Branching may be used when two lessons teach to the same objective, but each lesson uses a different content or methodology. Branching allows the teacher to decide which instructional approach is more appropriate for an individual or group of students.

In Figure Five all students must complete activities A, C, and D, but students may be directed to complete either B_1 or B_2, but usually not both. B_1 and B_2 teach to a common objective, but each lesson uses a different body of content and methodology to reach that objective. B_1 and B_2 are investigations of pendulum motion.

The objectives for B_1 and B_2 are stated as follows:

At the end of this lesson, students will be able to:

B_1. *identify the independent variable responsible for periodic motion of a pendulum.*

B_2. *write a statement describing the relationship between the significant independent variable and the dependent variable.*

Figure Five

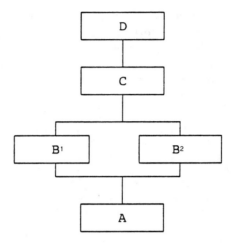

Activity B¹ directs students to setup an experiment using a string attached to a frame and washers for weights. Students are directed to identify, one-by-one, an independent variable (examples: number of washers, height of release, length of the string), and systematically change its value, while noting any effect on the dependent variable, the rate at which the pendulum swings (example: number of swings per ten seconds). Activity B² directs students to pages in a textbook where pendular motion is discussed and illustrated.

Branching may also be desired when no preferred sequential order for some specific groups of objectives is required, but a linear order is necessary for others. Branching allows the teacher to select the order between two or more branched learning experiences.

Figure Six is an example of branching written as part of a curriculum guide. The guide uses a flow chart pattern to illustrate the sequencing of enabling objectives for the terminal objective on the topic, **Adding Fractions**.

In this example all enabling objectives, not yet mastered, must be taught to reach the terminal objective. However, the ordering of enabling lessons is open to some choice. For example, it does not matter if lessons a and b are taught before or after lessons c and d, so long as a, b, c, and d are taught before e. Lesson e must precede lesson f. Either g or h, may be taught next. After teaching g and h, lesson i is taught. Either lessons k, l, m, n, or lesson j may follow. Finally lesson o is mastered and the unit is complete.

Figure Six

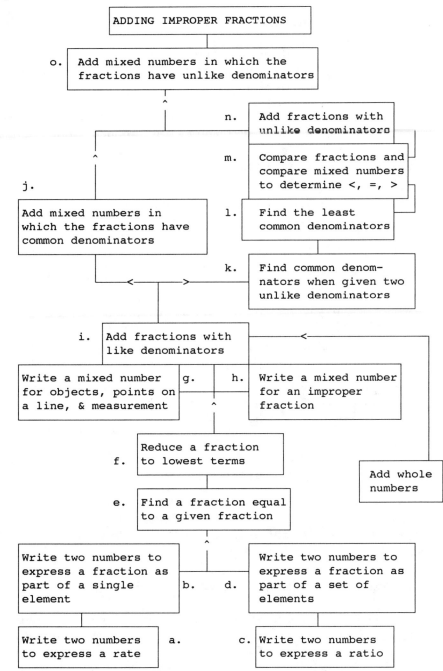

Large Group -- Small Group Designs

Figure Seven displays an instructional model that requires yet another set of curriculum components begins with large group instruction and ends with individual and small group instruction. Unit construction begins by planning whole class instruction designed to teach basic understandings as defined by the unit objectives.

Following basic instruction, students are tested to measure the level of competence reached by individuals. Data supplied from the test are used to group students into remedial, practice, or enrichment subgroups. Students who demonstrate mastery of the unit's objectives

Figure Seven

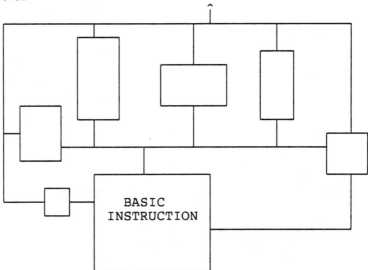

prior to instruction are assigned enrichment experiences rather than participate in the initial whole class instruction. This model is applicable to many instructional contents, but has generally been proposed for skill/process oriented studies.

A Diagnostic-Prescriptive Program As Design

Criterion referenced objectives are valuable when a clear definition of outcomes is desired. Instructional programs may be written which require behaviors with specific criteria of acceptability to be stated. Such is the case when progression to higher level competencies is based on mastery of lower level competencies, or when instructional content selection is based on non-mastery of objectives as measured by a pretest.

The curricular model, diagnostic - prescriptive - teaching (DPT) is a highly structured program that attempts to identify specific needs of students and then provide instruction to meet those needs. The four parts of DPT as described by Charles (Charles, p.95) are:

1. **Establishing objectives,** which in DPT are extensive groups of criterion referenced behavioral statements describing educational intents. Everything else in DPT relates back to this group of objectives.

2. **Diagnosis,** which is the process of ascertaining which objectives students have already reached and which they have not.

3. **Prescription,** which is the process of describing activities to be undertaken that will lead to objectives as yet not reached.

4. **Criterion measurement**, which is the process of determining whether students, after completing prescribed activities, have reached intended objectives.

DPT is a criterion referenced type of instruction. The behavioral objectives establish the criteria to be met. Pretests, written to measure the mastery level of objectives, prescribe instruction. Following instruction, criterion referenced posttests check to see if objectives not satisfied by the pretest are now mastered.

The Mastery Learning Program As Design

The mastery learning curriculum design also includes within it an implementation plan. The discussion which follows is one example to show the interplay between instructional content and instructional method.

The decade of the 70s saw evolution of a curriculum innovation called Mastery Learning. This instructional design is based on the assumption that all students can learn as well as the best students, if the constructed curriculum is organized and implemented in a manner that allows all students adequate and appropriate opportunity to learn well. The mastery learning model is an attempt to maximize the number of students who have this unique kind of learning opportunity.

The plan, as formulated in the writings of Benjamin Bloom, (Bloom) has been adopted and implemented in several American and foreign public and private school systems. The writers of the Chicago Mastery Learning Reading program explain that

> "Master Learning differs from traditional instruction primarily by the systematic and regular use of formative or diagnostic testing within each instruction unit, and the use of remedial instruction for those who fail to master the learning units. The mastery learning strategy is based on group instruction, supplemented by individual assistance" (Chicago).

Materials written for mastery learning are adaptable to a variety of teaching and learning styles. An instruction cycle begins with group instruction, where all students in the class are taught the same materials, followed by individual and/or small group activities. Teaching is directed toward mastery levels as defined by criterion referenced instructional objectives. Mastery learning uses a four step instructional progression.

1. Group instruction
2. Criterion-referenced formative testing
3. Correctives/Extensions
4. Criterion-referenced summative testing

Figure Eight and the discussion that follows depict the several steps of the mastery learning program developed by the Board of Education, City of Chicago (Chicago).

Figure Eight

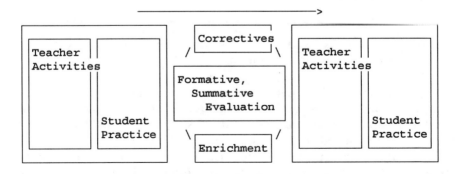

Step 1: Group Instruction

The first step utilizes a whole group instructional format. Teacher directed oral activities which introduce, develop, and/or review a skill or concept are the major expository emphasis. Students respond to teacher instruction through activities and exercises designed to provide independent learning toward objectives as part of the whole group teaching arrangement.

Step 2: Criterion-Referenced Formative Tests

Each unit uses a formative evaluation as a feedback/diagnosis tool to identify student mastery or non-mastery of the specific learning defined by the criterion referenced instructional objectives. Test items parallel objectives so that student performance reflects the specific mastery levels intended. Formative tests identify individuals requiring special assistance or additional practice, as well as those who have mastered the required competency.

Step 3: Correctives/Extensions

Those students failing mastery will require corrective-remedial instruction in the form of additional activities which use alternate learning materials and strategies. For this level the curriculum constructor needs to develop activities that match the variety of learning styles students exhibit. Multi-media materials which utilize different senses should be considered.

Some students seem to learn better through one sense than another. Some are readers, others listeners; some need physical materials, some reason well from pictures of physical materials, and others abstract from descriptions of physical materials.

Curriculum writers also need to consider multi-modal options. Materials should be available for use in both individual and small group settings. Students should be encouraged to help each other succeed. Those who understand may become tutors of those who need individual help. Cooperation among students should become the hallmark of successful learning. Students who achieve mastery on the formative tests are offered rewarding, productive activities as horizontal enrichment. These activities are usually completed independently, by individuals or small groups, allowing time for the teacher to focus major attention to helping the non-mastery students complete the remedial activities successfully. Mastery students may be directed to serve as tutors, thus giving them additional opportunity to test their level of understanding. Serving as a tutor often proves to be a challenging, but excellent method for strengthening and sharpening the tutor's grasp of the concept or process.

Step 4: Criterion-Referenced Summative Tests

When it is reasoned that the vast majority of the class has reached a mastery level, a final evaluation which parallels the formative evaluation used earlier is given. Students are again compared to the standard as defined by the criterion referenced instructional objectives.

Following administration of the final test, students are re-assembled for whole group instruction and the next learning sequence begins. Mastery learning progresses linearly as it cycles through the four-step learning process: whole group instruction, diagnostic evaluation, corrective/enrichment in individual and small group settings, and summative evaluation.

Scope and Sequence As Part of Design

The phrase, scope and sequence, is generally used when discussing the range or breadth and the ordering of content within a specific instructional program. Questions such as:

* Does the grade one mathematics program include a study of geometry?
* Should poetry be included as part of the formal reading program?
* What elements of organic chemistry should be incorporated into the Chemistry I course?

are scope oriented problems.

Sequence is concerned with order of presentation. Elementary school addition may sequence from:

1. adding a one digit number to a one digit number, to
2. adding a one digit number to a two digit number with no renaming, to
3. adding a two digit number to a two digit number with no renaming, to
4. adding a one digit number to a two digit number with renaming, to
5. adding a two digit number to a two digit number with renaming, to ... .

* "Should long vowel sounds be taught before short vowel sounds?
* Is there a preferred order to teaching consonant sounds?" and
* "When should alphabet names be taught?"

are sequence oriented questions.

In order to explore further the problem of vertical and horizontal organization within a curriculum program we will examine curricula for English and social studies.

Scope of an English Language Arts "Mastery Curriculum"[1] (Glatthorn)

A recommended curriculum for grades kindergarten through four employs a whole language approach. It is fashioned to include a literate environment that:

a. stimulates and supports the use of language;
b. integrates language arts skills and knowledge by requiring their use in real situations;
c. emphasizes the pupil's own oral language;
d. uses children's literature to develop an interest in reading and broaden reading horizons; and
e. stresses the functional uses of language.

A curriculum built on the six strands,[2] literature, language, writing, speaking and listening, critical thinking, and vocabulary development provide the recommended structure for grades 5-12.

Literature

Concepts: simile, metaphor, image, symbol, theme, irony, rhyme, rhythm, character, plot, setting, tragedy, comedy, short story, novel,

---

[1] This section is based on recommendations provided by Allan Glatthorn. Mastery curriculum was presented in chapter one.

[2] See Figure Nine for diagram of a spiral curriculum structure.

poem, drama, biography, autobiography, essay.

Classics: Greek and Roman mythology, Odyssey, the Bible as literature, Huckleberry Finn, Moby Dick, Julius Caesar, Great Expectations, Macbeth, the Canterbury Tales, Oedipus Rex.

Language

Grammar: noun, pronoun, verb, adjective, adverb, preposition, conjunction, subject, predicate, direct object, indirect object, predicate adjective, predicate noun, linking verb, transitive verb, verb, verb be, intransitive verb, participial phrase, prepositional phrase, adjective clause, adverb clause, sentence.

Special Units: Language Change, Languages of the World, History of the American Language, History of the English Language, The Dialects We Speak, Sexism in Language.

Writing

Types of Writing: exposition, persuasion, writing about literature, academic writing, practical and applied writing, personal and creative writing.

Speaking and Listening

Special Units: Group Discussion Skills, Presenting the Class Report, The Job Interview, The College Interview.

Critical Thinking

Special Units: Critical Listening, Critical Reading, Critical Viewing, Critical Use of the Mass Media, Information Processing, Language and Thinking.

Vocabulary Development

Special Units: Using Context Clues, Using Roots and Prefixes to Unlock Meaning, Taking Vocabulary Tests.

Scope of Social Studies Programs Since 1930

The scope of the instructional content for social studies programs has changed dramatically since pre-World War II days (Ellis).

Coining The Term, Social Studies

The term, social studies, which means an interdisciplinary, integrated approach to the various social sciences, was coined during the thirties. However, it did not become an established school subject until after World War II. Before then, elementary school students studied history, geography, and civics as separate entities. Even the history and geography of the United States were taught as separate disciplines.

The social studies of the 1940s and 1950s was generally narrative and descriptive. Learning of names, places, people, and events tended to proceed without interpretation or analysis. Textbooks usually ignored such developmental considerations as children's need to be actively involved in learning. The assimilation of content was considered of greatest importance.

The curriculum design was known as **Widening Horizons**. This meant that primary-grade students studied families, neighborhoods, and communities. Intermediate-grade students studied regions, the nation, and the western hemisphere. Upper-grade students studied Europe, Asia, Africa, Australia, and American history and government.

The New Social Studies

The New Social Studies gained prominence in the 1960s as part of the disciplines curriculum movement. The scope of interest and content base was broadened to include all of the social science disciplines: history, geography, political science, economics, anthropology, sociology, and psychology. Inquiry learning, based on the premise that students should discover knowledge for themselves as opposed to being passive receivers of descriptive information, became the dominant thrust. The emphasis on process of learning had as its goal:

1. To learn the bodies of knowledge social scientists know (economics, geography, history, political science, sociology, anthropology, psychology), and
2. To investigate issues as social scientists do (state problems, select data sources, gather data, process data, make inferences from data).

The Relevant Social Studies

During the 1970s, partly as a consequence of our involvement in Vietnam, the question of values emerged as a dominant concern. Values clarification programs found their way into social studies curricula as teachers tried to help students through self- analysis, self-expression, and other clarification of personal processes. Students were encouraged to work on **real-life** problems.
One attempt to develop a **real-life** problems curriculum was found in the elementary school program, Unified Science and Mathematics for Elementary Schools, (USMES) funded by the National Science Foundation. Social problems that affected students directly, such as noise and food waste in lunchrooms, behavior on the playground, or **real-life** economic concerns such as manufacturing and market-

ing a product produced by students in the school, determining which of several commercially produced products (paper towels, breakfast cereals, potato chips) is the best buy, were included as complementary units to the standard social studies program.

Back To The Basic Social Studies

As the 1980s approached, social studies educators felt pressures from a back to the basics movement. More emphasis was given to teaching basic communication skills. Teaching reading skills became an important part of the social studies teachers' tasks. Of particular interest were programs for the exceptional child and social studies curriculum as it related to main streaming and other special education programs.

The Focus: Responsible Citizenship

As the 1990s emerged there appeared the beginnings of a definite emphasis on moral education leading to responsible citizenship. During the 1980s, moral instruction was generally regarded as a task beyond the school's jurisdiction. As the 1990s emerged many persons began to feel a vacuum of moral and responsible citizenship attitudes on the part of young people. These persons clamored for schools to instruct toward correct attitudes and behaviors, those associated with American values. Moral education and citizenship education are two titles associated with the new focus for social studies education.

Each of these stages in social studies development left its mark on today's programs. The social studies curriculum of the 1990s attempts to employ an interdisciplinary, integrated approach to learning, which emphasizes the process approach, shows increased concern for student values, and seeks to strengthen basic academic skills.

Sequencing Social Studies Programs

Textbook publishers have traditionally used a widening horizons organization to sequence their content in elementary school social studies series. A K-6 program begins by focusing on local interests and expands its boundaries wider and wider as it reaches to upper grade levels. A widening horizons social studies series may have grade level textbooks with the following titles:

A Widening Horizons Curriculum

Kindergarten	Me
Grade One	My Family
Grade Two	My Neighborhood

Grade Three	Our Community
Grade Four	Our State (or)
	Regions Near and Far
Grade Five	The United States and
	Its Neighbors
Grade Six	Lands Across the Sea

A Traditional Junior and Senior High School Social Science Program

Most junior and senior high schools follow a fairly standard order of social studies offerings across the six grades that focuses on history, geography, and political science. A representative sequence is:

Grade Seven	Our World
Grade Eight	American History
Grade Nine	Civics
Grade Ten	World History
Grade Eleven	United States History
Grade Twelve	Problems in
	Democracy, and/or
	Economics, Sociology,
	Geography,
	Psychology, and more.

Generally, curriculum guide writers will identify courses for each grade level by naming a broad topic for study. Each broad topic is then broken into sub-topics. A grade five widening horizons curriculum guide might list social science topics related to study of the United States; perhaps adding Canada, Central, and South America. Curriculum for grade six may include topics related to a study of Europe, Asia, Africa, and Australia. A grade seven program might encourage a global perspective by asking students to examine topics such as agriculture, mineral resources, climate, and land formations around the world. Most eighth grade courses place their focus on American history.

Selection and sequencing options available when planning a study of United States history demonstrate choices unique to that social science study. Organization choices include:

a. Sequencing by following a strict chronological order.
b. Organization through a topical approach by selecting a few themes and developing them as topics for study. Examples include: Our Land, Our Economy, Our Government, Our Great Men and Women.
c. Combining a chronological and topical approach (Treat history chronologically through the Civil War, topically from Civil War to World War I, and chronologically

through to the present).

d. **Posthole** by important events/issues. Select **Major** events/issues to be studied indepth and give cursory consideration to **minor** events/issues.

Spiral Curriculum Structure

A curriculum structure that has been accepted at varying levels as an organizational structure in a number of subjects/ disciplines, including mathematics, science, and social studies, is the spiral curriculum shown as Figure Nine. This construct assumes that within a discipline or subject an implicit and basic framework exists, composed of concepts and processes, which is adaptable for use in organizing learning experiences.

Figure Nine

The Spiral Curriculum

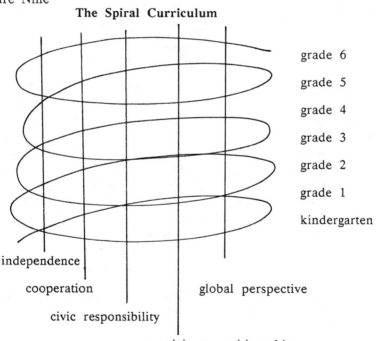

grade 6

grade 5

grade 4

grade 3

grade 2

grade 1

kindergarten

independence

cooperation   global perspective

civic responsibility

participatory citizenship

In a spiral curriculum, learners are introduced to a concept or process at a very simple level and the concept or process is visited again and again over the grades, each time at a progressively higher level. Each reteaching is based on what the student has previously learned and provides a more sophisticated study of the concept/process. Figure Nine illustrates one structure of a spiral curriculum as applied to elementary school social studies. Each strand may be thought of as a program goal. As the spiral connects with the vertical lines it graphically demonstrates how at every grade level each goal becomes a focus for planning one or more instructional units, each unit for grades 1 through 6 building on related learning from the previous year.

California History -- Social Science Framework

The state of California has developed a framework for its public school that uses history and geography as content themes (California). Titles for grades, K-12, are listed below.

Kindergarten	Learning and Working Now and Long Ago
Grade One	A Child's Place in Time and Space
Grade Two	People Who Make A Difference
Grade Three	Continuity and Change
Grade Four	California: A Changing State
Grade Five	United States History and Geography: Making a New Nation
Grade Six	World History and Geography: Ancient Civiilizations
Grade Seven	World History and Geography: Growth and Conflict
Grade Eight	United States History and Geography: Growth and Conflict
Grade Nine	Elective Courses in History -- Social Science
Grade Ten	World History, Culture, and Geography: The Modern World
Grade Eleven	United States History and Geography: Continuity and Change in the Twentieth Century
Grade Twelve	Principles of American Democracy (one semester) and Economics (one semester)

Articulation As Part of Design

Horizontal and vertical articulation generally inquire as to how the various elements of the curriculum are put together and how a coherence among studies within a given discipline or subject field may be improved. When relationships are sought between and among various disciplines or subject fields, the term, horizontal articulation, applies. Examples of horizontal articulation include: integrating the social sciences to form the elementary school social studies program; fusing certain areas of physical science and geography to form an earth science course; and correlating American history and American literature so that the literature of a specific period is studied at the same time the history of that period is examined.

As educators attempt to improve the coherence between elementary and secondary social studies, or among freshman general science, sophomore biology, junior chemistry, and senior physics they are concerned with vertical articulation. Questions, such as

* What topics should be covered over the grades, K-8, science?
* Does the eighth grade mathematics program present desired topics to those students entering freshman algebra?
* At what grade levels should American history be taught?
* If history is taught at elementary, junior high, and senior high, what content should be included at each level?

represent concerns identified with vertical articulation.[3]

Methods of Instruction As Part of Design

The teaching methods you should select are those which best support the objectives students are expected to master, and the instructional content they will learn. Before you can make decisions about methods you will need to understand the developmental level of your students as it applies to the structure of the subject matter.

At this point behavioral research carried on by people such as Piaget, Bruner, Gagne, Kagan, Maslow, Ausuble, Skinner, Watson, Rogers, Bloom, Erikson, Dienes, and others will become your focus of interest.

Research into psychological development and learning theories may be among the most important inquiries you complete. The information learned can significantly affect how you organize the instructional content, as well as what teaching strategies you use. This most important inquiry should receive high priority as prerequisite to any design decisions.

---

[3] It should be noted, however, that preference of terminology cited above is largely arbitrary, and often overlapping. The question of American history content for elementary, junior, and senior high is both a vertical and horizontal articulation concern. When discussing a widening horizons developmental ordering of the social sciences to form the social studies content for elementary school -- family, neighborhood, community, region, nation, western hemisphere, world -- educators may correctly decide to use the words, scope and horizontal articulation or sequence and vertical articulation, interchangeably.

Two examples will help you understand how educational research is used to answer the question: What teaching methods should be selected? Our first example will investigate instruction and mathematical understanding as applied in early childhood education.

Early Childhood Mathematics (Mueller, 1984, p.19-23)

Piaget, Dienes, and others have contributed significantly to our knowledge of intellectual development and mathematical understanding. Piaget regarded the development of the logic and reasoning of mathematics as indistinguishable from the development of intelligence in general. Therefore, it is argued, as cognitive development proceeds, mathematical growth should also proceed. Such is, however, not always the case.

Many intelligent children do not develop adequate mathematics concepts. They never understand the **real** meaning of mathematics and how it is structured. The problem does not appear to lie within the children themselves. Rather, the **improper kind of instruction** offered to children appears to be the villain; the broken link between continuous cognitive and mathematical growth.

The problem becomes obvious when one compares how mathematical understanding develops and traditional teaching is practiced. Traditional practices impose the formal, abstract structure of mathematics on pre-primary and primary grade children. They are required to work with numerals before these representations have been totally internalized and distinguished from their antecedents. The meaning of numerals and other mathematics symbols cannot happen unless they grow out of experience with objects. Matching pictures with written numbers is matching symbols with more symbols. Both are representations, a level of abstraction.

Before children can understand relations at an abstract level, they must experience relations at a concrete level. They must pair cup to saucer, milk carton and straw to student, and more.

It is not unusual to find a group of five year old kindergarten children attempting answers to addition or subtraction worksheet assignments without fully comprehending either process. Before children can understand representations of mathematical operations they must understand the operations themselves. They must experience processes which join a set of objects with a second set of objects; separate a set of objects into subsets. Otherwise operations are nothing more than manipulation of symbols -- a fallacious understanding -- and mathematics is reduced to memorization of what is meaningless content.

Wadsworth[4] (1978, p.162,168,174,175) cites three Piagetian principles that should be considered as an early childhood mathematics program is structured.

1. Mathematics concepts can be constructed by children **only** from spontaneous action of children on objects.
2. Children can comprehend the representations of mathematical processes only after they comprehend how symbols are used.
3. Children should possess comprehension of mathematical concepts **before** they are encouraged to deal with mathematical concepts symbolically (i.e., use numbers).

If one agrees that mathematical concepts can **only** be constructed out of children's actions on objects, those activities which encourage such action will be the **core** of the curriculum. Therefore, assignments such as worksheets which show a set of objects to be matched with a numeral will be rejected as both introductory work or basic developmental material.

If an understanding of the sentences 4 + 6 = [ ] and 6 - 2 = [ ] can follow only after comprehension of use of these symbols, activities will grow out of, and get meaning from, experiences where sets of objects are joined together, sets are compared to see if they have the same amount, and sets are separated into subsets.
Finally, early childhood mathematics curriculum builders should **religiously** adhere to the third principle: children should have comprehension of mathematical concepts **before** they are encouraged to deal with mathematical concepts symbolically.

Dienes   developed a teaching strategy which supported the above

---

[4] From *Piaget for the classroom teacher* by Barry J. Wadsworth. Copyright c 1978. By Longman Publishing Group. Reprinted by permission of Longman Publishing Group.

principles. He postulated three stages in development of concept formation:

a.   The play stage
b.   The semi-structured stage
c.   The fixing and application of concept stage.

Wadsworth discussed the development of mathematics concepts as outlined by Dienes when he stated:

> According to Dienes, in a proper educational environment, the development of each mathematical concept moves from the initial **free play** stage where children act on objects that the teacher has placed in the environment. These objects contain mathematical features relevant to a concept. As children come to know the materials and their properties, they begin to see regularities and start to make predictions about the objects and their actions on them.
>
> Eventually, after experiencing a variety of materials, children begin to detect commonalties or similarities between different games or actions on different objects (blocks can be ordered by size, coins can be ordered by size, stones can be ordered by size, adding 2 blocks to 5 blocks produces the same result as adding 2 stones to 5 stones). Children begin to construct the abstract notion that mathematical operations can be applied to any materials.
>
> Once the abstractions (concepts) are built from concrete experience, the child is ready to begin to represent the abstraction graphically, and shortly thereafter, in terms of signs (numbers and mathematical symbols). With the use of signs to represent the constructed mathematical operation, children have developed part of a formal system.
>
> Dienes' approach to mathematics instruction is a structured method based on the actions of the child on concrete objects. It leads gradually to the use of conventional numbers after comprehension of concepts has been built up.

Wadsworth clearly separates traditional teaching from research based teaching when he concludes:

> Traditional instruction that begins with numbers is the **wrong approach**. Numbers are abstract signs and have no meaning. Mathematical concepts can be built up only from the child's actions on objects. Active learning should be the **major** component of mathematics instruction in the initial stages and

until children develop formal operations.[5]

To permit children to play mathematical games or work with colored rods[6] after they finish their worksheets is the wrong idea.

> **Active learning should not be a supplement to work with symbols; work with symbols should be an outgrowth of active learning** (bold added) (Wadsworth).

The one stage in concept development often overlooked, even by those who espouse active learning through actions on objects,
is an opportunity for children to pursue activities without specific teacher direction. This opportunity for **messing about** provides a time to explore, formulate, hypothesize, and check hypotheses. It may be, finally, the most productive of learning times if properly supervised.

Cooperative Learning (Johnson, 1989)

As a second example we will consider Cooperative Learning as a learning structure with potential to improve academic and social learning across all grade levels. Cooperative Learning is an instructional environment designed to guide students toward collaborative small group work, ensuring that all members master the assigned material. It promotes positive interdependence among group members while maintaining individual accountability.

> "Positive interdependence is the perception that you are linked with others in a way so that you cannot succeed unless they do (and vise versa), and that their work benefits you and your work benefits them. It promotes a situation in which individuals work together in small groups to maximize the learning of all members, sharing their resources, providing mutual support, and celebrating their joint success"(Johnson, p. 59).

> Individual accountability requires each student to be accountable for both learning the assigned material and helping other group members learn.

An important non-academic goal of cooperative learning is development of appropriate collaborative skills and processing skills.

Social skills are of primary importance to successful coopera-

---

[5]Refers to Piaget's fourth state of cognitive development.

[6]Colored rods are commercially produced sets of rectangular rods of varying length that may be used to represent number.

tion. However, children and adolescents are not born with these skills. They must be taught. Cooperative learning situations are structured to help students develop and use the social skills necessary for successful group activity. Within a heterogeneous group structure students learn to accept roles as the **reader**, the **checker**, the **encourager**. Acceptance, support, trust, and liking are valued.

The final structure, processing, is designed to help students evaluate how well they have worked together cooperatively, and to assist them with plans for collaborative skill improvement. Students question their behaviors to determine what each member did that was helpful for the group and what each could do to make the group better during the next lesson.

> There is nothing more basic than learning to
> use one's knowledge in cooperative interaction
> with other people.

The major differences between traditional and cooperative learning groups are highlighted below.

Cooperative Learning Groups	**Traditional Learning Groups**
Positive interdependence	No interdependence
Individual accountability	No individual accountability
Heterogeneous	Homogeneous
Shared leadership	One leader appointed
Shared responsibility for each other	Responsibility only for self
Task and maintenance emphasized	Only task emphasized
Social skills directly taught	Social skills assumed and ignored
Teacher observes and intervenes	Teacher ignores group functioning
Groups process their effectiveness	No group processing

Summary

Articulation is concerned with relations among design components. Horizontal organization deals with relationships among topics within a program. Vertical organization deals with relationships among past, present, and future learning components.

Determination of instructional strategies should result from an examination of objectives and instructional content, as well as an understanding of students. Curriculum is the product of the tension between goals and instructional content, and their organization.

BIBLIOGRAPHY

Chicago Board of Education (1980). Chicago Mastery learning Reading. From *Excerpts From Chicago Mastery Learning Reading*™, 1980. Reprinted with permission of the Board of Education of the City of Chicago.

Dienes Z. P. (1971). Building up mathematics. London: Hutchinson Educational.

California Department of Education (1988). History -- Social studies framework. Springfield, IL.

Charles, C. M. (1980). Individualizing instruction. St. Louis: C. V. Mosby Company.

Ellis, A. K. (1981). Teaching and learning elementary social studies. 2nd.ed. Boston: Allyn and Bacon, Inc. Reprinted with permission.

Glatthorn, A. A. (September, 1988) What schools should teach in the English language arts. Educational Leadership. Alexandria, VA: Association for Supervision and Curriculum Development. 44-50. Reprinted with permission of the Association for Supervision and Curriculum Development. Copyright (c) 1988 by ASCD. All rights reserved.

Johnson, D. W., Johnson R. J. & Holubec, E. J. (1989) Circles of learning, 3rd. ed. 7208 Cornelia Drive, Edina, MN 55435: Interaction Book Company.

Mueller, D. W. (1984). Mathematics for early childhood. Concordia University, River Forest, Illinois 60305: Concordia University Bookstore.

Wadsworth, B. J. (1978). Piaget for the classroom teacher. New York: Longman, Inc.

Chapter Six

Putting the Parts Together

Writing and organizing the many parts that are a curriculum design is a highly complex process.

The complete document will direct teachers to implement a multitude of separate instructional experiences, each connected to and affected by other instructional experiences -- by their content and by the way they are sequenced and organized, by resources available, and more.

As you design your curriculum you will be concerned that optimal instructional experiences are provided for students so that the desired learning actually happens. This chapter will guide you through the steps that lead to a completed written document.

Looking At the Big Picture

Since goals and objectives are statements that declare the **learning outcomes** of a curriculum, we will treat them as the force that drives decision making.[1]   The rule of thumb will be:

Determinations about what will be provided as learning experiences for students will be made by matching proposed learning experiences with the established goals and objectives.

When the curriculum product is completed, it will appear as if goals and objectives are the basis for all other decision making. The process for decision making is illustrated in Figure One where each narrower component appears to derive validity from the broader component above it. The model draws on a study of the cultural context to determine its generalized curricular purpose and in a step-by-step progression reduces this generalization to more specific statements of curricular intent.

---

[1] Since subject-centered and theme-centered are the two most commonly used curriculum designs, our focus will be limited to their analysis.

Figure One

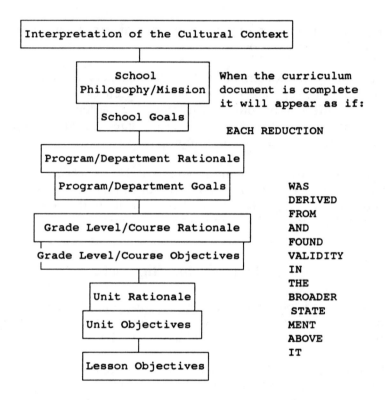

A Brief Reflection

Remember what you learned in college in educational foundations courses. Foundational concerns focus on interpretation of the cultural context in which the school finds itself. Cultural context concerns include sociological/technological pressures, psychological/theoretical learning, and organized knowledge; philosophy of education; and the history of education.

Each of these is a force affecting curriculum choice. As you study these forces with respect to your particular subject area, a variety of inquiries may be appropriate. They may include examination of research findings of how persons learn and develop, test results, census data, job trends, societal problems, economic considerations, speculations of futurists, as well as academic bodies of knowledge which provide content for instruction.

A study of the cultural context cannot be done in an intellectual and emotional vacuum. There is no such thing as totally objective inquiry. Each of us **sees** through the **eyes** of a personal philosophic bias. This value-set influences our decisions as we select data sources, gather and process data, and finally, as we interpret and apply data to our school settings.

Philosophy or Mission of the School and School Goals

The written documents that result from a study of the cultural context are a declaration of philosophic beliefs and school goals. These pronouncements, if written with clarity and precision, will provide a revealing description of your school to its potential clientele.

A more comprehensive treatment of schools' educational philosophies and school goals was found in Chapter Three. It may be that your school has a written mission statement or philosophy and has listed its school goals. These should be examined to see if they correctly reflect present values and purpose. If these statements have outlived their usefulness, document revision is required. If no philosophical or goal documents exist, the school's first order of business is their construction.

The school mission/philosophy statement and school goals once stated, provide the framework in which instructional program rationales and goals and high school department philosophies and goals are written.

Department Philosophy/Program Rationale

The department philosophy/program rationale is a declaration which serves as a defense for including its offerings as part of the curriculum. It shows how this particular part of the curriculum contributes to the total curriculum, how it articulates with other parts of the curriculum, and how it supports the philosophy statement of the school.

All programs should be headed with rationale that defend their inclusion in the curriculum. In a high school, each department will find it necessary to write a department philosophy to show how its several course offerings fit into, articulate with, and support the total school curriculum.

Co-curricular programs should also be prefaced with statements of rationale. All school sponsored programs should be able to show they are a desired, important, and necessary part of the school's total curriculum. A more complete discussion of program rationale was found in Chapter Three.

Department/Program Goals

Department/program goals are written to define broad, long range learning outcomes for each instructional or co-curricular program. When considering school sponsored co-curricular programs, goals are chosen that identify desired outcomes for those students who participate in the school sponsored activities. When considering instructional programs, goals give direction to learning; they identify strands or themes; they define instructional paths to be followed. A more comprehensive definition of programs goals was found in Chapter Three.

Constructing Subject Centered and Thematic Curricula

At this point your interpretation of the cultural context changes from discussion of theory and generalized learning outcomes to hard practical application. This is where the **rubber hits the road**. Our task now becomes one of thinking through the various steps leading to completion of a scope and sequence for a single instructional or co-curricular program.

A completed list of program/department goals becomes the source from which the mass of sub-components -- early childhood /elementary school/high school course objectives through unit/ lesson objectives -- and the variety of instructional content must be generated. The various competencies to be developed as progress toward program/department goal attainment is sought must be identified and positioned in proper relation with each other.

Curricula are usually developed for specific subject fields. For example, the products are designed for use within a specific program such as mathematics, natural science, social science, fine arts, language arts, or physical development and health. The discussion that follows entitled **"The Goal Analysis Approach"** describes this method of curriculum planning. You will be introduced to two goal analysis approaches. One assigns learning outcomes first, then instructional content, the other assigns instructional content first, then learning outcomes.

While much of "The Goal Analysis Approach" section can be used when developing thematic curricula, this chapter adds a section entitled **"Thematic Curriculum Designs"** which focuses on special concerns related to programs in which subject fields are crossed and mixed. Here you will be guided through two approaches to thematic planning, the "Topic Driven Theme Approach" and the "Discipline/ Subject Field Theme Approach."

The Goal Analysis Approach

The process of breaking down program/department goals into their elements is called goal analysis.

The implied direction of goal analysis is from broader to more specific definition of purpose. Figures Two, Three, and Four serve to illustrate, through use of diagrams, several structures resulting from goal analysis.

The task of selecting and organizing objectives and instructional content is a highly complex and multi-faceted process. Much of the effort is trial and error. Objectives and instructional content will be suggested, examined, rejected, and revised. Sometimes objectives will dictate instructional content; other times instructional content will suggest objectives.

There is no one strategy that can adequately describe the many processes used when completing a goals analysis. The approach used by one educator may be cumbersome to another. However, in an attempt to generically describe the points-of-view and approaches used as educators define the scope and sequence of an instructional program, we will explore this approach to curriculum writing from two perspectives:

Goal Analysis Approach # 1. Selection of learning outcomes first, then instructional content,

Figure Two   **DIAGRAMS SUGGESTING CURRICULUM ORGANIZATION**

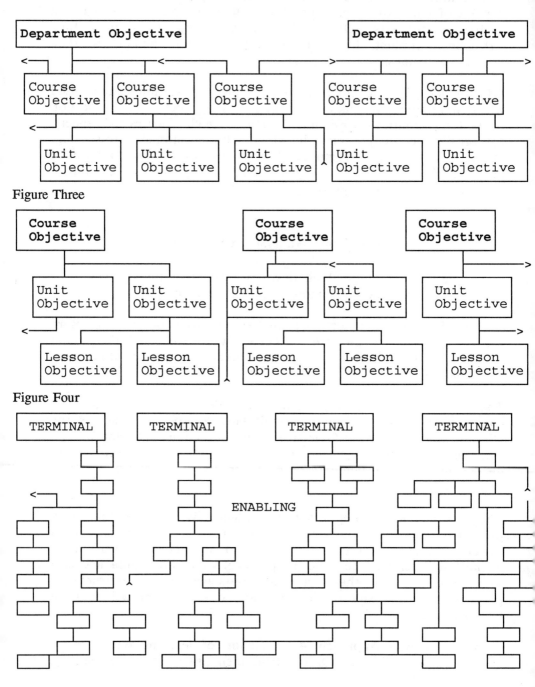

Figure Three

Figure Four

and
Goal Analysis Approach #2. Selection of instructional content
first, then learning outcomes.

Goal   Analysis   Approach   #1:   Selection   of   Learning Outcomes First, then Instructional Content

The first approach, selection of learning outcomes before instructional content is identified, will be examined as two separate strategies.

Strategy A.   Selection of --

a.   Program /High School Department goals, next
b.   terminal objectives,[2] next
c.   selection and ordering of enabling objectives,[3] then
d.   course/grade level assignment of the enabling objectives, and
finally
e.   assignment of instructional content appropriate to objectives.

Strategy B.   Selection of --

a.   Program/High School Department goals, next
b.   determination of courses/grade levels, then
c.   selection and ordering of course objectives through unit
objectives appropriate to each course/grade level, and finally
d.   assignment of instructional content appropriate to objectives.

An outline of the two approaches is listed below. Following each
outline is a detailed discussion of each approach.

Steps in Strategy A.

a.   Identify all program/high school department goals
b.   For each program/department goal, choose one or more
appropriate terminal objectives
c.   For each terminal objective choose appropriate enabling
objectives
d.   Continue the objective selection process to the most specific
objective level desired
e.   Order the objectives
f.   Decide on desired grade levels/courses for the program

---

[2] For a review of terminal objectives see Chapter Four.

[3] For a review of enabling objectives see Chapter Four.

   g. Place ordered sets of objectives into their appropriate courses
   h. Select instructional content designed to satisfy objectives
   i.   Revise, reorganize objectives and instructional content to form logical instructional units.

A goals analysis strategy based exclusively on learning outcome identification as the criterion for instructional content determination, begins with identification of the several program goals. The process of goal selection continues as each program goal is analyzed and broken into ... terminal objectives, enabling objectives, i.e.,   ... course objectives ... through to unit objectives/ lesson objectives.

Only after all objectives have been identified and positioned within the hierarchy that is the scope and sequence of the instructional program does the task of placing sets of ordered objectives within the school's grade levels/courses begin. Finally, after all objectives have been positioned within the courses, instructional content appropriate to each objective is sought, and organization of objectives and instructional content into teaching units is completed.

Below is a suggested procedure for implementing the strategy.

1.   Write a program rationale/high school department philosophy to show how the education unit fits into the total curriculum; how it articulates with the other parts of the curriculum; and how it supports the educational philosophy of the school.

2.   State the program/department goals as competencies toward which students strive as they matriculate through the total program.

3.   The program/department goals may identify learning strands, themes, or topics, then

   Ask: What knowledge, skills, or values should the learners know, be able to do, or feel when they have completed the total instructional program to demonstrate the competencies stated in each of the program goals that is being analyzed?

   *   Each response is a potential terminal objective
   *   Brainstorm to identify all possible terminal objectives

4.   Ask: What sub-knowledge, sub-skills, or values will the learners need to know, be able to do, or feel to demonstrate the competency stated in each of the terminal objective?

   *   Each response is a potential enabling objective
   *   brainstorm to identify all possible enabling objectives

5. Decide what will be the lowest level of objective constructed when considering the range: terminal objectives through lesson objectives.

6. Continue the procedure prescribed in #4 above for all remaining goal analysis steps through to the lowest competency level desired.[4]

7. Organize the objectives into topic sets.[5]

Each set should have these features:

   a. The objectives within each set are of approximately equal power (about the same in length, difficulty, and significance).
   b. The objectives are homogeneous in the way they are stated.
   c. As you process each item (a,b) above -- add, subtract, omit, collapse -- the objectives to find the best competency descriptors for achievement toward each goal statement.

8. Order the sets of objectives and order each objective within a set.

9. Decide on the desired grade levels/courses for the total program.

For Each Course:

10. Assign sets of objectives to their appropriate course and to topics within each course.

11. You may choose to write a brief rationale to show how the course fits into the total program; how it articulates with other parts of the program; and how it supports the rationale of the program.

12. Select instructional content designed to satisfy learning outcomes.

Sometimes this goals analysis process builds a structure that reminds one of a ladder. It suggests that the student begin at the lowest rung, and, in a step-by-step progression, climb to the highest rung.

----

[4] See Figure Three as an example beginning at the program level.

[5] Topic sets may be thought of as closely related instructional content offered at similar levels of proficiency. Examples include -- for social studies: learning outcomes related to mapping at a middle elementary level of difficulty; or for music: goal statements related to pitch at a junior high level of adeptness.

A K-6 Mathematics Program

This variation may be used when the scope and sequence of a K-6, mathematics program is defined. The goal analysis process begins by identifying mathematics competency strands. Examples of common mathematics strands are numeration, addition, subtraction, multiplication, division, measurement, money, time, and application.

Once the strands are selected, each is further clarified by defining the highest level of competency expected on that strand. Therefore, for each strand, an objective is written that states an observable behavior which clearly demonstrates the highest competency to be attained on that strand. Such a statement is said to describe a terminal behavior and is called a terminal objective.

An example of a K-6 division strand terminal objective is:

Given a two-digit number and a number less than 1,000,000, students will be able to divide the larger number by the smaller, using the compact division algorithm.

When the terminal objective for each strand is written, the process of identifying the range of enabling objectives begins.

When all enabling objectives are written and ordered, assignment to courses may need to be completed. The final task is selection of instructional content designed to teach mastery of the learning outcome requirement. The steps in construction of a K-6 mathematics program curriculum ladder may be sequenced as follows:

1. Write a program rationale for the mathematics program to show how it fits into the total curriculum; how it articulates with the other parts of the curriculum; and how it supports the educational philosophy of the school.

2. Select the mathematics strands upon which the program will be structured.

3. State the mathematics program goals to define each strand as long range targets for the K-6 program.

4. Write objective statements to clarify the highest level of competency desired within each mathematics strand. These are the terminal objectives for each strand.

5. Ask: What will each learner need to know or be able to do to master the competency in the terminal objective? Each

answer is a potential enabling objective.

Each time an enabling objective is constructed, ask: What must the learner know or be able to do as a prerequisite competency, before instruction toward mastery of this objective can be successfully attempted? and What is the next logical higher level of competence desired?

Thus you continue the process, assigning to each enabling objective another objective that leads directly to its fulfillment, and/or one that is the logical next step in competency development toward the terminal goal.

6. Decide on the lowest level of mastery needed within each strand. Complete the range of enabling objectives from lowest to terminal goal. Order all objectives to form a logical sequence of learning experiences.

7. Ask: What competencies from other strands are necessary to reach the terminal goal in the strand being processed? Where do these other competencies enter this strand?

8. Organize all enabling objectives into a matrix as shown in Figure Five to demonstrate relationships of goals to each other.

   Rewrite the statements so each has these features:

   a. Each enabling objective is of approximately equal power (about the same in length, difficulty, and significance).
   b. The objectives are homogeneous in the way they are stated.

9. If there are to be grade level divisions, assign sets of ordered objectives to each grade level.

10. You may choose to write a rationale to show how the grade level objectives fit into the total program, how they articulate with other parts of the program, and how they support the rationale of the program.

11. Select instructional content designed to satisfy each of the objectives.

Steps in Strategy B.

   a. Identify all program/high school department goals
   b. Decide on desired instructional levels (courses) for the program
   c. For each course choose appropriate course (terminal) objectives
   d. For each course objective, choose appropriate enabling

     objectives

e. Continue the enabling objective selection process to the most specific objective level desired

f. Order objectives within each course

g. Select instructional content designed to satisfy learning outcomes

h. Revise, reorganize objectives and instructional content to form logical instructional units.

This goals analysis strategy also begins with identification of goals and follows with selection of instructional content. It differs from the first in that after program goals are in place, the program is divided into courses. For each course a list of course objectives is written and ordered. Since objectives are the determiners of instructional content, selection of instructional content is delayed until all objectives are in place. After the total number of objectives has been identified, instructional content is selected that will best help students reach these objectives.

The progression in this goals analysis -- instructional content selection strategy is as follows:

1. Write a program rationale/high school department philosophy to show how it fits into the total curriculum, how it articulates with other parts of the curriculum, and how it supports the philosophy of the school.

2. State program/department goals as competencies achieved upon completion of the program.

3. Divide the total program into courses.

For Each Course:[6]

4. Ask: What is the proper contribution of this course to the total program?

You may choose to write a brief rationale to show how the course fits into the total program, how it articulates with other parts of the program, and how it supports the rationale of the program.

5. You may choose to identify learning strands, themes or topics and

Ask: What do the learners need to know or be able to do at

---

[6] See Figure Three as an example beginning at the course level.

the end of this course to perform at an acceptable level, the behaviors stated in the program/department goals?

Each response is a potential terminal course objective.

* Brainstorm to identify all possible terminal objectives.
* Select terminal objectives most appropriate as extensions of the program/department goals.

6. Organize the terminal course objectives so each set has these features:

   a. The terminal objectives are of approximately equal power (about the same in length, difficulty, and significance).
   b. The terminal objectives are homogeneous in the way they are stated.
   c. Ask: Do terminal objectives in one course level relate well with terminal objectives in another course level (Do objectives for the Literature I class articulate well with those of Literature II and III?).
   d. Ask: When terminal objectives from all courses are considered together, do they represent a complete and thorough analysis of program/department goals?
   e. As you process each item (a-d) above -- add, subtract, omit, collapse -- the objectives to find the best competency descriptors for achievement toward each program goal.

7. Ask: What knowledge, skills, or values do the learners need to know, be able to do, or feel to demonstrate the competency stated in each of the terminal course objectives which is being analyzed?

   * Each response is a potential unit objective.
   * Brainstorm to identify all possible unit objectives.

8. Organize the unit objectives into topic sets so each set has these features:

   a. The unit objectives are of approximately equal power (about the same in length, difficulty, and significance).
   b. The unit objectives are homogeneous in the way they are stated.
   c. As you process each item (a,b) above -- add, subtract, omit, collapse -- the objectives to find the best competency descriptors for achievement toward the several course objectives.

11. Order the sets of objectives and order the objectives within each set.

12. Assign sets of related unit objectives to their appropriate position within the course.

13. Select instructional content to satisfy each goal.

A 9-12 Mathematics Program

Goal selection for many secondary school programs will necessarily place course identification early in the planning process. Consider a 9-12 mathematics program. A priority decision is identification of the several course offerings.

Examples include: algebra, advanced algebra, geometry, and trigonometry.

Each course will be examined to determine its proper contribution to the goals of the 9-12 mathematics program. When the course objectives are identified, the next step may be selection of mathematics topics. Each topic may be thought of as a major unit of study. Terminal goals may be written to define the expected competency within each topic. Selection of content will follow placement of all goal statements.

One possible sequence for planning an algebra course is as follows:

A High School Algebra Course

1. Write a rationale for the algebra course to show how the algebra course fits into the Mathematics Department's Program; how it articulates with other courses offered by the Department; and how it supports the rationale of the Department.

2. Select topics as major units for study.

3. Define each topic by stating the terminal behaviors expected on completion of the course. An example of a terminal objective for the topic, polygons, is:

   + *Students will be able to use the various congruences, postulates, and theorems in proofs involving overlapping triangles.*

The several terminal objectives will be the list of course objectives.

4. For each topic, select the range of enabling objectives necessary

to reach mastery of the terminal objective. Examples of enabling objectives are:

+ *Name a polygon and identify its parts*
+ *For a regular polygon, find the measure of each interior and exterior angle*
+ *Use the AAS Theorem in proving triangles congruent*

5. Order the enabling objectives within each topic.

6. Select instructional content appropriate to satisfy each enabling objective behavior.

Interior Decorating

The course, Interior Decorating, an offering of a Home Economics Department, may be organized by following the construction of the rationale and course objectives with selection of a set of study topics such as:

* Principles and Elements of Design
* Furniture Arrangement
* Color
* Floors
* Wall coverings

Following selection of each topic, a statement that clarifies the intended outcome of a study of the topic is written. For example, under the topic, Principles and Elements of Design, the terminal behavior is:

+ *Students will be able to describe the mood presented in a decorated room and defend that description by relating it to the interaction of design principles and elements.*

Three of the several enabling objectives for this topic are:

+ *Label definitions of the principles and elements of design*
+ *Choose the type of decorative design represented by a pattern example*
+ *Contrast how different uses of each element of design affects the decor of the room*

The final step in constructing this course curriculum is selection of activities that lead to competency in each objective.

Selecting the Range for Analysis

The process of goal analysis could continue through a large number of successive analyses, ultimately establishing learning objectives for behaviors like:

+ *The learner is able to add 2 + 2, or,*
+ *The learner is able to name each of the ghosts that visited Scrooge.*

Not only is such a complete analysis unnecessary, but it is also undesirable because the final product is of little use. It is too cumbersome and detailed. When deciding on the power of the final product, these suggestions are offered:

a. If you are beginning at the program goal level and working down, decide to end up at a level no lower than unit objectives (perhaps units which take several weeks to complete) as opposed to lesson objectives or single learning activity objectives.

b. If you begin at a course objective level such as Fifth Grade Mathematics, or Introduction to Computer: Basic Language, a breakdown to the unit level may also be sufficient.

c. When a goal analysis begins at the unit level and is processed as -- Goals First, Then Instructional Content -- it should include identification of learning objectives appropriate for individual lessons.

d. Restrict the number of competencies which can be identified at any level. This forces the identification of competencies with power.

Goal Analysis Approach #2: Selection of Instructional Content First, then Learning Outcomes

The second goal analysis strategy is useful when organized bodies of knowledge or established programs of activity require content or concept identification before determination of learning outcomes, This process begins with subject matter selection.

Selection of instructional content first dominates when the instructional content is prescribed. Such is the case with courses in which specific readings are part of the syllabus, as with literature or history, or in those cases where the course content is determined by the content of one or more textbooks.

For example, a junior or senior high school history course syllabus might be constructed by:

1. Selecting content appropriate for a chronological survey of American history.

2. Selecting learning outcomes that are both desirable and compatible with specified content.

3. Adapting -- through emphasis, addition, omission, treatment -- content, so that it becomes a natural and reasonable vehicle leading toward desired learning outcomes.

A more detailed description of a --

Selection of Instructional Content First, Then Learning Outcome Selection -- strategy follows below:

1. Write a rationale for the program to show how the course fits into the curriculum; how it articulates with other parts of the curriculum; and how it supports the philosophy statement of the school.

2. State program goals as competencies achieved upon completion of the total program.

3. Construct a scope and sequence that outlines the instructional content of the total program.

Textbooks and supplementary materials may provide the scope and sequence for the instructional content of the program, or a school may have available a variety of commercial and/or teacher developed materials for instructional use. When the instructional content is specified through use of a set of textbooks, selection of new textbooks may, at this time, become a major concern.

Textbook selection will go hand-in-hand with development of steps 1-13. Steps 1-7 should normally be completed before actual selection of a textbook or series of textbooks. Steps 8-13 may be a logical response to the organization of the textbook selected.

In cases where the instructional content is not specified as it is in a textbook, but where it is deemed desirable to determine the instructional content before identifying goals and objectives, the task of constructing a scope and sequence is a major challenge.

You are encouraged to read the section, "Organization of Curricular Programs," found later in this chapter, and review the section, "The British Approach to Thematic Teaching" in Chapter Two, as well as, a good foundations in educations book for guidance.

4. Examine the scope and sequence and determine how to divide the instructional content into courses.
    Ask: What instructional content divisions will provide an acceptable packaging when considering the perspective of subject matter specialists, the needs of society, and the developmental level of students?

    Divide the instructional content into courses. Identify each course content division with a title. Write a summary of the instructional content for each course. If textbooks and/or other instructional materials are selected, identify each for easy reference.

For Each Course:

5. Ask: What is a proper contribution of this course to the total program?

    You may choose to write a brief rationale to show how the course fits into the total program; how it articulates with other parts of the program; and how it supports the rationale of the program.

6. Ask: What are desired learning outcomes that could reasonably be expected from a study of the instructional content of this course?

    *   Each response is a potential terminal course objective.
    *   Brainstorm to identify all possible terminal course objectives.

    Select terminal course objectives most appropriate as extensions of the rationale.

7. Organize the terminal course objectives so each has these features:

    a. The course objectives are of approximately equal power (about the same in length, difficulty, and significance).
    b. The course objectives are homogeneous in the way they are stated.
    c. Ask: Do course objectives at one level relate well with course objectives at another level? (Do fourth, fifth,

sixth, seventh, and eighth grade social studies objectives articulate well with each other?).

d. Ask: When course objectives from all courses are considered in total, do they represent a complete and thorough analysis of the program goals?

e. As you process each item (a-d) above -- add, subtract, omit, collapse -- the objectives to find the best competency descriptors for achievement toward the several program goals.

8. Ask: What topic separations[7] will provide the best instructional organization for the course?

   Identify each topic with a title. You may choose to write a brief rationale to show how each topic fits into the course; how it articulates with the other parts of the course; and how it supports the rationale of the course.

9. Write topic objectives as enabling objectives to the course objectives, using the criteria stated in #6,7 above.

10. Ask: What subtopics will provide the best instructional organization for each topic?

    Identify each subtopic with a title. You may choose to write a brief rationale, using the criteria stated above.

11. Write subtopic objectives as enabling objectives to the topic objectives, using the criteria stated in #6,7 above.

12. Continue the breakdown to the lowest level desired.

13. Adapt the instructional content -- through change of emphasis/treatment, addition/ omission of content -- so it becomes the appropriate vehicle to satisfy the desired learning outcomes.

Social Studies Program

An example of a goals analysis in which instructional content is identified before learning outcomes are chosen is a social studies program, K-12. The analysis process is described below.

A. At the program to course level --

---

[7] Topics, subtopics, divisions, units, chapters are commonly used names for portions of an instructional content. The terms used above are arbitrary rather than definitive.

a.   Write a rationale for K-12 social studies program.

b.   List the program goals.

c.   Construct a scope and sequence that outlines the instructional content of the   total program.

d.   Write a brief summary of the social studies content for each course. Identify the text and/or other instructional materials that will be used.

(Textbook titles: Kindergarten, Me; Grade 1, My Family; 2, Our Neighborhood; 3, Our Community; 4, Exploring Regions Near and Far; 5, Exploring the United States; 6, Exploring Canada and Latin America; 7, Exploring Europe, Asia, and Australia; 8, The Story of Our Country; 9, Our Government; 10, Our World Heritage; 11, Our American Heritage; 12 Living in A World Community).

e.   You may choose to write a brief rationale for each course.

f.   Select terminal objectives appropriate for each course.

B.   At the course to unit level -- The title, Our American Heritage, identifies a senior high school course to satisfy social studies program goals, K-12.

a.   Examine the rationale and terminal course objectives selected for the American History course.

b.   Examine the instructional content (textbook) selected for the course.

Ask: Into what sub-levels is the content separated? Each sub-level may be classified as a period of history.

(Examples include: The Period of Exploration, The Colonial Period, The Revolutionary War Period).

c.   For each period, ask: What are desired and appropriate learning outcomes that could reasonably be expected from a study of this instructional content?

   *   Each response is a potential objective.
   *   Brainstorm to identify all possible enabling objectives.
   *   Select those objectives most useful when considering desired student change.

d.   Each period may be divided into units.

(Examples of unit titles include: For The Colonial Period -- The Northern Colonies, The Middle Colonies, and The Southern Colonies.

e. For each unit, ask: What are desired and appropriate learning outcomes that could reasonably be expected from a study of this instructional content?

* Each response is a potential unit objective.
* Brainstorm to identify all possible enabling unit objectives.
* Select those goals most useful when considering desired student change.

f. Continue the breakdown to the lowest level desired.

g. Adapt prescribed instructional content to facilitate attainment of desired learning outcomes.

Elementary School Science Program

A second example of instructional content selection before goal selection can be found when considering a conceptually oriented elementary school science program.

A. At the program to course level --

a. Write a rationale for the 1-6 science program.

b. List the program goals.

c. Construct a scope and sequence that outlines the instructional content for the total program.

d. Write a brief summary of the concepts to be learned in each course. Identify the instructional materials that will be used.

(Instructional materials in the form of kits: Grade 1, Organisms and Material Objects; 2, Life Cycles and Interactions; 3, Populations and Relativity; Grade 4, Environments and Subsystems; 5. Communities and Systems; 6, Ecosystems and Energy).

e. You may choose to write a brief rationale for each course.

f. Select terminal objectives appropriate for each course.

B. At the course to sub-course ... unit level --

The title, Ecosystems, identifies a grade six offering to satisfy 1-6 science program goals.

a. Examine the rationale (if provided) and terminal course objectives selected for the course, Ecosystems.

b. Examine the instructional content selected for the course. List concepts which support an understanding of the generalization, Ecosystem.

(Examples include: Biosphere, Water Cycle, Food Chain).

c. List desired and appropriate objectives for each concept listed above.

d. Identify sub-concepts for each concept above.

(Examples include: For Food Chain -- Carnivore, Herbivore, Omnivore).

e. List desired and appropriate objectives for each sub-concept listed above.

f. Adapt prescribed instructional content to facilitate attainment of desired learning outcomes.

In the examples above the instructional content was identified with topic or concept titles. Objectives were used as definitions of learning outcomes for each title. Major titles were divided into series of sub-titles. Objectives were then selected for each sub-title. The final step matched instructional content with established objectives.

A High School Music Education Course

As a third example of determining instructional content before goal selection, we will look at a freshman level general music education course.

The instructional content was selected first and the learning outcomes were identified second.

This is an example of a curriculum construction task in which the instructional content was not specified by a textbook. The writer had to determine both the instructional content and the learning outcomes.

The freshman level course is divided into eight units and covers thirty-six weeks of instruction. A time limit is suggested for each unit. The unit and sub-unit titles are listed below.

Freshman Music

I. The Elements of Music   3 weeks

    A. Dimensions of tone
    B. Basic elements
    C. Design elements
    D. Performance media and interpretation

II. Popular Music   3 weeks

    A. The rise of popular music in America
    B. Basic-- tin pan alley to rock
    C. Music analysis of pop-rock idiom

III. Classical Music   17 weeks

    A. Early music through the Renaissance
    B. Baroque music
    C. Rococo and pre-classical music
    D. Music of the classical period
    E. Romanticism and post-romanticism
    F. Music of the twentieth century

IV. Jazz   4 weeks

    A. General characteristics
    B. Traditional jazz styles
    C. Big-band styles
    D. Modern jazz styles

V. Folk and Ethnic Music   4 weeks

    A. The oral tradition
    B. Ethnic music of the United States
    C. Music of Asia
    D. Music of Africa
    E. Folk music of Europe
    F. Music from the Eastern countries

VI. Music Theatre   2 weeks

    A. Operetta
    B. Musical comedy
    C. Musical play

VII. Synthesis: A Review of Music   3 weeks

    A. Rhythm
    B. Melody
    C. Harmony

D. Form
E. Performance
F. Interpretation
G. Style

The next necessary step is assignment of terminal course objectives. Then unit and sub-unit enabling objectives need to be written. These enabling objectives will be matched to the titles so they define the intended purpose of each instructional content.

Assuring A Usable Product

If the goal analysis begins at the program level, a breakdown to a course or unit level may be sufficient. If the analysis begins at a unit level, instructional content and objectives for lesson planning should be included. As you assign learning outcome statements to the various levels of instructional content, ask:

a. Do the more specific learning outcome statements support the broader learning outcome statements?
     (Does it appear that the sub-statements were derived from the broader statements?)

b. Do all objectives define expected outcomes from content, or do some objectives appear to be forced into the curriculum?
     (Do all objectives fit the instructional content or does it appear that some objectives were artificially put into the curriculum, rather than representing a natural outcome of instructional content?)

As you examine the rough draft of your written curriculum document, ask: How can it be improved. Consider modification through emphasis/treatment, addition/omission, until the subject matter becomes the appropriate vehicle to satisfy desired learning as defined in the outcome statements.

An Eight Step Curriculum Writing Plan for High Schools

A simple, straight forward, step-by-step plan for writing a curriculum guide can simplify construction. The principal of Walther High School provided each instructor with an eight step strategy for writing a course syllabus.

1. Carefully read the school and department philosophies.
2. Carefully read the school and department goals.
3. Write a course rationale.
4. Write course objectives.
5. List course units.
6. Write unit objectives.
7. Write or select content and activities.
8. Write evaluations for units and the course.

Imagine yourself developing a syllabus for a course, Consumer Economics. Each step you would follow is discussed below.

Step #1 -- Examine the School and Department Philosophies

Step #1 should be studied to assure that you know what the school and your department consider important considerations when reasoning the purposes of education.

Step #2 -- Examine the Program Goals

Step #2 will provide an understanding of the major thrusts in your school's education program and the strands which structure your department program.

School Goals:

Because of their schooling, students will develop

1. ... 2. ...

3. knowledge, skills, and attitudes to becoming worthy citizens.

...

Department Goals:

Because of learning from the Social Science Department, student will be able to:
A. ... B. ... C. ... D. ...

E. Develop the basic knowledge, skills, and attitudes

required to live and function effectively within a capitalistic society.

...

Step #3 -- Write A Course Rationale

You reason that the course, Consumer Economics, should be added as a social science offering to fill perceived citizenship need in today's economy. An explanation of the course's unique contribution to the total program is the rationale. Portions of it read:

Rationale:

> Consumption is a process in which all people are continually and actively engaged. It takes place everywhere persons happen to be, in space or on earth. ... To maximize satisfaction while minimizing costs is the fundamental concept of consumer economics. ...

> Consumer economics is therefore concerned with helping each student reach the economic goal of becoming an economically literate citizen.

Step #4 -- Write Course Objectives

The question, What knowledge, skills, and attitudes should students possess when completing the course? is answered by writing a series of course objectives. Some of the objectives read:

Objectives:

> *By the end of this course, students will be able to:*
>
> 1. *State and describe at least five ways in which consumer economics plays a vital role in their lives as consumers.*
> 2. *Define, apply, and describe the role of economic goals to consumer behavior.*
> 3. *... 4. ... 5. ...*
> 6. *Calculate simple statistics, mathematics problems, ...*

*which are necessary for making rational choices both
as individuals and as members of family units.*

Step #5 -- List Course Units

Units are the building block of courses. Fifteen units are selected
to complete the consumer course offerings. The unit titles:

The Basic Four Food Groups; A Balanced Meal; The Best
Buy; Good Food and Junk Food; Are Brand Names Better?
Why Pay for Water and Air? Additives; Grading Foods;
Bargain Hunting; Generic Brand Foods; The Consumer Price
Index; Annual Food Budget; Sales Gimmicks; Discount Food
Stores; and Food Fraud, make up the course offerings.

Step #6 -- Write Unit Objectives

Each of your units contributes to one or more of the several course
goals. Nine of the units --

The Best Buy; Good Food and Junk Food; Why Pay for
Water and Air? Grading Foods; Bargain Hunting? Generic
Brand Foods; Sales Gimmicks; Discount Food Stores; and
Food Fraud, --

contribute directly to either course goals #2 or #6, or to both #2
and #6. One unit that teaches toward both goals #2 and #6 is
"The Best Buy." This unit, described by a single objective and two
class activities, is presented on the following page.

You develop goal correlations beyond unit and course objectives.
Connections between course objectives and department goals are
also demonstrated. Course objectives #2 and #6 support department goal E. You show relationships among "economic goals and
consumer behavior" (course objective #2), "calculating to make
rational choices as consumers" (course goal #6), and "will develop
the basic knowledge, attitudes, and skills required to live and
function effectively within a capitalistic economy" (department
goal E). Department goal E upholds the school goal #3, "will
develop knowledge, skills, and attitudes to becoming worth
citizens." While identification of specific relationships should not
be considered a requirement for curriculum guide construction, it
is useful to note what relationships do exit.

Unit Objectives:

By the end of this unit, students will be able to:

   a. prepare shopping lists that represent the greatest food value per dollar spent.

   b. judge the worthiness of purchasing at various stores.

   ...

Step #7 -- Write or Select Content and Activities

School Goal   # 3   Unit: THE BEST BUY
Department Goal   E
Course Objective   # 2, # 6

Objectives: Activities:

By the end of this unit, students will be able to:

Students prepare high and low priced menus, write grocery shopping list, shop for foods using ads and store visits to determine best buys for each item on the list.

a. prepare shopping lists that represent the greatest food value per dollar spent.

Compare stores to find best value store.

b. judge the worthiness of purchasing as various stores.

Discuss feasibility of shopping at several stores to get best buys.

Discuss factors other than price that determine where food is purchased.

...

...

Culminating Activity: Class develops poster for display in school atrium -- 20 Ways to Waste Money Buying Food. -10 Ways to Save Money Buying Food.

Step #8 -- Write Evaluation

A list of items used to check student progress includes assessment of activities, written assignments, and tests. A description of the assessment process is prepared.

Consumption of food is an active process and consequently a large portion of the student's evaluation will be directed toward activities and processes. The following scheme will be employed:

Activities -- 50%

>   Listing menus
>   Planning menus
>   Reports
>   Taste testing and ranking
>   Supermarket and other store visits
>   Role playing

Tests -- 50%

>   Written   25%
>   Defining the basic four food groups
>   Interpreting labels
>   Describing the unit pricing process
>   Describing product differentiation fallacies
>   Describing the use of grading as buying guides
>   Calculating the CPI
>   Describing Gimmicks
>   Describing food frauds

>   Consumer Decision Making Tests   25%
>   Tests using displays will be set up and students will be asked to choose the best buy on the basis of information supplied with each display.

>>   Example: Three menus displayed by pictures of food products. Which one is best?

>>   Four brands of a certain kind of food will be displayed. Students must choose the one which provides the greatest value.

Thematic Curriculum Designs

Thematic curriculum designs cross and mix subject fields. A theme is chosen and students are guided to investigate topics suggested by their association with the theme.

Topics are generally conceptual titles. Many titles have an identification with social studies or science. Conceptual topics lend themselves to study because they are by definition abstract. Concepts such as structures, energy, wars, travel, foods, electricity, connections, dependencies, communities, and countries have proven effective organizing centers. Events such as WWII, westward movement, dating, vacations, and birthdays can also be used.

Two approaches to thematic design are (a) the topic driven theme approach and (b) the discipline/subject field driven theme approach.

Topic Driven Theme Approach

Topic driven theme designs totally dispense with subject matter lines. No effort is made to assign topics to subject fields. Nor do designers ask, "To what subject matter is this topic related?" Once the theme is selected, topics related to the theme are listed and relationships from theme to topic and topic to subtopic are highlighted. Figure Five graphically demonstrates this relationship. As you read the descriptions that follow, try to imagine how their parts could form diagrams as shown in Figure Five. The figures, Heat, page 23, Space, page 24, and Flight, page 26 are specific examples of the topic driven theme approach.

Our Ecosystem

Students visit a wood lot and pond. They bring back an assortment of wriggly specimens for an aquarium, as well as crawly creatures for a terrarium. Student curiosity leads to a widening array of study-topics that range across titles such as:

> mosquitoes, daphnia, eggs and tadpoles, brine shrimp; sink or float, clay boats, properties of liquids, pollution; ants, mealworms, butterflies; earthworms, reptiles, mammals; bone structures, human body; plant identification, leaf mounting; taping outdoor sounds, outdoor art, song about nature; ...

Exploring Our Community

The topic, Exploring Our Community, begins with a mapping project to define locations of roads, streets, rivers, railroads, and natural features.

Figure Five

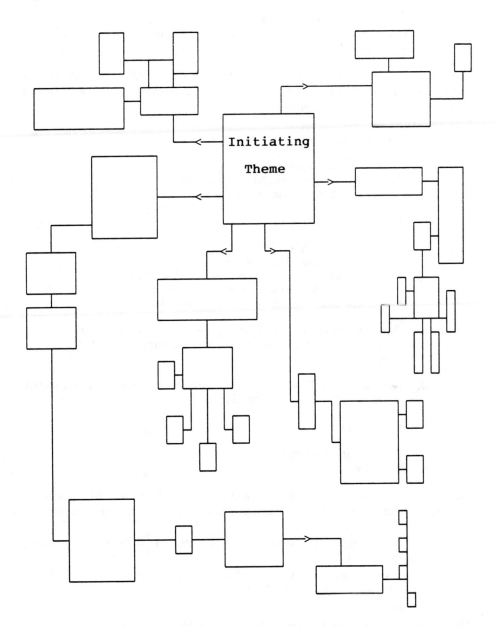

Further inquiry leads to identification of locations for:

> gas stations, fast food restaurants, stores of various descriptions; factories, warehouses; single family dwellings, condos, town houses, apartments, mobile homes; schools, churches and synagogues; ...

The question, Why is each of the above located where it is? opens a plethora of discussions and investigations. Examples of additional questions for research include:

    a.   For service businesses, stores, etc., ask --

         *   who owns them?
         *   what do they sell/offer as a service?
         *   who are their customers?

    b.   For industries, ask --

         *   who owns them?
         *   what are their raw materials?
         *   from where do the raw materials come?
         *   what do they make with them?
         *   where are the finished products sold?

    c.   How are these businesses/industries connected to other parts of the country/world?   (re-examine a and b above)

    d.   How are the following industries/service organizations connected to other parts of the country/world?

         *   agriculture
         *   religious communities
         *   education communities
         *   other

When constructing thematic curricula, identification of learning outcomes follows selection of desired study-topics. In many cases

  * a set of basic objectives that relate to skill development, together with
  * a set of general objectives that relate to knowledge and attitude is all that's desired.

Discipline/Subject Field Driven Approach

Themes may be developed using disciplines or subject fields as the organizing construct. An integration by disciplines or subject fields begins with identification of an organizing center. The teacher/school staff selects, as a unifying construct, a theme from which a variety of related ideas can be easily generated. Following identification of the theme, disciplines or subject fields to be examined are selected. Listing theme related topics under each discipline or subject field is then begun.

Constructing Discipline/Subject Thematic Units

The several disciplines or subject fields into which the school's curriculum is divided may become the categories for selecting and locating the various thematic topics. Typical selections include mathematics, language arts, social studies, science, the fine arts, and physical development and health. Since many themes associate with moral and "world view" questions, philosophy/theology may be an added subject heading.

The planning process for one faculty began by naming the school's subject fields as shown in Figure Six. Figure Seven lists the thematic topics that were generated under each subject field.

Figure Six

THEMATIC UNIT

Subject Field Concept Model

Figure Seven

THEMATIC UNIT

Subject Field Concept Model

A Unit on Africa

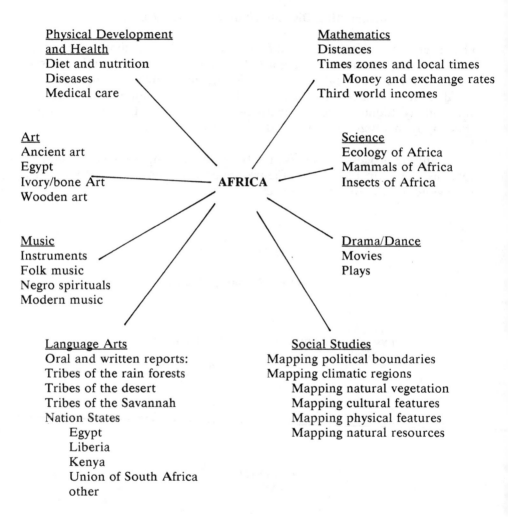

Physical Development
and Health
Diet and nutrition
Diseases
Medical care

Mathematics
Distances
Times zones and local times
Money and exchange rates
Third world incomes

Art
Ancient art
Egypt
Ivory/bone Art
Wooden art

AFRICA

Science
Ecology of Africa
Mammals of Africa
Insects of Africa

Music
Instruments
Folk music
Negro spirituals
Modern music

Drama/Dance
Movies
Plays

Language Arts
Oral and written reports:
Tribes of the rain forests
Tribes of the desert
Tribes of the Savannah
Nation States
    Egypt
    Liberia
    Kenya
    Union of South Africa
    other

Social Studies
Mapping political boundaries
Mapping climatic regions
Mapping natural vegetation
Mapping cultural features
Mapping physical features
Mapping natural resources

Brainstorming may be used to encourage many and varied topics from which to examine the unit theme. Four brainstorming rules are:

a. No suggestions may be criticized during the session.
b. "Free-wheeling" is encouraged. Creative ideas are encouraged.

c. Many ideas are desired. Evaluation of ideas is delayed.
d. Piggy-backing on ideas is encouraged. Two or more sug-
    gestions may be collapsed into a single new or revised
    idea.

It is often wise for participants to write a few ideas on paper prior to group
sharing as a way to start the brainstorming process.

The array of brainstormed associations from the web now needs to be
organized. One strategy directs teachers to formulate a series of questions
that guide student investigations. Figure Eight lists questions that were used
to direct inquiry on the topics listed under Mathematics.

A final step was listing methods to resolve each question or direction and
materials necessary for their resolution. The example in Figure Nine shows
how resolution of the question, "What is the distance from Cairo, Egypt to:
... ," was pursued.

Figure Eight

THEMATIC UNIT

Subject Field Concept Model

Africa

Mathematics

What is the **Distance** from: Cairo, Egypt to Monrovia, Liber-
                                        ia; to Cape Town, South Africa;
                                        to Nairobi, Kenya; to Lagos, Ni-
                                        geria; to New York; to Tokyo; etc.

How many **time zones** are there in Africa?

When it is noon in Chicago, what is the **time** in Cairo, Monrovia,
Cape Town, Nairobi, Lagos, etc.?

What are the names for **money** in Egypt, Liberia, South Africa,
Kenya, Nigeria,...?

How much Egypt, Liberia, South Africa, Kenya, Nigeria, ...
currency could you **exchange** for an American dollar?

What is the average family **income** in Egypt, Liberia, South Africa,
Kenya, Nigeria ...?

Figure Nine

THEMATIC UNIT
Subject Field Concept Model
Africa

<u>Mathematics</u>

What is the flying **Distance** from: Cairo to Monrovia, Cape Town, Nairobi, Lagos, New York, Tokyo, Moscow?

Methods

1. List African disembarkation cities.

2. Use ruler to measure length from Cairo to disembarkation cities.

3. Compute distance using map mileage scale.
    Compare scaled miles per inch with actual inches measured to find actual mileage between cities.

Example:

$$\text{Scaled } \frac{\text{miles}}{\text{inch}} = \frac{\text{Actual miles}}{\text{Measured inches}}$$

$$\text{Scaled } \frac{100 \text{ miles}}{1 \text{ inch}} = \frac{\text{Number of miles}}{\text{measured inches}}$$

$$\frac{100 \text{ miles}}{1 \text{ inch}} = \frac{(600 \text{ miles})}{6 \text{ inches}}$$

4. List non-African cities of disembarkation.

5. Use string to measure length on globe.

6. Match length of string with rule to determine length of string.

7. Compute distance using globe mileage scale.

Materials

U.S. map with mileage scale
ruler
globe with mileage scale
string

Jacobs[8] (p. 53-65) offered alternate strategies for exploring the topics listed under each discipline or subject field. A unit on flight for elementary school children generated the web shown as Figure Ten. Questions that moved from fundamental to complex issues were used to shape the unit. They were:

1. What flies?
2. How and why do things in nature fly?
3. What has been the impact of flight on human beings?
4. What is the future of flight?

Figure Twelve shows how Bloom's taxonomy was used by the elementary school teachers to ensure the cultivation of higher-level thought processes.

When constructing the unit on intelligence shown as Figure Eleven, a high school team devised the following questions to organize their study:

1. What is intelligence?
2. How is human intelligence measured?
3. How did human intelligence evolve?
4. Is intelligence a solely human quality?
5. How is creative intelligence expressed?

Figure Thirteen demonstrates how the problem solving model was used to direct high school student inquiry. An agreed-to format may be preferred to guide teacher teams with their unit planning. The form shown as Figure Fourteen may encourage easier sharing with colleagues.

Many interdisciplinary units culminate as students report their findings. Students may have organized as small cooperative groups, large groups, or worked individually.

A variety of sharing forms can be employed. Students may be asked to write and read, speak, debate, draw, paint, sing, dance, or dramatize. They may construct centers, galleries, or dioramas. The full gamut of a learning repertoire is available.

---

[8] Reprinted with permission of the Association for Supervision and Curriculum Development. Copyright (c) 1989 by ASCD. All rights reserved.

160

Figure Ten

**Interdisciplinary Concept Model
A Unit of Flight - Steps 1 and 2**

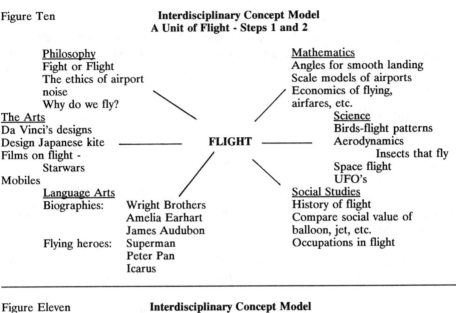

Philosophy
Fight or Flight
The ethics of airport
noise
Why do we fly?

Mathematics
Angles for smooth landing
Scale models of airports
Economics of flying,
airfares, etc.

The Arts
Da Vinci's designs
Design Japanese kite
Films on flight -
    Starwars
Mobiles

FLIGHT

Science
Birds-flight patterns
Aerodynamics
    Insects that fly
Space flight
UFO's

Language Arts
Biographies: Wright Brothers
                Amelia Earhart
                James Audubon
Flying heroes: Superman
                Peter Pan
                Icarus

Social Studies
History of flight
Compare social value of
balloon, jet, etc.
Occupations in flight

Figure Eleven

**Interdisciplinary Concept Model
A Unit on Intelligence - Steps 1 and 2**

Science
The evolution of intelligence
The structure of the brain (chart)
How the brain works: memory
Animal intelligence: training
Genetic influences
Left brain/right brain
mice/rats

The Arts
How ideas are expressed in art
The relationship of creativity to
intelligence
Abstraction in thought and in art
Biographies of geniuses
                mice/rats

Philosophy
Read essays on thought, intelligence
syllogism/premises
Compare novel-short stories in terms
of intellectual and emotional qualities

INTELLIGENCE

Language Arts
Of Mice and Men by
Steinbeck
Differences between
cleverness and wisdom
in writing
Logic of Sherlock Holmes

Mathematics
Measuring intelligence - tests
Dimensions of the brain
Mathematical logic

Social Studies
Anti-intellectualism as a culture
phenomenon
Problems of being a genius
What is philosophy
Rational and irrational behavior
Power of thought in the media
Environmental effects on intelligence

Figure Twelve

Processes

Unit: Flight	Knowledge	Comprehension	Application	Analysis	Synthesis	Evaluation
1. How does nature fly?	Identify bird's flight patterns	Recall principles of bird flight	Chart the movements of bird flight	Compare to man-made flying machines		
2. How and why do people fly?	List principles of aerodynamics	Translate these principles to: balloon jet hand glider	Illustrate the principles as they apply to space flight	What are the historical reasons for change in flying preferences? Write in essay form	Create a new flying machine in blue print	Appraise the machine's effectiveness
		Read the biography of Lindburg and Earhard	List modern-day counterparts to these fliers	Compare similarities & differences between past & modern flight heroes	Write a biography of a fiction flying hero of the future	

162

PROCESS/INQUIRY QUESTION MATRIX

UNIT INTELLIGENCE	GATHERING DATA	ANALYZING THE DATA	DESIGN SOLUTIONS
1. ...			
2. How can intelligence be measured?	Write a summary of the methods and considerations that psychologist and measurement experts use when designing tests.	Analyze the following tests for elementary students: WISC, Otis, Lennon, CTBS. List any areas that might prove problematic. Use items from the tests to support your arguments.	Design an intelligence test based on behavior characteristics for students in your class. It should predict success in the class.
3. How has intelligence evolved?	Chart the evolution of animal and human intelligence on a timeline. Use illustrations when appropriate.	On the basis of what we know about the hemispheres of the brain, analyze the dominant hemispheres you use in home and school functions.	Design an anatomical diagram of the brain of human beings ten thousand years from now. You should be able to support any changes in the brain on the basis of past evolutionary trend.
4. ...			
5. ...			

Figure Fourteen

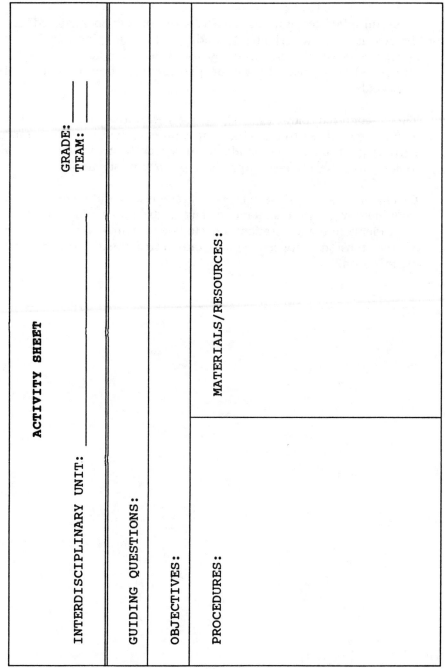

ACTIVITY SHEET

INTERDISCIPLINARY UNIT: _____

GRADE: _____
TEAM: _____

GUIDING QUESTIONS:

OBJECTIVES:

MATERIALS/RESOURCES:

PROCEDURES:

Summary

A useful plan for guiding construction of subject-centered curricular designs is a goal oriented paradigm. In this plan, goal statements appear to become the driving force for decision making. Subject matter selection may follow or precede selection of course through unit goals.

Theme-centered paradigms allow for innovative and creative choices at the time of writing and during implementation. These approaches encourage teachers and students to select from an array of possible topics those topics most appropriate for investigation.

Determination of instructional strategies should result from an examination of goal statements and instructional content, as well as an understanding of student development. Curriculum is the product of the tension between goals and instructional content and their organization.

BIBLIOGRAPHY

Jacobs, H. H. (1989). Interdisciplinary concept model: A step-by-step-approach for developing integrated units of study. Interdisciplinary curriculum; Design and implementation. Alexandria, VA: Association for Supervision and Curriculum Development. 53-65.

Chapter Seven

Evaluation of Learning Outcomes

The four basic parts of an instructional plan are:

a. objectives,
b. content,
c. methods, and
d. evaluation.

These four, organized into instructional programs, courses, units, and lessons are the **nuts and bolts** of curriculum planning. Evaluation provides a measure for judging student mastery of objectives.

In this chapter we will define evaluation and show how it is linked with learning outcomes.

The term, evaluation, is frequently misunderstood. It is important to realize that evaluation is not the same as testing. Evaluation is a three part process that includes obtaining information, forming judgments, and making decisions based on those judgments. When evaluation is considered as part of curriculum writing, it means:

1. obtaining information about student performance toward objectives,

2. forming judgments about student mastery of objectives based on the information obtained, and

3. making decisions about future objectives as they relate to judgment of student performance.

Evaluation is the ever present companion of objectives. If education is the process of changing students, then objectives are the description of students after the change has been completed, and evaluation is obtaining information about desired change, judging of the degree to which the change took place, and making decisions for future action.

Ellis (1986), when discussing instructional planning at a daily level, identifies three components:

* objectives,
* activities, and
* evaluation.

Objectives describe student competence following instruction; activities, as a composite of content and methods, detail the process used to change students; and evaluation provides the process for assessment, determination of and comparison to standards, and resolution of future action.

Figure One

Objectives

stated in behavioral terms become realized in

Activities

designed to help students develop knowledge,
skills, and values, which are examined through

Evaluation

to enable students, teachers, and
parents to assess learning outcomes,(objectives)
judge if an acceptable level of competence
was reached, and decide future action.

Ellis (p.293-294) showed relationships among the three components by example:

Objective: Students will be able to state ways in which two artifacts are alike and different.

Activities: Students discuss and record similarities and differences between two artifacts in small groups. Student groups share their analysis with the class. The teacher helps students to consider the physical properties, form, and potential uses of artifacts.

Evaluation: The teacher gives groups two new artifacts and asks them to record differences and similarities, then judges if students met the learning outcome as stated in the objective.

Referents for Judging Progress

The evaluation reported above used the objective as the specific referent for judgment. In all evaluation a referent for determining judgment must be agreed to.

TenBrink[1] (Cooper) identified three types of referents which correspond to three types of judgments that result from their use:

* norm referenced judgments,
* criterion referenced judgments, and
* self referenced judgments.

Norm Referenced Judgments

Norm referenced judgments have a long history in American education. This form of valuative interpretation developed from a desire to differentiate among individuals, or to discriminate among the individuals of some defined group, on whatever was being measured. Norm referenced judgments are made by comparing information about an individual on some task with information about a group of similar individuals on the same task. Norm referenced judgments show how well an individual performs in comparison with the individual's peers or some other selected group (Cooper). The individual's position in the normative group is the concern; thus the comparison is relative rather than absolute. When the concern is whether students have mastered specific skills and knowledge, norm referenced judgments are less appropriate.

Norms are defensible references because they are a relational measure of learning outcome attainment. Much of the subject matter students are expected to learn is not reduced to criterion referenced competence statements. For example, educators have not usually reduced the content called American history to lists of criterion referenced objectives. Yet, it is understood that the body of content identified as American history is to be studied and learned as well as each student is able. It is also accepted that all students will not (and perhaps should not) be expected to attain to the same level of understanding. A norm referenced judgment assumes that a few will master most of the content, many will master some of it, and the remainder will master little of it. Those who master **some** of the content represent the **average** student.

---

[1] Parts of this section reprinted by permission of D.C. Heath and Company, Lexington, MA.

Norm referencing generally compares each student with the **average** student. The amount of difference between a student's score and the middle score is an indication of how great the student's mastery of the content differs from the norm.

Norm referenced judgments are used when teachers grade on **the curve**. When grading on the curve the teacher selects a score value from the range of score values to represent the midpoint and assigns a grade, perhaps a C or B-. Intervals are determined and the range of grades, A - F, is fixed to sets of scores. It is usually assumed that the score-group with the most students in it will be graded with the mid-point grade, and there will be an equal number of students graded higher and lower than the mid-point grade.

Most standardized achievement tests are designed primarily for norm referenced interpretations. Norms are generated from the scores of groups of students that have taken the test. Most often the scores of the normative group represent a typical or average performance. Standardized tests such as the Iowa Test of Basic Skills provide national norms for grade equivalent scores. These are converted scores computed from raw scores earned by the norm generating students. Grade equivalent scores specify a grade level and a month of that grade level for each student's raw score. For example, a grade equivalent score of 93 means the student performed as a **typical** ninth grader during the third month of the school year.

Percentile norms are also provided for comparing students with their grade level peers. For example, a student whose raw score converts to a percentile score of 69 has scored higher than 69 percent of the normative group for that grade level on that test.

Criterion Referenced Judgments

Criterion referenced judgments require comparisons to be made between an individual's attainment of a goal and a behavioral description of that goal. This type of judgment is concerned with level of competence achieved on a criterion, rather than performance in comparison with others. Criterion referenced judgments are made by comparing the information of student performance with statements of performance criteria. In most cases the criteria are behaviors stated in observable and measurable terms. TenBrink (Cooper) offers the following examples of criterion referenced judgments:

    a.   A typing teacher graded students on how many words they typed per minute. Sixty words per minute = A, 50 words per minute = B, etc.

b. A junior high school English teacher gave passing grades to students who produced at least six of the ten basic sentence patterns studied during the unit on a final test.

c. A shop teacher graded one test on the basis of the number of tools students could correctly identify out of the total number of tools tested.

d. A high school history teacher graded students by comparing the number of course objectives they successfully completed with the total number available for mastery.

In the above examples, information about students was compared with information concerning the instructor's expectations for the students. None of the judgments required student's performance to be compared with that of peers. A student's performance or position within a group will tell the instructor little about what skills and content the student has actually mastered. A student could rank high within a group and yet not have met the objectives set for that student. Conversely, a student could score low on a test and have met the objectives, providing the criterion did not require a high level of mastery.

With certain curriculum designs the instructor is interested in how well the student has met specific instructional objectives. Attainment of instructional objectives at some level of acceptability, perhaps mastery or partial mastery, then becomes the criterion for judging achievement. This level of achievement measurement may be used when decisions about whether students should exit from a study of the present subject matter and proceed to another level of learning are made.

Criterion referenced programming assumes all student achievement will be part of a continuum of achievement ranging from no proficiency at all to perfect performance. When using criterion referenced instruction programs, standards are chosen which represent points along achievement continuum. One point is selected as the minimal subject matter mastery level for allowing students to pass on to further stages of learning. The criterion is usually determined prior to actual instruction. This standard of acceptability may be stated in the instructional objective or as a supplement to the stated objective.

The criterion referenced objectives defined in chapter four include within them the condition under which students are measured, the specific task students will attempt, and the minimal acceptance level for mastery. Thus the objective --

> *   *By the end of this unit, given a paper on which 20 basic addition facts are written in the form, x + y = [ ], students will correctly write the sum of at least 18 basic addition facts in three minutes, --*

includes all of the three criteria necessary for determining mastery of the objective. The objective (Nicholls) --

> *   *By the end of this unit, students should show increased sensitivity towards other people, --*

is an example of a statement which needs considerable further definition before satisfactory evaluation is possible. A discussion which follows under the heading, "Objective Clarity and Precision Related to Assessment," shows one strategy for aiding interpretation and assessment of this objective.

Sometimes a percent correct on a test of an objective is established as the criterion. Eighty percent is a frequently used acceptance level. If an 80 percent correct criterion is used, it means that a student who has scored 80 percent or more correct on a measure of an objective is judged to be sufficiently competent in that objective to move on in the instructional sequence.

Criterion judgments are human decisions. As such, they are subject to frequent re-evaluation and adjustment based on their appropriateness as transition points.

Diagnostic Prescription Teaching as described in Chapter Five requires the use of carefully written criterion referenced objectives. The Mastery Learning Program described in Chapter Five and the modularized instruction program and modular example, Learning About Shapes and Sizes, found in Chapter Nine, are final examples of curricula which might profitably use criterion referenced goal judgments.

Self Referenced Judgments

When information about an individual is compared with other related information about that individual, a self referenced judgment is made. This type of judgment can be useful when the instructor wishes to assess individual student change such as gains in achievement, attitude adjustments, behavior improvements, and the like.

Judgments are usually based on assessment of change from a previous assessment of performance. If information is available about a student prior to instruction, that information can be compared with newly gotten information following instruction. In this way the instructor can determine to what degree the student has changed with respect to the objectives toward which the instruction was intended.

TenBrink (Cooper) states that it is important to note that self referenced judgments are often formed on the basis of previously formed norm referenced or criterion referenced judgments. An instructor might decide that a student has made a great deal of progress because on the last test the student's percentile rank in class was low but now it is high. In this case a comparison between two norm referenced judgments formed the basis for a self referenced judgment.

Progress may also be a judgment of achievement on a continuum. A student may be judged to make excellent progress because the student moved from almost no proficiency in a particular skill to a moderately high level of proficiency as shown on a continuum defining the skill. In this case a self referenced judgment based on a comparison of two criterion referenced judgments was made.

Objective Clarity and Precision Related to Assessment

Curriculum makers attempt to construct learning experiences which give students the best chance to make progress toward stated objectives. Student progress toward objectives is the main criterion for determining the success of a curriculum.

Some objectives are not easily measured. Grade level/course objectives may not be measurable until schooling is completed. There are few satisfactory classroom techniques for measuring attainment of objectives that are concerned with interests, attitudes, and values. Yet it is the responsibility of educators to assess all intended learning in an attempt to determine growth of students and worthiness of curricula.

Evaluation must be directly connected to instructional objectives. Since there is such a close relationship between evaluation and objectives, an adequate statement of instructional objectives is a prerequisite for conducting evaluation. However, during the initial writing of objectives the curriculum maker should not be unduly concerned about their measurement. The first purpose of objectives is to target intended student change. The second purpose is to direct evaluation of intended change.

Objectives should, however, be written with clarity and precision. Well written objectives offer the best guarantee that worthwhile assessments will follow.

Below are four examples based on work by Audrey and Howard Nicholls (Nicholl, p.72-76) to demonstrate how clarity and precision can be written into the objective statement.

> Example #1: *By the end of this lesson, students should be able to name in French articles of common use in the classroom.*

The objective is fairly clear and provides sufficient guidance for course planning, but greater clarity is necessary for careful assessment. A decision must be made regarding how many articles students must name before it is ruled that the objective has been achieved.

A revised objective might read:

> *By the end of this lesson, students should be able name in French at least twelve articles of common use in the classroom.*

> Example #2: *By the end of this unit, students should be able to write reports of National Geographic video specials.*

This objective indicates that any report, however short or badly written, is acceptable as evidence of achievement. One could expect that such is not the intention.

A more desirable objective might read:

> *By the end of this unit, students should be able to write reports of National Geographic video specials. The reports will include the purpose of the video, the main findings, and the conclusion to be drawn*

from the findings. Correct spelling, punctuation, and capitalization are required.

Example #3: *By the end of this unit, students should show increased sensitivity towards other people.*

This objective, as written, does not offer sufficient clarity for guidance in course planning. How is one to interpret sensitivity toward other people? It is necessary to define more clearly and precisely the intent of the objective.

The objective could be expanded by including:

> *By the end of this unit, students should show increasing sensitivity towards other people as demonstrated by five observable behaviors.*
>
> a. *Listen to the opinions of others in their group.*
> b. *Help members of their group to carry out tasks.*
> c. *Take part in community service activities.*
> d. *Criticize social practices which show lack of consideration for individuals.*
> e. *Propose alternative practices to those in (d) above.*

While the above statements provide sufficient guidance for course planning, they need to be more precise when considering assessment. Is it sufficient that a student display a behavior once or twice? What are minimal expectations?

A revision of the five observable behaviors to include judgments for assessment is shown below.

> a. *Increased listening to the opinions of others in their groups.*
> b. *Increased helping of members of their group to carry out tasks.*
> c. *Take part in community service activities on at least three occasions during the year.*
> d. *Increased criticism of social practices that show lack of consideration for individuals.*
> e. *Increased proposal of alternative practices to those in (d) above.*

Items a and b, listening and helping, could be assessed

through observation and recording. Item c, taking part in community services, will be measured by tabulation. Items d and e, criticizing and proposing, could be assessed by means of rating of pupils in discussion or by means or specially set written work, or even by dramatic means through role - playing.

Items a,b,d, and e will use a self referencing judgments. Item c will use a criterion referencing judgments.

Example #4: *By the end of this track season, the best students will be able to run the 100 yard dash in under 12 seconds.*

If form and style are not a consideration, the objective requires only the opportunity to demonstrate the behavior.

Matching Assessment Task with Objective Task

Chapter Four discussed the different levels of objectives using Bloom's taxonomy. If students are expected to master both high and low level learning, objectives must direct instruction to both levels. If objectives and instruction are directed to lower and higher levels of learning, evaluation should measure this same range of levels.

The range and proportion of low and high level objectives will vary depending on student population and subject matter. Young children's learning will probably include more objectives at knowledge, comprehension, and application levels than those of older students.

Instruction that introduces students to a subject matter will probably include fewer analysis, synthesis, and evaluation objectives than instruction which directs students to integrate earlier learning with other earlier learning.

When constructing tests on subject matter as part of student evaluation, the test maker must match the make-up of the subject matter with an appropriate evidence of mastery. Science subject matter may be product or process oriented. Science programs often emphasize a process approach where students are taught to observe, classify, measure, predict, process data, control variables, interpret data, and more. When student instruction is directed toward skill attainment rather than information acquisition, it is reasonable to assume that evaluation will direct students to demonstrate an ability to use the skill rather than verbalize a knowledge of the skill.

Thus an objective which states --

By the end of this course, students will be able to construct histograms using observed data, --

could appropriately be tested by asking them to construct a histogram using the data in Figure Two.

Figure Two shows a table of data collected during an experiment to see how long it took a white rat to travel a maze during a six day trial period.

Figure Two

Day	Time to Travel Maze (Seconds)
Monday	120
Tuesday	90
Wednesday	60
Thursday	40
Friday	30
Saturday	25

Construct a bar graph on your response sheet which illustrates these data. Be sure to label the axes.

Aligning Assessment Items with Objective Items

Not only must the test maker be concerned that the observed behavior is a behavior which truly assesses the objective, but concern must also be given that all objectives are included for measurement. Some objectives may be assessed through observation, demonstration, or other alternate means. Many will be measured through testing. When a test is written following a unit of study, care must be taken to assure that all objectives deemed appropriate for testing are assessed. This point is examined by Nichols for a high school science unit in Figure Three (Nicholls, p.177).

Figure Three _____

    BLOOD

    Objectives: By the end of this unit, students will, through use of final examination, demonstrate:

      1.   A knowledge of facts and principles

      2.   An understanding of facts and principles

      3.   An ability to apply principles to new situations

      4.   An ability to interpret data

_____

The major headings used to define the scope and sequence of the unit are:

    Subject matter: Unit outline --

      A. Composition of the blood
      B. Functions of the blood
      C. Circulatory system
      D. Lymphatic system

Each objective and outline heading could be broken down into further subdivisions, but for purposes of this illustration it is not necessary. When planning assessment, objectives and subject matter need to be brought together.

Figure Four shows one possible method. For example, of the sixty items, fifteen will test the objective: know facts and principles. Three of these fifteen test items are related to composition of blood, five to functions of blood, four to circulatory system, and three to lymphatic system.

As you can be see from the illustration, assessment forces the test maker to examine objectives in light of subject matter treated. As the curriculum constructor makes decisions about assessment, comparable decisions are made about objectives.

Evaluation and objective writing are inseparably locked together, for evaluation is essentially a matter of looking at students for evidence of progress toward objectives and making judgments and decisions based on that evidence.

Figure Four

OBJECTIVES

	1.Know facts and principles	2.Understand facts and principles	3.Apply principles	4.Interpret data
A Composition of blood	3	3	2	
B Functions of blood	5	8	5	4
C Circulatory system	4	7	5	4
D Lymphatic system	3	2	3	2
Total items	15	20	15	10

Alternate Assessment Strategies

A variety of assessment devices can be appropriate for school use. They include:

rating scales, teacher observations, diaries, written reports, student records, role-playing, interviews, questionnaires, examinations of work in art, crafts, music, and more.

Any device which shows evidence of the behavior indicated in the objective is an appropriate means of assessment (Nicholls).

As stated above, there is no one best way to assess student progress toward desired goals. Student differences, as well as desired goals will direct the curriculum maker to examine a number of alternate evaluation strategies. Ellis briefly examines nine assessment strategies used by teachers (Ellis, 1986, p.138-153).

* **I Learned Statements** give students an opportunity to self-select one or more learnings resulting from instruction.

* **Interviews** may be appropriate to use with student lacking reading or writing skills, and/or as ongoing diagnosis of student learning.

* **Observation** serves both ongoing and summative purposes. Data gathered through observation may purposely be shared with student and/or parent.

* **Summary Sheets** written by students allow them to synthesize learning over one or more instructional periods.

* **Written and Pictorial Assignments** in the form of essays, booklets, pictures, maps, charts, and the like provide evidence of a variety of learning.

* **Checklists** provide an organized record of subject matter encountered and/or mastered. Instruction can be divided into small parcels, each with an identity, and presented to students in sequence. As a student successfully completes a parcel, that accomplishment is noted on the checklist. An example of one checklist use is found in the description of an early childhood mathematics learning center found in Chapter Ten.

* **Essay Tests** provide indications of students' understandings and their ability to present ideas in a logical and coherent manner.

* **Attitude Scales** furnish the instructor with clues to how effectively students are learning and/or how meaningful they think the instruction is.

Summary

Evaluation is a three part process that includes obtaining information, forming judgments, and making decisions. If education is the process of changing students, then goals are a description of the student after the change is completed, and evaluation is the process for obtaining information about desired change, judging the degree to which change occurred, and making decisions about goals, students, and instruction based on that judgment.

Three types of evaluation referents correspond to judgments that result from their use. They are norm referenced judgments, criterion referenced judgments, and self referenced judgments. Goal selection, as well as assessment, should address high and low level learning. Objectives should be written with sufficient clarity and precision to guide evaluation.

There is no best way to assess student progress. The curriculum maker should examine alternate strategies to find those most appropriate for measuring selected instructional objectives when considering subject matter and student body.

BIBLIOGRAPHY

Cooper, J. M., General Editor (1977). Classroom teaching skills: A handbook. (Terry TenBrink, Chapter 10, Evaluation). Lexington, Mass.: D.C. Heath and Company, Lexington, Massachusetts.

Ellis, A. K. (1986). Teaching and learning elementary school social studies. 3rd.ed. Boston: Allyn and Bacon, Inc.

Nicholls, A. & Nicholls H. (1978). Developing a curriculum: A practical guide. Boston: George Allen and Unwin (Registered as Harper Collins *Publishers* Ltd (Scotland 1949 No. 27389), Westerhill Road, Bishopbriggs, Glasgow G642QT.

Part Two

Examples of

Curriculum Writing

Chapter Eight

The Curriculum Guide

A curriculum guide is a written document. Its purpose is to direct teacher instruction and student learning within a specific field of the total curriculum. Curriculum guides are usually written to define instructional programs or courses.

Examples of instructional programs include:

Language Arts, K-6; Mathematics, 1-8; Science, 9-12; Social Studies, K-12; Industrial Arts, 7-12; Music, 1-6; Physical Education, 7-9; Art, Pre-K.

Examples of courses include:

Trigonometry, American History, English I, Fifth Grade Mathematics, First grade Reading, Music for Kindergarten.

Curriculum Guide Examples

We will examine curriculum guides for use with early childhood centers, elementary schools, and high schools. They are the:

* Rantoul K-8 School Health Curriculum Guide

* State of Illinois Department of Education K-12 Guides

* Columbia Elementary School District Reading Curriculum Guide

* Agape Early Childhood Mathematics Curriculum Guide

The Structure of Curriculum Guides

Components included as part of curriculum guides vary according to purpose and focus, as well as to time, talent, and resources. To give you an idea of the comprehensive and varied character of fully developed curriculum guides beginning at the program level, and to sort out which components might be most useful to your specific case, the following outline will be followed:

* program rationale,
* program goals,
* program organization and/or instructional theory,
* course level/grade level objectives, or other organizer, and for some guides,
* unit objectives, lesson objectives, methods instructions, and evaluations strategies.

Program Rationale

Program level curriculum guides should begin with a statement of rationale. The rationale provides answers to questions such as:

1. How are the instructional program and the school's philosophy related?
2. How does this instructional program fit with other instruction programs?
3. What are contemporary views of the instructional content's value?

Program Goals

A statement of the program goals should follow the program rationale. This goal statement will show an obvious relationship to the school goal statement. It will identify the specific learning paths on which instruction proceeds. Learning goals are not concerned with specific levels of achievement at specified periods of time. They are, rather, the vertical learning strands upon which the series of specific outcome statements, learning objectives, are ordered. Learning objectives, then, mark progress along each learning goal.

Program Organization and Instructional Theories

You may need to explain how the curriculum was structured so the reader can readily interpret and implement it. You may select a specific design such as single subject, disciplines, correlated, integrated, thematic; and design configurations such as spiral, post hole, widening horizons; and analyses such as, selection of learning outcomes first, then instructional content, selection of instructional content first, then learning outcomes, a topic driven thematic approach, or a discipline/subject field driven thematic approach.

You may also need to explain contemporary views of how the instructional content should be taught. Perhaps the views of theorists such as Piaget, Gagne, Bruner, Erikson, Skinner, or others need to be explained so the reader will understand why specific content was selected and how content should be implemented.

Course Level/Grade Level Objectives

Curriculum guides should list learning objectives that specify intended learning outcomes following instruction. Each objective should show a direct and obvious linkage to the program goals.

Unit Objectives, Lesson Objectives, Methods Instructions, Evaluation Strategies

Some curriculum guides include information specific to instructional units, or sets of lessons or methods, or evaluation. These guides list unit, lesson or activity objectives, as well as suggest content, methods, and evaluation instructions.

Examining the Structure of One Curriculum Guide

The Rantoul School K-8 Health Curriculum Guide found on pages 191-201 uses a --

Selection of Learning Outcomes First, Then Instructional Content -

approach to curriculum building. The basic structures are

* a program rationale,
* program goals,
* grade level objectives, and
* unit level objectives, content, methods, and evaluation.

The program's scope and sequence is organized using a spiral curriculum structure. The nine program goals shown on pages 191-

193 are treated as vertical learning **strands.** Strands are encountered at every grade level as content is spiraled upward from kindergarten to grade eight. Grade level objectives are written for each strand and grade level intersection (see pages 194-197).

Cumulatively, the eight to nine vertical strands, intersected at nine horizontal levels, provide the organization for a comprehensive health educational program. Within each grade level these strands define objectives and suggest topics for study. Each objective provides the basis for constructing an instructional unit.

An examination of grade level objectives, K-8, (see pages 194-197) shows eight objectives for each grade level, K-6, and nine and ten objectives for grades seven and eight respectively. Since each grade level objective suggests a unit of study, the total curriculum will consist of seventy-five units of study.

Since course goals define the vertical strands, and each strand emphasizes a specific concept, the same concept is encountered and restructured as a unit at each grade level. Therefore, development of a single concept will progress systematically as units are written that spiral back to the same concept at every grade level (see diagram, page 193).

The Mental and Social Health Strand

Below are the grade level objectives for a single strand, Mental and Social Health, as they sequence over the nine grade levels.

Kindergarten: *Recognize self as a person of worth, others of the same age as different, yet persons of equal worth.*

Grade 1:   *Be able to demonstrate positive attitudes and behaviors toward getting along with others.*

Grade 2:   *Develop attitudes and behaviors that assist in understanding what a family is and what students can do to help themselves and others in their family be happy.*

Grade 3:   *Understand feelings and relationships of members within a group.*

Grade 4:   *Be aware of their own needs and the needs of others for good mental and social development.*

Grade 5:   *Recognize the importance and effects of feelings for themselves and others.*

Grade 6:	*Possess an awareness that behavior is an important variable for preventing, reducing, or avoiding stress.*
Grade 7:	*Understand the concepts: personality, emotion, maturity, values.*
Grade 8:	*Recognize that each person's values are unique, and accept others holding different values.*

The strand, Mental and Social Health, is concerned with helping students understand themselves and develop positive self concepts. To assist understanding of how course objectives can be developed as units of study, let us consider the two levels of **strand one**, kindergarten and grade eight.

Kindergarten

The kindergarten objective for strand one reads:

Students will recognize self as a person of worth, others of the same age as different yet persons of equal worth.

Page 198 entitled, Health -- Kindergarten, shows how a unit of study was structured to meet this unit objective. The unit objective is broken into three parts that reads:

By the end of this unit, students will be able to:

1. *Recognize self as a person of worth.*
2. *Recognize others as different.*
3. *Recognize others as persons of equal worth.*

The writer of this unit provides additional focus by including a statement which identifies the main thrust of the unit -- a statement of the Main Idea:

  *   I am special/Others are special.

The format chosen to develop this unit employs four headings: OBJEC-TIVE, CONTENT/CONCEPT, SUGGESTED ACTIVITY, MATERIALS/RESOURCES. The enabling objectives selected to satisfy the unit objectives are listed in the first column according to teaching order. Objective #1 assumes students will recognize that each person is a worthy individual.

The two concepts the teacher will try to develop as part of this objective is: I am a unique individual in appearance and I deserve to be liked by others. The activity, children draw and sign a self portrait and the class tells why they like each person, provides the vehicle for clarifying the concept, unique, and reinforcing the attitude of self worth. Column four identifies special materials necessary to carry out the activity.

Grade Eight

The eighth grade objective for strand #1 reads:

By the end of this unit, students will be able to:

    1. Recognize that each person's values are unique.
    2. Accept others holding different values.

The unit of study written for this objective (see page 199) begins with the same format used in the kindergarten unit (i.e., statements identifying the PROGRAM, STRAND, UNIT OBJECTIVES, and MAIN IDEA). Variation from the kindergarten format is found in the headings for the eighth grade unit. They were selected as: OBJECTIVES, LEARNING EXPERIENCES, RESOURCE, EVALUA-TION. By substituting EVALUATION for CONTENT/CONCEPT a tool is provided for measuring attainment of each enabling objective.

Following completion of the activity, COAT OF ARMS, students provide data which suggest how they view others' values by completing an evaluation entitled: What I Learned From This Activity. The activity uses a Likert scale to rate statements which depict other persons' values. A measurement of level to which students accept others with differing opinions and beliefs (objective #2) is attained as students respond to an evaluation entitled: How Can I Like You When You Won't Agree With Me?

The final section of the Rantoul K-8 Health Curriculum Guide, pages 200-201, lists resource materials. Kit #8, My Values and Me, provides much of the content for the eighth grade unit discussed above.

RANTOUL ELEMENTARY SCHOOL
HEALTH PROGRAM CURRICULUM GUIDE K-8

Rationale

The Health Program of Rantoul Elementary School is an integral and planned part of the total school curriculum. Health education has held a priority position in education goals since 1917 when it was listed as first of the Seven Cardinal Principles by the National Education Association. It is a primary consideration in Rantoul's Elementary School Goal Statement. One of the school's goals focuses on human physiology, health habits, and decision making relative to use of drugs and medicines.

Rantoul Elementary School is concerned with the total growth of each student. This growth begins by instilling proper attitudes toward self, family, and community. These attitudes are achieved through a planned health program that gives children the facts, concepts, and principles related to healthful physical, mental, and social life styles.

Program Goals

The following statements are cited as goals for the Rantoul Health Program. They will be achieved in varying degrees at different grade levels.

Because of the Rantoul Elementary School Health Program, students will have a functional knowledge of:

> a. *Mental and social health*
> b. *Growth and development*
> c. *Safety and first aid*
> d. *Diseases and disorders*
> e. *Nutrition*
> f. *Environment*
> g. *Health information, products and services*
> h. *Dependency causes and substances*
> i. *Health careers and health futures*

Each goal is described below:

A. MENTAL AND SOCIAL HEALTH

Deals with aiding students to understand themselves and develop a positive self-concept which in turn (a) helps them to have a positive relationship with others (b) helps them learn to adapt to pressures in their lives.

B. GROWTH AND DEVELOPMENT AND BODY HYGIENE

Concerns itself with physical, emotional, and social growth. Is concerned with changes in the body and related emotional development. Hygiene focus is on body cleanliness.

C. SAFETY AND FIRST AID

Includes discussion of safety procedures in many areas of life, prevention of accidents and first aid information and skill development.

D. DISEASES AND DISORDERS

Includes study of infectious disease, non-infectious disease, symptoms of common illnesses, and importance of self-care when sick.

E. NUTRITION

Involves how the body uses food, eating habits related to balanced diet, four food groups, function and interrelation of selected body systems.

F. ENVIRONMENT

Deals with caring for the home, school, neighborhood, and with various health problems caused by different types of pollution.

G. HEALTH INFORMATION, PRODUCTS, SERVICES

Studies responsibilities of various health workers. Discusses how to make intelligent decisions concerning health products.

H. DEPENDENCY-CAUSING SUBSTANCES

Emphasis at lower grades on misuse of home

medicine cabinet contents. Study of dependence on tobacco, alcohol, and chemical drugs a major concern at upper grade levels.

I.   HEALTH ORGANIZATIONS, LAWS, CAREERS, AND FUTURES (grades 7-8)

Explores local, state, and national health organizations. Explores laws concerning health and the environment. Explores health careers and health related problems of the future.

Organization of the Curriculum Guide

Since students do not fully master any subject on the first encounter, the health program employs a spiral-strand approach to the overall development of goals. Each goal is treated as a vertical strand. Strands are encountered at every grade level as the content is spiraled upward over the nine grades.

The goal-strands are introduced to the kindergarten at a simplified level. Subsequent encounters emphasize different aspects of each concept or give additional information relative to the concept. Knowledge and understanding are strengthened and expanded as students, through maturation and experience, apply content at progressively higher levels.

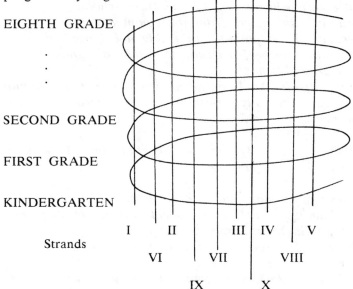

EIGHTH GRADE

.
.
.

SECOND GRADE

FIRST GRADE

KINDERGARTEN

Strands   I   II   III   IV   V

VI   VII   VIII

IX   X

GRADE LEVEL OBJECTIVES

KINDERGARTEN By the end of kindergarten, students will be able to:

1. Recognize selves as a person of worth, others of the same age as different yet persons of equal worth.
2. Recognize the importance of good health habits.
3. Describe what accidents are and act to prevent and control them.
4. Recognize the difference between being sick and well, and name common diseases that affect children.
5. Realize that good nutrition is necessary for proper growth and development.
6. Assist maintenance of a clean, neat, safe, and quiet classroom.
7. Understand the role of the school nurse.
8. Identify medicines and drugs in their lives and realize that only sick people may need drugs.

GRADE ONE   By the end of grade one, students will be able to:

1. Demonstrate positive attitudes and behaviors toward getting along with others.
2. Demonstrate healthful attitudes towards personal grooming and body cleanliness.
3. Practice care when going to and from school.
4. Protect self and others from the common cold.
5. Understand the importance of eating a balanced diet.
6. Assist maintenance of a clean, neat, safe, and quiet environment in and around school.
7. Identify different kinds of health workers in the community.
8. Recognize commonly consumed drugs, medicines, and diet supplements.

GRADE TWO   By the end of grade two, students will be able to:

1. Demonstrate attitudes and behaviors that assist in understanding what a family is and what students can do to help themselves and others in their family be happy.
2. Understand the role rest and exercise play to help healthful growth.
3. Identify safety factors at home, school, and during recreation.

4.   *Understand the function of eyes and ears and their care.*
5.   *Identify foods that belong in the four food groups and state their value.*
6.   *Identify factors involved in a healthful environment and conservation of resources.*
7.   *Appreciate doctors, dentists, and pharmacists as people who help maintain health.*
8.   *Practice the safe use of drugs, medicines, and diet supplements in their homes.*

GRADE THREE   By the end of grade three, students will be able to:

1.   *Understand feelings and relationships of members within a group.*
2.   *Practice good hygiene and dental behaviors.*
3.   *Recognize behaviors relevant to personal safety and to the safety of others.*
4.   *Protect self and others against common illnesses.*
5.   *Plan menus that represent a balanced diet.*
6.   *Recognize neighborhoods, their care and changes.*
7.   *Appreciate people who work in health and safety related jobs.*
8.   *Practice safe use of common drugs found in the home.*

GRADE FOUR   By the end of grade four, students will be able to:

1.   *Demonstrate alertness to their own needs and the needs of others for good mental and social health.*
2.   *Possess a positive attitude to their own bodies.*
3.   *Assist first aid for minor injuries.*
4.   *Practice rules for preventing and controlling communicable diseases.*
5.   *Practice behaviors that assist in maintaining a satisfactory level of nutrition.*
6.   *Explain the importance of pure air and water preservation in our environment.*
7.   *Recognize the need for good health information when developing attitudes about health related behaviors.*
8.   *Recognize abuse of drugs and the need to fight drug abuse.*

GRADE FIVE   By the end of grade five, students will be able to:

1.   *Recognize the importance and effects of feelings for themselves and others.*

2. *Understand that the growing process involves physical, mental, and social changes.*
3. *Provide first aid for minor injuries and be aware of safety practices in recreational activities.*
4. *Identify chronic diseases and their causes.*
5. *Realize the importance of nutrients and the problems of junk food.*
6. *Recognize the effects of air pollution.*
7. *Use information to aid choosing health products and services.*
8. *Understand the effects and problems of alcohol and smoking.*

GRADE SIX   *By the end of grade six, students should be able to:*

1. *Understand an awareness that behavior is an important variable for preventing, reducing, or avoiding stress.*
2. *Identify changes in their own physical, emotional, and social growth during adolescence.*
3. *Describe simple first aid procedures used in emergencies.*
4. *Appreciate their nervous system and begin to establish practices for controlling and preventing disorders.*
5. *Possess a beginning knowledge of body systems and how the body uses food.*
6. *Recognize the value and dangers of pesticides.*
7. *Discriminate when finding, choosing, or using health aids.*
8. *Understand the term, drug abuse.*

GRADE SEVEN   *By the end of grade seven, students will be able to:*

1. *Understand the concepts, personality, emotion, maturity, values.*
2. *Understand the various stages of human growth and development from conception to adulthood.*
3. *Assist first aid for emergencies and develop an awareness of cause of unsafe behavior.*
4. *Describe the nature and treatment of infectious diseases.*
5. *Understand the function of the digestive and respiratory systems.*
6. *Demonstrate ways to improve the quality of the local environment.*
7. *Understand the importance of being a wise shopper when purchasing health products.*
8. *Recognize improper use of dependency-forming drugs such as alcohol, tobacco, and marijuana.*
9. *Demonstrate concern about current health problems and an interest in community health and about health needs.*

GRADE EIGHT   By the end of grade eight, students will be able to:

1.   *Recognize that each person's values are unique, and accept others holding different values.*
2.   *Describe factors contributing to various aspects of a person's physical, social, and mental growth and development.*
3.   *Apply first aid procedures used in common emergencies.*
4.   *Recognize the nature and treatment of non-infectious diseases.*
5.   *Understand function and relationships among various body systems to convert food and oxygen to energy, cellular material, and waste product (digestive, circulatory, urinary systems).*
6.   *Recognize the major problems that upset the balance between humans and the environment.*
7.   *Recognize quackery and consumerism in light of one's responsibility for protecting healthful behaviors.*
8a.   *Understand the proper and improper use of barbiturates, narcotics, alcohol, amphetamines, hallucinogens.*
8b.   *Make wise and intelligent decisions about the use of drugs.*
9.   *Appreciate the role of various health organizations and health careers.*

A GUIDE FOR CURRICULUM WRITERS

Program: **Health -- Kindergarten**

Strand: I -- Mental and Social Health

Unit Objectives: By the end of this unit, students will be able to recognize:

     a.   self as a person of worth,
     b.   others the same age as different,
     c.   others as persons of equal worth.

Unit Idea: I am special / Others are special

Objective	Content/Concept	Suggested Activity	Materials/Resources
a. Self as person of worth	Each human being is unique in appearance and is a person of worth	Children draw self portrait and write name below. Display and tell	Colored pencils, crayons, markers, paper, pencils, etc.
	Non-living things, plants, and animals possess different attributes	Display pictures of living and non-living things. Discuss	Kit 12
b. Others as different	Each person is physically different in height and weight	Take heights and weights of students and graph them	Ruler or yardstick, scale, paper for graphing
	Children come in different shapes and sizes	Students lie on backs and trace each other on butcher paper. Decorate	
c. Others of equal worth	Students should regard themselves as being liked by others	Class guess whose picture each is. Tell decoration. Class tells 3 good things about each student	Butcher paper, markers, paint, etc.
	Students should demonstrate a liking for other students		

CHAPTER 8: THE CURRICULUM GUIDE

Program: **Health -- Grade Eight**

Strand: I -- Mental and Social Health

Unit Objectives: By the end of this unit, students will be able to recognize:

    a.   that each person's values are unique

    b.   accept others holding different views

Main Idea: Examine personal values and compare with values of others

Objectives	Learning Experiences	Resources	Evaluation
a. Recognize uniqueness of each person's individuality	Prepare a personal COAT OF ARMS. Use pictures only in sections 1-5 A.Complete: Activity sheet. B.Complete: What I Learned from This Exercise	Kit 8 Teacher made	Examination of responses on: What I Learned from This Exercise
	Values Continuum exercise sample: It is all right to steal food from a grocery store if you are very, very hungry and have no money. strongly agree disagree	Kit 8	
b. Accept others with differing views	Exercise: How Can I like You When You won't Agree with Me?	Kit 8	Examination of responses on paper: How Can I Like You When You Won't Agree with Me?

TEACHER RESOURCE MATERIALS

A. Materials housed Media Center

    1. "Death and Dying Education Curriculum Guide"
    2. "Drug Education Curriculum Guide"
    3. "Sex Education Curriculum Guide"
    4. Card Catalog Listings:

       a. Community Resources
       b. Games and Simulations -- Health and Nutrition
       c. Health Education Media -- Regional Library

B. Available from School Nurse

    1. Film -- "Becoming a Woman"
    2. Film -- "Becoming a Man"
    3. Charts -- Male sex organs, female sex organs
    4. Sample box of Kotex, Tampons

C. Available from the National Dental Society, Bloomingville, New Jersey

    1. Tooth paste
    2. Tooth brush

D. Supplementary Health Kit Materials

Grade K-1   Kit 12   I AM ME & YOU ARE YOU

    Helps children see themselves as worthy individuals in a community of other worthy individuals. 32 exercises with picture cards, 1 video cassette, activity sheets.

Grade 2   Kit 25   MY FIVE SENSES

    An awareness of the sensory system of the human body. 3 video cassettes and discussion guide.

Grade 3   Kit 16   CARING FOR MY BODY

    Awareness of body care and hygiene. 3 filmstrips with cassettes and discussion guide.

Grade 4   Kit 24   THE HUMAN BODY

Explores body parts. Shows body as functional and graceful. 4 filmstrips with audio cassettes.

Grade 5   Kit 3   SHOULD I EAT JUNK?

Explores importance of nutrients and problems of junk food. 1 Video cassette and discussion guide.

Grade 6   Kit 9   THE BODY SYSTEMS

Develops an awareness of functions of various body systems to use food and oxygen. 8 prints, 3 filmstrips with cassettes, worksheets.

Grade 7   Kit 14   WHAT MAKES ME - ME?

Explores personality, emotion, maturity when entering puberty. 5 filmstrips with audio cassettes, 18 copy masters, 12 idea cards, 3 values exercises.

Grade 8   Kit 22   DRUGS - SHOULD I OR
                              SHOULDN'T I?

Explores proper and improper use of barbiturates, narcotics, alcohol, amphetamines, hallucinogens. 3 video cassettes, 8 worksheets, 5 value activities.

               Kit 8   MY VALUES AND ME

Challenges students to examine values related to behavior choices. Series of values issues and dilemma exercises, some developed through video cassette. 1 video cassette and teacher's manual.

State of Illinois Department of Education Curriculum Guides[1]

The State of Illinois Department of Education Guides provide a straight-forward and reasonable approach to organizing curricula. The guides use a --

> Selection of Learning Outcomes First, Then Instructional
> Content --

approach to curriculum construction. The Department of Education has written a series of six curriculum guides for use with early childhood, elementary, and secondary education. Learning outcomes are expressed as program goals and grade level objectives.

The six school instructional programs are identified as:

 a. Language Arts
 b. Mathematics
 c. Social Sciences
 d. Biological and Physical Sciences
 e. Fine Arts
 f. Physical Development and Health

Each instructional program begins with one or several paragraphs that might be entitled, The Rationale. Learning paths are written as program goals and followed by a clarification of goals and grade level objectives.

We will examine the six curriculum programs by looking at these four components. In each program we will consider:

 a. The Rationale,
 b. The Goals for Learning,
 c. A Clarification of **one** of the Goals for Learning, and
 d. The Objectives related to **that learning goal for one** of the grade levels: 3, 6, 8, 10, 12.

LANGUAGE ARTS

Rationale:

Language arts includes the study of literature and the development

---

[1] For more information write to Illinois State Board of Education, 100 North First Street, Springfield, Illinois 62777.

of skills in reading, writing, speaking, and listening. The most effective instruction occurs when the skills are stressed across the learning areas at all grade levels with the students learning to use skills appropriately in a variety of contexts, applying skills in increasingly complex situations and identifying alternative ways to accomplish purposes. The emphasis in language arts is on skills, not content areas.

The skills and knowledge of the language arts are essential for student success in virtually all areas of the curriculum. They are also central requirements for the development of clear expression and critical thinking. The language arts include the study of literature and the development of skills in reading, writing, speaking, and listening.

The Rationale is followed by a listing of Goals for Learning. The Goals for Learning are the program goals. They define competencies students should strive toward as they progress through the curricular program. It is understood that student growth within these paths will vary.

Goals for Learning

As a result of their schooling, students will be able to:

1. *read, comprehend, interpret, evaluate and use written material;*
2. *listen critically and analytically;*
3. *write standard English in a grammatical, well-organized and coherent manner for a variety of purposes;*
4. *use spoken language effectively in formal and informal situations to communicate ideas and information and to ask and answer questions;*
5. *understand the various forms of significant literature representative of different cultures, eras, and ideas.*
6. *understand how and why language functions and evolves.*

Clarification of Goals for Learning

A goal statement, because it is a single statement, may need clarification. The teacher may ask, "What specific knowledge and skills are to be included?" The example below shows how a specific Goal for Learning, **goal number 3**, was clarified.

Learning Goal 3

As a result of their schooling, students will be able to write standard English in a grammatical, well-organized and coherent manner for a variety of purposes.

This goal is clarified through an introductory paragraph and a listing of the knowledge/skills associated with it.

Clarification:

As a result of instruction in language and composition, students should write compositions demonstrating appropriate levels of complexity.

General Knowledge/Skill Related to Goal 3

The following knowledge and skills are related to this Goal for Learning:

A   Use of appropriate language and style in writing for a variety of purposes and audiences.

B   Ability to develop and maintain a focus with a clear thesis, a main idea, theme, or unifying event.

C   Use of specific information or reasons to support and elaborate the main point.

D   Clear, coherent, logical organization of ideas within the appropriate major discourse structures.

E   Use of standard written English conventions.

F   Ability to revise, edit, and proofread.

Grade Level Objectives

Objectives are written to define the expected outcomes for each of the Learning Goals at a specific grade level. In a completed curriculum program, objectives are written for each of the Learning Goals and at each of the grade levels, K-12. Since there are six Learning Goals for Language Arts, there need to be six sets of objectives written at each grade level.

The grade level selected as an example is **grade 8**. The expected learning outcomes for **Learning Goal 3 at grade level 8** are listed as 12 objectives. Each objective is keyed to a General Knowledge/ Skills Related to Learning Goal 3, A-F.

Grade Eight Learning Objectives

Learning Objectives for Learning Goal 3

By the end of Grade 8, students should be able to:

A1. Know the purposes of public and personal writing.
A2. Use the various forms of public and personal writing.
A3. Write for various audiences.

B1. Focus clearly upon one central idea or event when writing.

C1. Use descriptive details, reasons for an opinion, concrete examples of solutions to a problem and/or an authority's viewpoint to support the main idea.

D1. Write in narrative, expository, descriptive, and persuasive styles.
D2. Use varied methods of paragraph development.
D3. Use appropriate transitions within paragraphs and between paragraphs.

E1. Write using conventional forms of standard English.
E2. Use the dictionary or other resources when unsure about the spelling of a word when writing.

F1. Correct fragments and run-on sentences.
F2. Revise written work to correct spelling, punctuation, grammar, and to meet the needs of audience and purpose.

MATHEMATICS
Rationale:

Mathematics provides essential problem-solving tools applicable to a range of scientific disciplines, business, and everyday situations. Mathematics is the language of quantifying and logic; its elements are symbols, structures, and shapes. It enables people to understand and use facts, definitions, and symbols in a coherent and systematic way in order to reason deductively and to solve problems.

Goals for Learning:

As a result of their schooling, students will be able to:

1. perform the computations of addition, subtraction, multi-

plication, and division using   whole numbers, integers, fractions, and decimals;

2. understand and use ratios and percentages;
3. make and use measurements, including those of area and volume;
4. identify, analyze and solve problems using algebraic equations, inequalities, functions and their graphs;
5. understand and apply geometric concepts and relations in a variety of forms;
6. understand and use methods of data collection and analysis, including tables, charts, and comparisons;
7. use mathematical skills to estimate, approximate, and predict outcomes and to judge reasonableness of results.

Clarification of Goals for Learning

The Goal for Learning selected as an example is **goal 5.**

Learning Goal 5

As a result of their schooling, students will be able to understand and apply geometric concepts and relations in a variety of forms.

Clarification:

The study of geometry is the study of size, shape, and position. It promotes a deeper awareness and understanding of the real world and contributes to the attainment of important problem-solving processes such as exploring, conjecturing, testing, confirming, and refuting. It also provides opportunities for students to examine the processes of defining, classifying, and deducing. The study of geometry is not only fundamental to a full understanding of mathematics for the scientifically oriented, but it is also fundamental for the understanding of real-world situations by the general population. As such, the concepts of geometry are essential for all students at all grade levels, not just for the college-bound student in high school.

General Knowledge/Skills Related to Goal 5

The following knowledge, processes, and skills are related to this Goal for Learning:

A   Simple geometric figures and patterns of relationships in two and three dimensions.
B   Application of symmetry and transformations.
C   Application of concepts of congruence and similarity.

D   Application of the Pythagorean Theorem and common right triangle relationships.

E   Definition of common geometric figures and methods of using deductive reasoning to relate properties of those figures.

Grade Level Objectives

The grade level objectives selected as an example is **Grade Three** Learning Objectives.

Learning Objectives for Learning Goal 5

By the end of Grade 3, students should be able to:

A1. Sketch circles, squares, triangles, and rectangles.

A2. Identify cubes, spheres, cylinders, cones, and pyramids.

A3. Count the number of vertices and sides of plane figures and the number faces, edges, and vertices of simple solids.

A4. Know the polygons with 3, 4, 5, 6, and 8 sides.

B1. Identify figures that have lines of symmetry.

B2 Draw symmetry lines in figures that have them.

C1 Identify congruent figures.

SOCIAL SCIENCES

Rationale:

People, both collectively and individually, are the focus of the social sciences.   The dimensions of this focus are historical, political, geographic, economic, sociological, and psychological. The social sciences may include the study of historical events, government functions, natural resources, business cycles, group behavior, and individual personality to understand better the past, the present, and the possible future of human society.

The study of the social sciences in our school has this same goal of better understanding human society, with an additional goal of education for citizenship.   While citizenship education is a goal of the entire educational community, social sciences have a special role. A democracy demands citizens who are knowledgeable concerning human affairs and who can apply this knowledge effectively in the critical task of self-government.

Social sciences provide students with an understanding of themselves and of society, prepare them for citizenship in a democracy, and give them the basics for understanding the complexities of the world community.   Study of the humanities, of which social sciences are a part, is necessary in order to preserve the values of human dignity, justice and representative processes. Social sciences include anthropology, economics, geography, government, history, philosophy, political science, psychology, and sociology.

Goals for Learning

As a result of their schooling, students will be able to:

1. *understand and analyze comparative political and economic systems, with an emphasis on the political and economic systems of the United States;*
2. *understand and analyze events, trends, personalities, and movements shaping the history of the world, the United States, and our state;*
3. *demonstrate a knowledge of the basic concepts of the social sciences and how these help to interpret human behavior;*
4. *demonstrate a knowledge of world geography with emphasis on that of the United States;*
5. *apply the skills and knowledge gained in the social sciences to decision making in life situations.*

Clarification of Goals for Learning

The Goal for Learning selected as an example is **Goal 4**.

Learning Goal 4

As a result of their schooling, students will be able to demonstrate a knowledge of world geography with emphasis on the United States.

General Knowledge/Skill Related to Goal 4

The following knowledge and skills are related to this State Goal for Learning:

Location: Position of the Earth's Surface

A Location of physical and cultural features of the local community, the state, the nation, and the world.
B Use of maps and models as primary geographic tools.
C Influences of physical and cultural features on the locations of objects and places.

Place: Physical and Human Characteristics

D Ways in which people define, name and alter places.

E   Different ways in which various groups within society may view places.

F   Positive and negative effects of human actions or natural processes on places.

Relationships within Places: Human and Environments

G   Ways people inhabit, modify and adapt culturally to different physical environments.

H   Habitats as complex ecosystems which may have been modified by human action.

I   Ways people depend on, evaluate, and use natural environments to extract needed resources, grow crops and develop settlements.

Movement: Humans Interacting on the Earth

J   ways people depend on products, information, and ideas that come from beyond their immediate environment.

K   Ways people move themselves, their products, and their ideas across the earth's surface.

L   Concept of region in physical and cultural terms.

M   Cultural and physical geography of each of the world's regions.

N   Basic physical and cultural geography of the United States.

Grade Level Objectives

The grade level objectives selected as an example are **Grade Twelve** Learning Objectives.

Learning Objectives for Learning Goal 4

By the end of Grade 12, students should be able to:

Location: Position on the Earth's Surface

C1. Analyze ways in which physical and cultural features influence the location of objects and places.

Place: Physical and Human Characteristics

E1. Understand how various groups within society may view places differently.

Relationships within Places: Human and Environments

G1. Understand ways by which people inhabit, modify and adapt culturally to different physical environments.

Movement: Human Interactivity on the Earth

J1. Analyze ways people depend on products, information, and ideas that come from beyond their immediate environment.

K1. Understand ways in which people move themselves, their products, and their ideas across the earth's surface.

Regions: How They Form and Change

L1. Understand the concept of region in physical and cultural terms.

M1. Understand the cultural and physical geography of each of the world's regions.

BIOLOGICAL AND PHYSICAL SCIENCES

Rationale:

Science is the quest for objective truth. It provides a conceptual framework for the understanding of natural phenomena and their causes and effects. The purposes of the study of science are to develop students who are scientifically literate, recognize that science is not value-free, are capable of making ethical judgments regarding science and social issues, and understand that technological growth is an outcome of the scientific enterprise.

Goals for Learning:

As a result of their schooling, students will have a working knowledge of:

1. *the concepts and basic vocabulary of biological, physical, and environmental sciences and their application to life and work in contemporary technological society;*
2. *the social and environmental implications and limitations of technological development;*
3. *the principles of scientific research and their application in simple research projects;*
4. *the processes, techniques, methods, equipment, and available technology of science.*

Clarification of Goals for Learning

The Goal for Learning selected as an example is **goal 4**.

Learning Goal 4

As a result of their schooling, students will have a working knowledge of the processes, techniques, methods, equipment and available technology of science.

Clarification:

General Knowledge/Skills Related to Goal 4

The following knowledge and skills are related to this State Goal for Learning:

A   Observation.
B   Classification.
C   Inference.
D   Prediction.
E   Measurement.
F   Communication.
G   Data collection, organization and interpretation.
H   Operational definition development.
I   Question and hypothesis formulation.
J   Experimentation.
K   Model formulation.
L   Results verification.
M   Scientific equipment use.

Grade Level Objectives

The grade level objectives selected as an example is **Grade Six** Learning Objectives.

<u>Learning Objectives for Learning Goal 4</u>

By the end of <u>Grade 6</u>, students should be able to:

A1. Record data after observing objects and events.

B1. Use a classification key to place objects or events within a scheme.

C1. Distinguish between an observation and an inference.

D1. Confirm a prediction through experimentation.

E1. Use estimating as a means of gathering data.

F1. Understand the organization of a data table.

G1. Test an inference by collecting data.

H1. Recognize an operational definition.

I1. Use the results of an experiment to answer an appropriate question.

J1. Identify the variables in a simple experiment.

K1. Use works to create a visual image.

L1. Demonstrate consistency in repeated trials of an experiment.

M1. Use appropriate equipment to measure mass, distance, time, and temperature.

FINE ARTS

Rationale:

The fine arts give students the means to express themselves creatively and to respond to the artistic expression of others. As a record of human experience, the fine arts provide distinctive ways of understanding society, history, and nature. The study of fine arts includes visual art, music, drama, and dance.

Goals for Learning:

As a result of their schooling, students will be able to:

a. *understand the principal sensory, formal, technical, and expressive qualities of each of the arts;*
b. *identify processes and tools required to produce visual art, music, drama, and dance;*
c. *demonstrate the basic skills necessary to participate in the creation and/or performance of one of the arts;*
d. *identify significant works in the arts from major historical periods and how they reflect societies, cultures, and civilizations, past and present;*
e. *describe the unique characteristics of each of the arts.*

Clarification of Goals for Learning

The Goal for Learning selected as an example is **goal 2**.

Learning Goal 2

As a result of their schooling, students will be able to identify processes and tools required to produce visual art, music, drama and dance.

Clarification:

Students must recognize how the arts are produced. Studying processes and tools can be part of participating in the art form, as well as a way of aiding students in understanding the expressiveness of the work of art.

General Knowledge/Skills Related to Goal 2

The following knowledge and skills are related to this Goal for Learning:

Visual Art

A   Processes used to create various types of visual art (drawing, painting, graphics, sculpture, photography, crafts, architecture, computer art and film.)
B   How specific tools are used to create various types of visual art.

Music

C   Processes used to create solo, ensemble, choral, instrumental and electronic music.
D   How sound sources affect the creation of music.

Dance

E   Methods (practical and aesthetic considerations) used to create solo and ensemble dance composition and performance.
F   How tools (body, ideas, sound sources, props) are used to create dance.

Drama

G   Methods used to create solo and ensemble dramatic performances.
H   How vocal and body expressions, performance area, and technical elements of lighting, set, costuming and properties are used to create drama.

Grade Level Objectives

The grade level objectives selected as an example is **Grade Twelve** Learning Objectives.

Learning Objectives for Learning Goal 2

By the end of <u>Grade 12</u>, students should be able to:

Visual Art

A1. Understand or demonstrate processes used to create various visual art forms.

B1. Identify or use tools to create various visual art forms.

Music

C1. Understand or demonstrate processes used to create solo, ensemble, choral, instrumental and electronic music.

D1. Identify or demonstrate sound sources which create music.

Dance

E1. Understand or demonstrate methods used to create dance composition and performances.

F1. Understand or demonstrate how the body, sound sources, props and ideas are used to create a dance.

Drama

G1. Understand or demonstrate methods used to develop dramatic performance.

H1. Understand or demonstrate how body expression, performance area, and technical elements are used to create a dramatic piece.

PHYSICAL DEVELOPMENT AND HEALTH

Rationale:

Physical development and health is concerned with the total

well-being of students. This learning area encompasses interrelated studies in health and physical education programs and involves the cognitive and psychomotor domains. Physical fitness, motor skill development, general well-being and health promotion are the essential components. Basic concepts in physical development and health provide students with knowledge, skills, and experiences in body development, opportunities for obtaining and assessing their individual skills, opportunities for developing persona health/fitness plans, and skills and strategies in activities for lifelong participation and maintenance of wellness.

Effective human functioning depends upon optimum physical development and health. Education for physical development and health provides student with the knowledge and attitudes to achieve healthful living throughout their lives and to acquire physical fitness, coordination, and leisure skills.

Goals for Learning:

As a result of their schooling, students will be able to:

1. *understand the physical development, structure, and functions of the human body;*
2. *understand principles of nutrition, exercise, efficient management of emotional stress, positive self-concept development, drug use and abuse, and the prevention and treatment of illness;*
3. *understand consumer health and safety, including environmental health;*
4. *demonstrate basic skills and physical fitness necessary to participate in a variety of conditioning exercises or leisure activities such as sports and dance;*
5. *plan a personal physical fitness and health program;*
6. *perform a variety of complex motor activities;*
7. *demonstrate a variety of basic life-saving activities.*

Clarification of Goals for Learning

The Goal for Learning selected as an example is **goal 7.**

Learning Goal 7

As a result of their schooling, students will be able to demonstrate a variety of basic life-saving activities.

Clarification:

Participation in daily living tasks and a variety of movement activities demands the awareness and development of basic life survival skills.

General Knowledge/Skills Related to Goal 7

The following knowledge and skills are related to this State Goal for Learning:

A   Demonstration of life-safety skills of climbing, lifting, carrying, pushing, pulling, and falling.
B   Rescue skills appropriate to various life-threatening situations.
C   Essential skills and procedures for use in life-threatening situations.
D   Sources of training for cardiopulmonary resuscitation.

Grade Level Objectives

The grade level objectives selected as an example is **Grade Ten** Learning Objectives.

Learning Objectives for Learning Goal 7

By the end of Grade 10, students should be able to:

Physical Development

B1. *Know or demonstrate rescue procedures in aquatic emergencies.*
B2. *Describe safety precautions when removing themselves from a variety of life-threatening situations.*

Health

C1. *Know the four urgent actions to be taken at the scene of an accident.*
C2. *Know the four techniques for controlling severe bleeding in proper order.*
C3. *Understand the first-aid and rescue procedures for emergency situations.*
C4. *Recognize the local warning signals for natural disasters.*
C5. *Understand procedures to follow in case of natural disasters.*

D1. *Know location for CPR training in the community.*

Columbia Elementary School District
Reading Curriculum Guide

The Columbia Elementary School District Reading Curriculum Guide offers an organizational structure different from the Rantoul School Health Curriuclum Guide and the State of Illinois Department of Education Guides. The Columbia guide is divided into three parts: A Scope and Sequence Chart, Objectives for Individual Grade Levels, and a Concept/Skills Guide.

The Scope and Sequence Chart, page 219, outlines a total reading program, grade K-8, under six major headings: Readiness Skills, Decoding/Word Attack Skills, Comprehension Skills, Literary Skills, Reference and Study Skills, and Oral Reading Skills -- and their respective sub-categories. Four levels of instruction are defined: exposure, instruction, reinforcement, and mastery. The level of instruction of each concept/skill is coded for each grade level.

Objectives for Individual Grade Levels, page 220, are coded to correspond with the Scope and Sequence Chart described above. Therefore, the concept -- C.1.b, Simile -- on the Scope and Sequence Chart, is treated as an instructional objective:

* *The student will recognize the use of simile.*

The objective is taught at mastery level under Objectives for Grade Level -- Grade Eight.

A third chart, a Concepts/Skills Guide on page 221, correlates basal reading series to the school's objectives. Subject matter for teaching mastery of the concept, Simile, can be found in the eighth grade textbooks, #1, 3.

COLUMBIA ELEMENTARY SCHOOL DISTRICT
READING CURRICULUM GUIDE K-8

Rationale

Certain subjects are seen to possess the generative power necessary to accomplish the school's primary mission as described in the Statement of the School's Educational Philosophy. These are the subjects, once mastered that enable learners to master new subjects. First among those subjects that possess a generative power is reading. Mastery of the reading process is basic to most other learning; the dependent or self-terminating subjects, as well as the more complex developments related to the reading process itself. Therefore, reading must necessarily possess a dominant place in the elementary school curriculum.

Program Goals

As a result of their schooling students will:

1. *Successfully apply decoding and word attack skills.*
2. *Interpret what is read through application of comprehension skills.*
3. *Apply literary skills by identifying elements of stories, types of literature, and styles of writing.*
4. *Utilize effective reference and study skills.*
5. *Develop appropriate oral reading skills.*
6. *Develop attitudes that encourage life long reading habits.*

Organization of the Curriculum Guide

The Reading Curriculum Guide was developed for the purpose of providing each reading teacher with a guide to the skills taught at each level. This format was designed to be workable and useful in daily and long range planning. The guide is divided into three parts:

1. A Scope and Sequence Chart,
2. An Objectives for Individual Grade Levels, and
3. A Concepts or Skills Guide.

Reading Scope and Sequence Chart - Grade Eight

The Scope and Sequence Chart includes an outline of the major concept or skill areas as well as states the individual grade levels that are coded to show various stages of instruction.

Key to Level of Learning

| * Exposure | 0 Instruction | # Reinforcement | $ Mastery |

CONCEPTS OR SKILLS	K	1	2	3	4	5	6	7	8
I. ... II. ... III. ... IV. ...									
A. ...									
B. ...									
C. Elements of Style									
1. Figures of Speech									
a. Personification						*	0	$	$
b. Simile			*	*	0	#	$	$	$
c. Metaphor				*	0	0	#	$	$
2. Figurative Language									
a. Exaggeration-hyperbole					*	0	#	#	#
b. Idiom				0	0	#	#	$	$
c. Understatement							*	0	0
d. Play on Words/Pun					*	*	*	0	#
e. Slang					*	*	0	#	#
f. Parody							*	0	0
3. Flashback								*	0
4. Foreshadowing								*	0
5. Imagery								*	0
6. Point of View							*	0	$
7. Alliteration							*	0	0
8. Onomatopoeia							*	*	*
9. Irony						*	*	0	0
10. Satire						*	*	0	0
11. Humor						*	*	0	0
12. Suspense						*	*	0	0
A. Uses Basic Location Aids									
1. Page	*	0	0	#	#	#	#	#	#
2. Table of Contents	*	0	#	$	#	#	#	#	#
3. Alphabetical Order	0	$	$	$	$	$	$	$	$
4. Index				*	0	#	$	#	#
B. Locates/Interprets Book Features									
...									

Reading Objectives for Individual Grade Levels - Grade Eight

Objectives are coded to correspond to the Scope and Sequence. The first column states the appropriate objective number. The second column indicates the code previously given for that level of instruction. The third column states the instructional objective. The fourth column contains examples and/or definitions to help clarify the objective.

Key to Level of Learning

     * Exposure   0 Instruction   # Reinforcement $ Mastery

Number Code	Objective - Students will be able to:	Example
IV. C. 1. b. $	recognize the use of simile.	Definition: A comparison using "like" or "as". *soft as a lamb*
IV. C. 1. c. $	recognize the use of metaphor.	Definition: An implied comparison. *Thunderclouds were giant mushrooms.*
IV. C. 2. a. #	recognize the use of exaggeration-hyperbole.	*I'm so hungry, I could eat a horse.*
IV. C. 2. b. $	recognize the use of idiom.	Definition: A group of words containing both a literal and figurative meaning. *It's raining cats and dogs.*
IV. C. 2. c. 0	recognize the use of understatement.	*It is 102o in the shade. Is that hot enough for you?*
IV. C. 2. d. #	recognize the use of play on words.	*a chocolate 'moose' for dinner*
IV. C. 2. e. #	recognize the use of slang.	
IV. C. 2. f. 0	recognize the use of parody.	*Definition: Humorous imitation of something said or written by someone else*

Reading Concepts or Skills Guide - Grade Eight

The Concepts or Skills Guide correlates the basal reading series to the school's objectives. Proceeding from left to right, the first column is a teacher check-off area. The second column states the appropriate objective number. The third column states the concept/skill to be instructed. The fourth column indicates the instructional code. The remaining columns indicate the reading series used in the building. A number indicates where the topic can be found in a series. Space remains for supplementary materials to be listed as needed.

Key to Level of Learning

* Exposure	0 Instruction	# Reinforcement	$ Mastery

Objective Number	Concept or Skill	Code	SF	HM	SB	Supplementary
IV. C.1.b.	Simile	$	23		75	
IV. C.1.c	Metaphor	$	89-99		12,56	
IV. C.2.a.	Exaggeration/ hyperbole	#	64		6	
IV. C.2.b.	Idiom	$			109	
IV. C.2.c.	Understatement	0	33	47-52	205	
IV. C.2.d.	Play on words/ pun	#	167	34		
IV. C.2.e.	Slang	#	44-51		67-70	
IV. C.2.f.	Parody	0	125		78	
IV. C.3.	Flashback	0	45		88-89	
IV. C.4.	Foreshadowing	0	79-93			
IV. C.5.	Imagery	0	102-105		154-157	
IV. C.6.	Point of view	$	208-218		275-283	
IV. C.7.	Alliteration	0	106	175	89-93	
IV. C.8	Onomatopoeia	*	230	34-39	190	
IV. C.9.	Irony	0	234-244		154-163	

Agape Early Childhood Center
Mathematics Curriculum Guide

The Early Childhood Mathematics Curriculum Guide (Mueller, 1983) is organized by using a matrix to identify activities as intersections of seven mathematics processes with seven attributes of common objects. The *Early Childhood Mathematics Developmental Model* matrix is shown on page 224.

The first process, describing, is examined by using the attributes: color, shape, size, capacity, and mass. Similar activities are generated for the remaining processes: classifying, comparing, ordering, equalizing, joining, and separating.

The model provides both non-number and number activities. Number activities use measurement as the vehicle for teaching the counting process. The pages following the matrix provide sample activities for each cell in the model. Some examples of suggested activities are shown on pages 226-228.

Rationale

Early childhood educators agree that some type of mathematics experience should be part of an early childhood curriculum. They tell us that early childhood inquiries should emphasize a **concrete** hands-on approach. Mathematics should be considered a verb, growing from children's activities. Mathematics educators suggest that mathematics problems should result from children's inquiring activities.

The mathematics program offered at the Agape Early Childhood Center is one that encourages children to manipulate materials as they attempt to resolve mathematics problems. It is a program in which children explore and discover. It emphasizes an inductive approach to understanding the physical world. It allows children to do their own learning.

The program presents children with situations in which they experiment in the broadest sense of the word -- trying things out to see what happens, manipulating things, manipulating symbols, posing questions and seeking their own answers, reconciling their findings at one time with findings at another time, and comparing their findings with those of other children.

In order to encourage children's use of objects, the center provides as basic learning tools:

1. A table to hold water and a variety of containers for exploring capacity.
2. Sticks, string, tapes, plastic chain links, and similar tools for

exploring length.
3. Tiles, linoleum pieces, pattern blocks, tanagrams, and geoblocks to explore area, position, space, and shape.
4. A large pan balance and miscellaneous objects to explore mass.
5. A variety of objects such as a box of buttons, popsicle sticks, interlocking cubes, and more to encourage counting.

Program Goals

As a result of the Early Childhood Mathematics Program, children will grow in their ability to:

1. *Describe, classify, compare, order, and equalize objects on the attributes: color, shape, size (length, area), capacity, and mass without the use of number.*
2. *Describe, classify, compare, order, and equalize objects on the concept, how many.*
3. *Compare, order, equalize, join, and separate objects on the attributes length, capacity, and mass with use of number.*

Organization of Instructional Content

The matrix on page 224 shows the scope and sequence used for selecting activities which are the mathematical program. Sequencing of processes tends to move from top to bottom.

The general sequence of activities begins in the upper left hand corner and progresses toward the lower right hand corner. Non-number activities tend to come before number activities. However, many non-number activities (examples: ordering beads, classifying by shape) should continue after children are working with number.

Goal #2 of the Early Childhood Mathematics Curriculum is development of the concept, **how many**. Mathematics educators agree that exposure to several processes is prerequisite to children understanding **how many,** and using number to quantify **how many.**

The curriculum matrix directs children to use physical materials to explore the following processes:

*	describing	*	classifying
*	comparing	*	ordering
*	equalizing	*	joining
*	separating		

Goal #1 is encouraged as children employ the first five processes

Early Childhood Mathematics Development Model

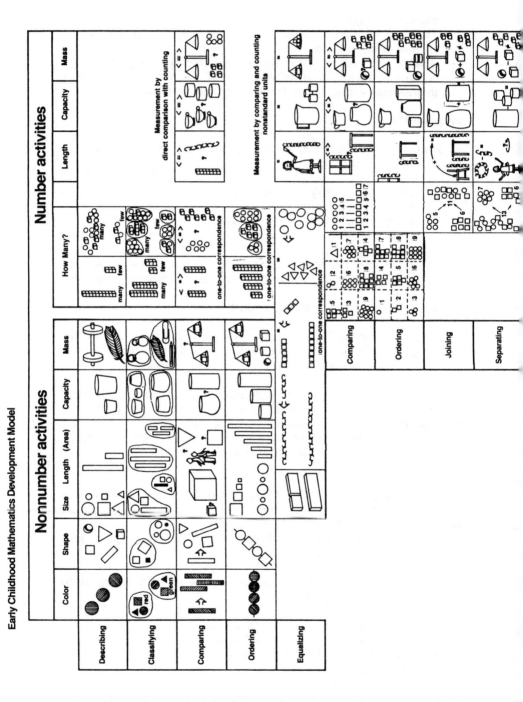

to examine the following attributes of objects without the use of number:

* color   * shape
* size (length, area) * capacity
* mass.

The processes, classifying and comparing, are subject to reverse ordering at times. There is no preferred sequence to selection of attributes. Describing two masses may properly precede describing two colors. Children may, however, prefer to compare two shapes before comparing two capacities. The question, How Many? and its processes leading to counting are specifically intended to assist teaching the relationship, number. These activities should follow some exposure to non-number activities in each process. Equalizing activities which require use of one-to-one matching are included as part of Non-number as well as How Many experiences. Matching one-to-one is a necessary and important part of number development.

Activities that use number to measure length, capacity, and mass are related to goal #3. These activities come after development of the number concept. Children who can successfully measure these three attributes using number, conserve length, capacity, and mass, as well as number.

After number is learned, the integrated processes, joining and separating, are explored.

Curriculum activities described in the examples use physical materials only. Activities that describe, classify, compare, and order events, or examine happenings or situations are not included. They should, however, be provided by the classroom teacher.

Consider as supplement, problems such as:

* How do you feel today?
* Sort the pictures as happy pictures and sad pictures.
* Mime the events required to brush your teeth.
* Order the pictures according to which happened first, which happened next.

Let the printed curriculum be a springboard for generating a broad, experiential based early childhood mathematics program.

The last section of the Agape Early Childhood Center's Mathematics Curriculum Guide (examples on pages 226-228) provides a host of sample activities which direct young children to investigate mathematics using physical materials. Each cell in the Early Childhood Mathematics Model is individually portrayed in this section. Each activity set highlights the intended purpose and use of each cell in the model. The activities selected below are a representation of the final section.[2]

NON-NUMBER ACTIVITIES

Process: Describing

Attribute: Color

After experiencing these activities, children will be able to name the color of objects and select objects by their colors, red, yellow, blue, green, purple, orange, white, black.

\#   Set out attribute pieces. Name a color (red, yellow, blue). Ask children to identify the object or the color.

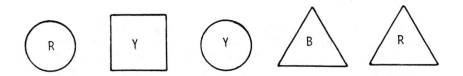

Point to a red piece.

*   Point to an object and ask children to name the color.

*   Direct a child to name a color. Ask another child to identify the object.

Process: Classifying

Attribute: Size

After experiencing these activities, children will be able to place objects into sets, using one or more sorting criteria.

\#   Set out attribute pieces, buttons, other. Children may sort by color, size, shape, weight, other.

*   Direct children to sort objects. Ask them to describe the criteria for sorting.

---

[2] A complete listing of activities is found in:
Mueller, D. W. (1984). River Forest, IL 60305: Concordia University Book Store.

I put the big buttons in one pile and the small buttons in another pile.

Process: Ordering

Attribute: Shape

After experiences these activities, children will be able to order objects on a simple criterion.

\# Set out colored stringing beads, attribute pieces, other objects that can be ordered by shape. Direct children to order by shape.

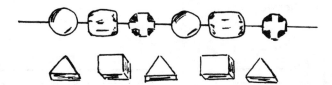

MEASUREMENT ACTIVITIES THAT REQUIRE USE OF NUMBER

Process: Comparing

Attribute: Length

After experiencing these activities, children will be able to count unit measures to compare two objects on length.

* Direct children to use links to find how tall they are.

I'm fourteen
links tall.

Direct children to use dominoes to measure the length of their feet.

Process: Equalizing

Attribute: Mass

After experiencing these activities, children will be able to count unit measures to equalize mass between two objects.

\# Set out two objects with differing masses. Select a set of lighter objects, each of equal mass, as the units for measure. Direct children to use the lighter objects to compare the masses of the heavier objects.

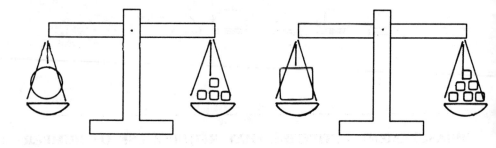

The cylinder is four block heavy.   The cube is six blocks heavy.

The cube is heavier than the cylinder.

Chapter Nine

Writing Units

A unit of study is an organization of various activities, experiences, and intended learning built around a central problem, theme, or purpose. Units may be identified as resource units, teaching units, learning or activity centers, learning activity packages, and more. Units of study vary with respect to genesis, specificity, and range of content. Some may be totally the result of teacher invention, while others may seek varying levels of commercial product input.

Some study units direct students along carefully prescribed paths while others offer a variety of options. Some attempt to integrate several subjects into a central theme (e.g., a social science unit may include activities which require reading, writing, spelling, music, art, physical education, science, or mathematics experiences) while other units construct walls which separate subject matter in an attempt to maintain the integrity of the discipline.

The components commonly included as part of unit construction are designed to ensure that the teacher:

1. Stated the rationale for teaching the topic under discussion.

2. Listed the major learning to be mastered by the students as instructional objectives.

3. Described and organized supporting instructional content required to meet mastery of objectives listed in item #2 above.

4. Described and sequenced learning experiences appropriate to item #3 above.

5. Listed aids, and their sources, which may be used in support of items #3 and #4 above.

6. Provided materials for evaluation of student progress toward objectives.

A limited selection of unit constructions used by teachers is examined on the following pages. They are the teaching unit, resource unit, learning center, and two individualized learning modules, Respiratory System and Math Fun. Thematic unit approaches were detailed in Chapter Six.

The Teaching Unit

Title

Level

I. Unit Rationale

II. Unit Objectives

III. Unit Scope and Sequence

IV. Initiating Activity

V. Developmental Activities

   A. Objectives
   B. Content
   C. Methods
   D. Evaluation

VI. Cumulative Activity

VII. Unit Evaluation

VIII. Bibliography

   A. Books

      1. Textbooks
      2. Teacher References
      3. Children's Books and References
      4. ...

   B. Audio-visual Materials

   C. ...

IX. Appendix

   A. Worksheets
   B. Handouts
   C. Bulletin Board Plans
   D. ...

The Teaching Unit Components

Each component of a teaching unit plan is discussed below.

I. Rationale

A rationale is written in which the purpose, emphasis, and value of the unit to students at a particular age/grade level are discussed. The rationale attempts to show how the unit fits in with and complements the purposes of the larger program. Below is a rationale written by one teacher to explain the significance of inclusion of the unit, *Economic Literacy*.

Economic education has been part of the American school curriculum for many years. In recent years it has become the recipient of renewed interest in our district. A major reason for renewed interest is increased awareness of a need for economic literacy among "inner-city" students.

Economics is the study of the production, distribution, exchange, and consumption of goods and services that people need or want. Economic Literacy concerns itself with helping students achieve an understanding of some of the basic relationships between our economic system and our way of life. The unit is built around basic economic concepts as applied to inner city realities. ...

II. Objectives

Three kinds of objectives are encouraged for many subject fields. Unit objectives should identify intended learning outcomes related to:

1. Understandings (processes, facts, concepts, generalizations, principals).
2. Skills (reading, writing, speaking, listening, mathematics, inquiry, library, map, athletic).
3. Attitudes (feelings, beliefs, values).

Unit objectives should satisfy the following criteria. They should:

a. be stated as learning objectives.
b. be stated as observable and measurable behaviors when possible and practical.
c. identify both higher and lower level outcomes.

Below are objectives written by an elementary school teacher to identify terminal behaviors of students following instruction of a unit entitled, **Families**.

By the end of this unit, students will be able to:

1. *Understandings*

    a. *tell how other families of the earth live.*
    b. *explain why family members are important to each other.*
    c. *compare differences and similarities among various family structures.*
    d. *describe structures that hold families together.*

2. *Skills*

    a. *construct a family tree.*
    b. *state the common relationship name between two relatives when members are identified on a family tree.*
    c. *construct a schedule showing before and after school experiences.*

3. *Attitudes*

    a. *express empathy toward feelings of other family members.*
    b. *express acceptance of family structures different from their own.*
    c. *express appreciation of family customs and values different from their own.*

Teacher Goals

Some units include as part of II. OBJECTIVES a section named TEACHER GOALS that define the teacher's role. Just as unit objectives state student competencies, teacher objectives focus on intentions and responsibilities of the teacher. Below is an example of teacher goals for the unit, **Banking**.

My goals as this unit is taught are:

1. *To increase student knowledge of the banking process.*
2. *To provide students opportunities for problem solving using*

critical thinking.

3. *To broaden student experience by integrating subject matter concepts and skills while using activity-centered learning situations.*

4. *To stimulate student respect for individuals regardless of occupation.*

5. *To develop in students an awareness of banking as an occupational interest.*

III. Scope and Sequence

An overview of the scope and sequence may be provided by --

A. listing a series of enabling objectives leading to the terminal objectives, or through a --

B. description of organization of content/concepts in the unit.

 A. A set of enabling objectives may be sequenced to provide the organizational structure for the unit. These objectives will direct selection of content for each subset of learning experiences. They will become the inclusions under the heading, Objectives, and thus provide direction for inclusions under the headings, Concept, Activities, and Resources, as in the developmental activities for the *Poetry* and *Dawn of History* units, pages 239 and 241.

 Below is a terminal objective and the supporting enabling objectives written by a primary grade teacher to teach the unit, **Telling Time.**

Unit Objective: *Student will be able to tell time to the nearest five minutes past the hour.*

Enabling Objectives: *By the end of instruction, students will be able to:*

8. *Look at a clock with the minute hand in a five minute interval position and write the time in terms of* ____:____.

7. *Look at a clock with the minute hand in a five minute interval position and say the time with the hour first, them minutes past the hour.*

6. *Look at a clock with 1/2 hour showing and write the*

time in terms of ___:___.
5. *Look at a clock with 1/2 hour showing and say,*
   _____-thirty.
4. *Count to 55 by fives.*
3. *Look at a clock in the hour position and write in*
   ___:00 terms.
2. *Look at a clock in the hour position and say time in*
   terms of o'clock.
1. *Assemble a clock with the numbers in the correct*
   position.

B. The scope and sequence may also be presented in outline
   form by writing headings and subheadings which suggest
   major points of emphasis. Headings may be written in
   topical or question style. The outline becomes the
   inclusion under the heading, Generalizations, and thus
   provides direction for the inclusions under the headings,
   Content, Teaching Procedure, and Materials, as itemized
   in the *Canada* unit, page 240. Below is an outline for
   inclusion under the heading, Generalizations, used to
   define the scope and sequence of a high school science
   unit, **Heredity**.

   I.   Mendelian genetics

        A. An introduction to probability
        B. The three laws of heredity
           a. vocabulary and problem solving
           b. experimental evidence

   II. Non-Mendelian genetics

        A. Sex linkage
        B. Sex determination

   III. Mutations

        A. Genetic
        B. Chromosomal

   IV. Human heredity

   V.   Allele frequencies and natural selection contemporary
        problems in genetics

A. Intelligence
B. Genetic engineering

VI.   Evaluation

IV.   Initiating Activity

An initiating activity introduces the unit and is used to:

1. Bridge any gap between where students presently are and where students should be before the new learning can begin.

2. Establish a rationale for students to answer the question, Why is this important to learn?

3. Arouse within students an excitement for beginning the new set of learning experiences.

4. Provide students with an overview of the unit's learning activities and expected outcomes.

Options Approach

Some unit plans provide descriptions of several initiating possibilities. The teacher is expected to select one or more for a particular class.

Below is a list of initiating activities appropriate for introducing the unit, *Our Nation's Capital.*

1. Several days before the unit is introduced, pictures of famous Washington structures can be placed on the bulletin board. Begin the unit by asking students to identify buildings, monuments, and memorials. Ask students to relate the importance of each structure.

2. Read the story, <u>A Visit to Our Capital</u>. See bibliography.

3. Show the film, <u>Our Nation's Capital</u>, or <u>Washington, A City of Shrines</u>. See bibliography.

4. Explain that students will soon be leaving for an imaginary trip to the capital city. Plan how arrangements will be made for the trip. Let the unit be a study of what will be seen and done while in Washington.

5. Pretend your class is a group of foreign students. Ask questions about Washington to find how much students already know.

First Day Lesson Plan Approach

Rather than provide a variety of options to initiate the unit, some teachers prefer to write a single, well thought-out lesson plan as the initial activity. They reason that a well structured and fairly detailed plan for the first lesson should probably be written anyway, and therefore should be provided by the author of the unit as part of a well written unit plan. Below is a one day lesson plan to initiate students to the unit, *Poetry*.

Objectives:

By the end of this lesson, students should:

1. *be motivated to learn more about poetry.*
2. *be acquainted with the earliest form of poetry -- the Psalms of David.*
3. *be able to describe a difference between poetic and non-poetic literature.*
4. *possess a general understanding of unit activities and expectations.*

Lesson:

Introduction --

Initiate a discussion by asking students what the word, poetry, calls to mind. (Typical responses will include rhyming words, nursery rhymes, etc.) Ask students to name poets they heard of; recite a poem they know. Read from an anthology of poems and/or play a recording of a poem.

Body --

Give a simple definition of what poetry is and explain briefly that contrary to popular belief poetry need not rhyme, but it must have rhythm; the beat or movement suggested by the words within the poem.

Note: There should be either a bulletin board display, series of charts, or some type of learning center relating to poetry in the room, and students should be directed to it during this class session as a means to motivate interest.

Ask when students think the first poems were created, ... or when were the first poems written down?

Introduce the Psalms from the Bible. Tell that these are among the first recorded poems. Read Psalm 23 by David, king of Israel. Explain that these poems were songs to God, either asking for help or offering praise or thanksgiving. Distribute Bibles or a handout of selected Psalms such as #1, 2, 23, 100, 117, 117, 130, 150. Listen to Psalm 1 and 23 from the record, The Poems of Israel. Read selected Psalms in class. Read individually and by using group reading responsively and as choral reading.
Conclusion --

Provide a brief overview of unit components. Explain that poetry is a special way of writing down the thoughts we wish to express, and that students, after learning more about poetry, will have opportunity to become writers of poetry.

Assignment:

Give handout, "Fun Poems," to students. Direct that each student select one poem for oral reading in class tomorrow. Counsel students to practice oral reading of the poems prior to class time.

Materials:
Bible
Poems for Young Adults (bibliography: books)
Verses for Listening (bibliography: records)
The Poems of Israel (bibliography: records)
"Fun Poems" (appendix)
Bulletin board display

V. Developmental Activities

These activities are the heart of the unit. It is through the development activities that objectives listed under II. UNIT OBJECTIVES will be satisfied. The format and information included under DEVELOPMENTAL ACTIVITIES may vary considerably.

Headings Structure

The format chosen for the unit *Poetry* on page 239 employs four headings, **Objectives, Concepts, Activities, and Resources**. Objective #9 requires students to be able to write poems in the selected forms: couplets, triangular triplets, and as Haiku/Haikon. The **Concept** column supplies a brief explanation of each form, while the **Activities and Resources** columns provide the means to achieve the objectives.

The unit *Canada* format on page 240 follows and organization that lists as headings, **Generalizations, Content, Teaching Procedure, and Materials**. Roman numeral VII focuses on the natural resources of Canada. Subheading A examines the fishing industry. **Content** is divided into four areas of interest. **Teaching Procedure and Materials** provide direction and resources to complete the study.

The unit plan for *The Dawn of History* unit on page 241 shows three headings: **Objectives, Activities, and Evaluation**. This format provides a systematic comparison of purposes, means, and ends. It assists the teacher who asks, Were my objectives for each lesson met by the students?

You will note that the DEVELOPMENTAL ACTIVITIES for the two units *Poetry* and *Canada* do not separate into daily lesson segments. The poetry example could cover from one to several days of teaching, depending on teacher preference and student interest.

An examination of the plan for teaching about Canada's fishing industry will show four fields of content and five suggestions for teaching procedures that could provide from three to six or more one-day lesson plans. In contrast, the unit plan for *The Dawn of History* offers a format that suggests divisions into one lesson each.

Lesson Plan Structure

Some DEVELOPMENTAL ACTIVITIES sections are written as a series of one-day lesson plans. An example of a one-day lesson plan format is provided in the section on INITIATING ACTIVITIES, pages 236-237. This lesson plan is divided into three sections: **Objectives; Lesson -- Introduction, Body, Conclusion, Assignment; and Materials**.

A second example is shown on page 242 as part of the unit *Advertising*. It is one of several daily lesson plans included as part

Objectives	Concept	Activities	Resources
9. At the end of this unit, students should be able to write original poems in selected forms:	1. Couplets are poems of two lines. 2. Both lines follow the same meter and rhyme scheme.	1. Listen to examples of couplets; name the rhyming words. 2. Use given rhyming words (i.e. heat, shredded wheat) to write a humorous couplet. 3. Make a booklet of *Couplet Cuties*.	Record: *Poetry Listening for Young People.* Volume I. *Fantasies*, p.89,99
a. Couplets			
b. Triangular triplets	1. A triplet is a poem of three lines which rhyme. 2. The lines are arranged around a triangular shape to form a triangular triplet. 3. The lines can be read in any order and still make sense.	1. Read/discuss examples of triangular triplets. 2. "Follow-the-Leader" triplet; one line from each person. 3. Compose your own triangular triplet; illustrate it.	*Fantasies*, p.105,106 Appendix, p. III
c. Haiku/Haikon	1. Originated in Japan in ancient times. 2. Popularity is due to its simple form. 3. Haiku contains 17 syllables in 3 lines, 5-7-5. 4. Haiku need not rhyme.	1. Listen to examples of Haiku; note the number of syllables. 2. With your class, compose several Haiku poems. 3. compose your own Haiku; Form a Haikon by writing your Haiku around your illustrations.	*Fantasies*, p.110 *Innovative Activities to Stimulate Children*, p.36 Appendix, p. IV

Unit: *Canada*

Developmental Activities

Generalization	Content	Teaching Procedure	Materials
VII. Canada's natural resources are extensive	1. Fishing grounds of Newfoundland and Nova Scotia	1. Locate fishing areas on maps	Wall map of Canada from Media Center
A. Fishing is an important industry	2. Salmon fishing in British Columbia	2. See video *The Grand Banks*. Discuss importance of Gulf Stream	Videos: *The Grand Banks*
	3. Fishing in the Great Lakes	3. See video *The Story of Salmon*	*The Story of Pacific Salmon*
	4. Sport fishing as an industry	4. Discuss salmon life cycle	Textbook: p. 89-100,107, 109-110
		5. Committee oral reports:	Children's books:
		a. processing cod	Bibliography #6, 8, 13, 17, 18
		b. fishing in the Great Lakes	
		c. bush pilots and sport fishing	

Unit: *The Dawn of History*

Developmental Activities

Topic C

Paleozoic Ares: Later Periods

Objectives	Activities	Evaluation
At the end of this unit, students should be able to:		
C¹ recognize names of the later period of the Paleozoic Era	C¹ Students skim textbook pages 118-123 and write name and description of later periods	C¹ Given a list of period names of the chalk board, students will match names with description of the period (appendix 5)
C² explain how oil and petroleum are formed	C² Students view video *Formation of Fossil Fuels.*	C² Given a picture of a swamp forest, students will explain in a written paragraph how coal and petroleum could have formed beneath its waters
C³ classify characteristics of the Paleozoic Era into the proper periods	C³ Students view projection of fossils and illustrations of plant and animal forms from each period	C³ Given a worksheet, students will classify various characteristics into the appropriate period (Appendix 6)

of a senior high school unit. The major components of this lesson plan are **Objectives, Materials, Lesson, and Evaluation**.

One Day Lesson Plan As Part of Developmental Activities

<u>Unit: Advertising</u>

Objectives: *By the end of this lesson, students will be able to:*

Understand how products are sold by --
    a. emphasizing the positive characteristics of the product, and by
    b. understanding the audience to be persuaded.

Materials: None

Lesson: 1.   Have students list ways to discourage potential freshmen from attending Blasingame High School.

    2.   Discuss use of bias when persuading others.

    3.   Ask: Suppose you were trying to encourage potential freshmen to attend the school, how would your presentation change?

    4.   Identify major positive characteristics of the school.

    5.   Select one or two major points and write an ad selling the school to freshmen.

    6.   Read advertisements orally and discuss language, style, etc.

    7.   Discuss how presentation might differ if the prospect was a child, a parent, the president of a potential new industry.

Evaluation: Have students rewrite their commercials by specifying a different audience and directing the commercial to that audience.

Options Structure

DEVELOPMENTAL ACTIVITIES can be described in still another way. Units written for early childhood programs often itemize a variety of subject fields with a list of activities appropriate to each field. A unit entitled **Fruit** written by an early childhood teacher identified eleven subject fields, each followed by a listing of activities. A few of the suggestions are shown below.

Reading -

* Have names of pictures of fruits on separate cards. Children match name to fruit.
* Make a bingo game using names of fruit.

Mathematics -

* Draw outlines of fruit on hardboard. Cut out foam shapes to match outlines. Children map shapes to outlines.
* Set out plastic fruits of various sizes. Have children order them by size.

Science -

* Make a list of noises made while chewing different fruits.
* List forms in which fruit is sold. (juice, frozen, canned, fresh, dried) Bring examples to class for tasting.

Art -

* Draw pictures of fruit. Color the picture.
* Make a fruit basket.

Physical Education -

* Play fruit basket upset

VI. Culminating Activities

Suggestions for culminating activities aid the teacher as the unit is brought to a close. This part of the unit may address itself to several of the following questions:

1. Where did we start?
2. Where have we been?
3. Where are we now?
4. What did we learn?

Several alternate suggestions for culminating activities are frequently offered. Emphasis is on higher order objectives such as analyzing, synthesizing, and evaluating. A suggested list of culminating activities for the poetry unit is shown below.

Culminating Activities -- *Poetry*

Present to class, school assembly, or parents:

Work done by individuals or groups
Performance by individuals or groups
Poetry Fair

A. Independent Activities

1. Construct a booklet entitled, My Book of Poetry, to contain:

   a. the student's own definition of what poetry is, based on what was learned in the unit, and
   b. two examples of each style of poetry presented in the unit; one example from an established poet, and one example of the student's own attempt at writing.

2. Construct a booklet entitled, My Favorite Poet, to contain at least five poems written by the poet the student enjoyed or admired. The poems shall be copied by the student, exactly as they appear in print, and each poem is to be illustrated. There shall be a brief biography of the poet, as well as an identification of the particular style(s) of poetry that poet has written.

3. Recite from memory an original poem or a poem by an established poet.

   ...

B. Group Activities

1. Plan a bulletin board or display/exhibit dealing with poetry in general, or a particular aspect of poetry.

2. Participate in choral reading group performance.

...

VII. Evaluation

Evaluation is an attempt to measure how the student has changed as a result of the unit experience. Measurement instruments are directed at the unit objectives with focus on the unit's understandings, skills, and attitudes. Evaluation is a continuous teacher activity. Measurement of students' attainment of some objectives may be made as the teacher interacts with children during the instructional part of the unit. Other objectives may be evaluated as the teacher critiques students' written and oral contributions. Finally, some evaluation may take the form of a written examination. An example of part of the final examination used for the poetry unit is shown below.

Evaluation -- *Poetry*

Three kind of evaluation strategies are used:

a. Daily observation and grades from daily assignments,
b. grade for the Culminating Activity projects, and
c. grade for the final examination.

Final Examination -- Poetry

Name_____ Date_____

I. Turn these sentences into refrains:

1. The star light bright

_____

...

II. Poetry styles:

Name five different styles of poetry discussed in class.

1._____   2._____

3._____   4._____

5._____

...

III. Changing narrative to poetry

Find the nouns, adjectives, and descriptive verbs in these prose sentences. Re-write some of these thoughts as a poem. Use at least one example of alliteration. Use your own choice of poetic style. Name the style, and follow the line, shape, structure, capitalization and punctuation of that style. (do not use free style)

I like morning. It is fresh and cool. The sun is shining, warming and lighting the sky. I can hear birds and insects. The feeling of exhilaration from these moments will not stop until the evening comes.

...

VII. Bibliography

This portion of the unit plan lists sources for textbooks, library books, films, filmstrips, pictures, video and computer sources, teacher constructed materials, maps, transparencies, bulletins, kits, artifacts, resource persons, and other aids to learning not included in the appendix. It should include all materials identified or referred to in the unit but not part of the appendix. It is important that complete bibliographic data of all resources be included to facilitate ready retrieval. An example of a partial listing of resource materials is shown on page 247.

IX. Appendix

It is not uncommon for resource units to include an appendix. Included as appendix information are suggestions for displays; all prepared work sheets and handouts; aids such as maps, pictures, graphs, articles; and a host of other support materials which are not readily available, but which are needed to successfully teach the unit. An example of a poetry unit appendix appears on page 248.

Bibliography -- *Poetry*

BOOKS

.

.

.

Kasper, Wilfred (1987). <u>Writing aids for high school</u>. New Bay, IL: Laabs Printers.

Wunrow, Jewel (1990). <u>Poems for young adults</u>. Forestville, WI: Lau Publications.

.

.

.

FILMSTRIPS

.

.

.

<u>Fun with limericks</u> (1989). Maplewood, CA: AV House, Inc.

<u>Great American poets</u> (1987). Teske, MI: Teske Woods.

<u>Nineteenth century English poetry</u> (1972). Teske, MI: Teske Woods.

.

.

.

RECORDS

.

.

.

<u>American folk songs</u> (1985). Chicago, IL: Concordia University Sales.

<u>The poems of Israel</u> (1975). Chicago, IL: Concordia University Sales.

<u>The poems of Walt Whitman</u> (1965). Hilbert, WI: Lemke Records.

.

.

.

Bulletin Board Displays -- *Poetry*
(for displaying students' work)

Students write poems on
a chosen theme for
display on appropriately
decorated bulletin.

Selected Poems Appropriate for Use with Developmental Activities

from <u>The Adventures of Isabel</u> by Ogden Nash

Isabel met an enormous bear,
Isabel, Isabel didn't care.
The bear was hungry, the bear was ravenous,
The bear's mouth was cruel, big and cavernous.
The bear said, Isabel, glad to meet you,
How do, Isabel, now I'll eat you!
'Isabel, Isabel, didn't worry;
Isabel didn't scream or scurry.
She washed her hands and she straightened her hair up,
Then Isabel quietly ate the bear up.

.
.
.

The Resource Unit

A useful form of unit construction is the resource unit. It is a written document that serves as a resource for several teachers as they prepare a teaching unit to fit their specific instructional setting. Each teacher is expected to use the resource unit as a fountain head for ideas, information, and materials. Resource units include more suggestions for approaches, activities, and materials than a teacher would normally use with one class.

Most resource units written for elementary and secondary programs include a rationale, objectives, and information on scope and sequence. Suggestions for instruction may begin with an initiating activities section. Resource units usually offer a variety of initiating activities choices. Any of the several developmental activities offered as part of the Teaching Unit, pages 230-248, are appropriate for resource units.

A resource unit usually lists a wide variety of activity choices to meet the unit objectives. Each listed suggestion should be sufficiently detailed to assure an interested teacher will know the lesson objectives, activities, evaluation, and materials. The degree to which variety, novelty, and wealth of useful ideas pervades the resource unit pages is a significant determiner of how useful it will be to other teachers. An annotated bibliography can be a major help.

Selection of components to be included in a resource unit and organization of these components will vary according to the particular educational focus. A unit designed to aid an early childhood teacher could be organized quite differently and might include a number of components not found in one written for a senior high school setting.

Early childhood programs emphasize thematic interdisciplinary unit construction in which a variety of subject fields are represented. Special attention is given to room arrangement, interest centers, individual activities, large group activities, and large group presentations. An outline for an early childhood resource unit follows. The pages of the resource unit that follow the outline would detail each of the items listed in the outline.

The content of a resource unit should improve over time as each year outdated materials are discarded and new materials are added to enrich instruction. A supportive principal will encourage that

Early Childhood Resource Unit Plan

I. Background information

    A. Rationale
    B. Goals
    C. Objectives
    D. Age level

II. Environment

    A. Room arrangement
       1. Bulletin boards
       2. Teacher desk
    B. Center
       1. Blocks
       2. Art
       3. Housekeeping
       4. Discovery
       5. Manipulatives
       6. Book
       7. Music and rhymes
       8. Woodworking
       9. Water, sand
      10. Balance
      11. Large muscle area

III. Activities

    A. Individual (free choice)
       1. Art
       2. Manipulatives
       3. Science
    B. Group
       1. Large group activities
       2. Group time presentations
          a. concept development
          b. movement
          c. social studies
          d. language and pre-reading
          e. science
       3. Finger play
       4. Cooking and snacks

IV. Extended activities

    A. Resource people
    B. Field trips

V. Bibliography

resource units and their instructional materials be housed in a central location available to all teachers, and provide the assistance necessary to maintain and expand the resource curriculum center.

As is now obvious, there is no one best way to construct units. All units will have some components in common, but variations tend to be the rule. As you plan to write a unit, select the organization that best fits your needs. Perhaps your unit will contain some organization which is usually identified with resource units and other organization which reminds one of a teaching unit. In the final analysis, you must be the judge. The structure you choose should be the one that provides the desired support for successful teaching.

The Learning Center

"A learning center is a designated area of a classroom that contains a variety of instructional materials and activities organized around a topic, theme, concept, or skill. Several learning centers can be in operation in the classroom simultaneously. The purpose of the learning center can be to introduce, develop, explore, or reinforce a concept, or to facilitate development of skills.

A learning center should provide activities that accommodate different interests and learning styles. If activities are properly structured, individual students or small groups of students can work independently or with a minimum of teacher supervision. The learning center should:

1. Contain a varied and extensive collection of materials related to fundamental concepts or skills.
2. Provide for the needs, interests, and learning styles of the students.
3. Be designed to provide specific learning experiences, carefully sequenced, when necessary, and packaged within practical time limits.
4. Seek to stimulate interest and encourage active learning.
5. Be related to and build on past experiences or provide readiness for new learning experiences.
6. Seek to develop problem solving, creative thinking, and valuing.
7. Provide an opportunity for exploration, discovery, and student interaction.
8. Accommodate a wide range of abilities.

It is unlikely that every learning center that is developed will encompass all these characteristics. However, these suggestions should provide useful guidelines to consider when developing learning centers for a classroom" (Johnson, 1978, p 5,6).

Learning centers are used in many early childhood centers. A model useful for constructing and implementing learning centers will be illustrated for you through a narrative entitled, Mrs. Winkie.

Mrs. Winkie[1]

Mrs. Winkie, a first grade teacher at Luther Elementary School, was deeply concerned about individual differences in children. She spent part of August reading each student's cumulative file from the kindergarten year. It soon became obvious to her that there was a wide variance in mathematics competence within the new class of first graders. She decided to talk with Miss Heine, the kindergarten teacher. The discussion confirmed her fears. She would need more than a textbook to teach mathematics this year.

Mrs. Winkie decided that after the first week of school she would test those children who seemed to have the poorest understanding of mathematics. She constructed a test that measured children's knowledge of concepts associated with number development and space relationships.

The test results showed all children could identify shapes and colors quite well. Del, however, could not count beyond four. Dorleen counted to nine, but seemed to have no real understanding of number beyond six. Arnold and Frieda showed an ability to conserve when tested using seven red checkers and eight black checkers, but did not conserve on any other attribute. Nora counted to twenty-five, but did not conserve number beyond six. Walter and June conserved number, length, and mass, but did not conserve area and capacity.

---

[1]This section is based on content from:

Mueller, D. W. (1984). <u>Early childhood mathematics</u>. River Forest, Illinois: Concord University Book Store.

Mueller, D. W. (1980). <u>Building foundations in mathematics</u>. New Jersey: Silver Burdett Company.

Mrs. Winkie chose not to measure the remainder of the class. Testing took time, and she felt enough valuable time had already been taken from the regular teaching schedule. She was thankful for at least some indication of where the lower achieving students were in mathematics understanding.

But now what was she to do? If the rest of the class -- those who were not tested -- differed as much as did the tested children, how could she generate a mathematics program appropriate for all? Should she invent a separate program for each child? Obviously some children were not ready for the required mathematics textbook. Mrs. Winkie puzzled and worried. Finally she decided what she would do.

> "I know I can't provide individual programs for each of my twenty-two children," she asserted. "I just don't have the time or talent. Perhaps I can begin by making some lessons for my lower achieving students and continue to use the regular textbook with the rest of the class. Maybe I should examine the use of learning centers. Perhaps they will help. I could follow the plan I used for my nature center. I'll put it on the corner table."

As preparation for construction of a learning center, Mrs. Winkie read several articles on early childhood mathematics. One article described an early childhood instructional model that used measurement as the vehicle to teach beginning number work. It was entitled, THE EARLY CHILDHOOD INSTRUCTIONAL MEASUREMENT MODEL. The model shown on page 254 divides instruction into three sections and each section into two columns.

The first section, DIRECT COMPARISON, guided teachers to:

a. direct the student to compare directly, using no numbers, and
b. require the student to count to compare.

Section two, EQUALITIES, guided teachers to:

a. designate the non-standard unit to be used when measuring an attribute, and
b. require the student to select an appropriate unit for measuring an attribute.

EARLY CHILDHOOD INSTRUCTIONAL MEASUREMENT MODEL

	DIRECT COMPARISON inequalities		NON STANDARD UNITS equalities		NON STANDARD UNITS inequalities	
	NON NUMBER	NUMBER	UNIT ASSIGNED	SELECT UNIT	UNIT ASSIGNED	SELECT UNIT
LENGTH	Which rod is longer?	Which is longer, 8 links or 6 dominoes?	How many links does it take to go around your neck?	Select a unit and find: the length of the chalkboard.	Use links to find who has the biggest neck.	Select a unit and find: which is longer, the chalkboard or the table.
AREA	Which shape is bigger?	Which is bigger, 4 squares or 7 triangles?	How many persons can stand on the rug?	Select a unit and find: the area of the counter top.	Use people to find which is bigger, the rug or the mat.	Select a unit and find: which is bigger, the counter top or the desk top.
CAPACITY	Which holds more?	Which holds more, 4 cups or 3 glasses?	How many cups does the bowl hold?	Select a unit and find: the capacity of the pitcher.	Use cups to find which holds more the bowl or the pitcher.	Select a unit and find: which holds more, the pitcher or the carton.
MASS	Which is heavier?	Which is heavier, 5 blocks or 9 dominoes?	How many dominoes does the cube weigh?	Select a unit and find: the mass of the cube.	Use dominoes to find, which is heavier, the cube or the pyramid.	Select a unit and find: which weighs more, the cube or the box of crayons.

348

Section three, INEQUALITIES, guided teachers to:

a. designate the non-standard unit to be used when comparing an attribute between two or more objects, and

b. require the student to select an appropriate unit to use when comparing an attribute between two or more objects.

Mrs. Winkie decided to build centers based on the concept progression of that model. Each center would focus on a single cell in the matrix. Task cards called challenges would be used to direct student learning. She decided that each challenge should include the following information:

*   number of the challenge,
*   materials needed, and
*   directions to complete the task.

Mrs. Winkie used drawings to help children understand the task. She began by preparing a set of twenty task cards. After demonstrating their use before the class, she set them on the learning center table along with the objects for comparison. A colorful placard invited children to accept the challenges.

She decided to have the children work in pairs. Her first set of cards required children to compare lengths using non-number, direct comparison. Ten cards of the twenty card set are shown on page 256. Mrs. Winkie colored the rods and blocks to help children identify color names. Children were directed to circle the correct answer in the response book, **My Measurement Book**. A sample of the response book is shown on page 261.

Several more sets of task cards were prepared using the EARLY CHILDHOOD INSTRUCTIONAL MEASUREMENT MODEL as a guide. A second set of investigations asked students to count to compare lengths.

*   Which is longer, a row of 5 black rods or a row of 4 brown rods.
*   Which is longer, a row of 5 dominoes or a row of 3 purple rods?
*   Which is longer, 8 chain links or a row of 6 red rods?
*   Which is taller, a tower of 7 checkers or a tower of 3 locking cubes?

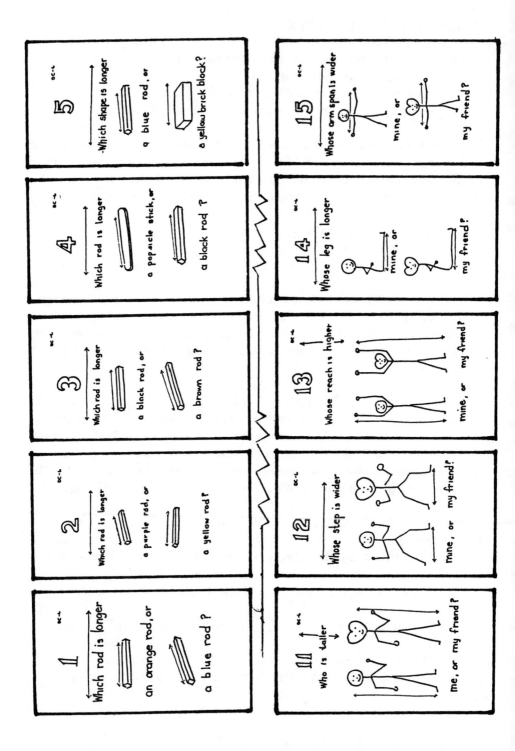

* Which is taller, a tower of 10 checkers or a tower of 9 dominoes?

A third investigation asked students to use teacher specified, non-standard units to measure a given length.

* How many links are as tall as the table?
* Use dominoes to find the length of the table.
* How many links does it take to measure around your waist?
* Use orange colored rods to find the length of the bench.
* Make a train of four orange colored rods. Use yellow rods to measure its length.
* How many books long is the classroom?

Mrs. Winkie decided to include tasks which required students to select the unit appropriate to measure the length of a given object.

Select from the interest center a unit to measure:

* How tall you are.
* How far you stretch from finger tip to finger tip.
* The length of our rug.
* The length of your shoe.
* The width of the bathroom doorway.
* How long your little finger is.
* The length of your finger nail.

A fifth set of task cards for length required students to use teacher specified, non-standard units to compare between two or more lengths.

* Choose a partner and use links to find who has the longer arm.
* Use links to find which is higher, the green chair or the blue chair.
* Choose a partner and use links to find who is taller.
* Use dominoes to find which doorway is wider.
* Use dominoes to find which is longer, the table or the bench.

A final set of task cards for length required students to select the unit appropriate to compare between two or more unequal lengths.

* Find the taller table.
* Find the tallest bookcase.
* Find the widest window.
* Which is taller, the table or the bookcase?

Mrs. Winkie left the first set of cards out for one week. This allowed time for the children to become acquainted with the format of challenges. She then placed the cards into a box and encouraged children who still needed practice to use the appropriate card from the box.

During the next several weeks Mrs. Winkie created challenges to measure area, capacity, and mass. She decided to continue using the format suggested by the EARLY CHILDHOOD INSTRUCTIONAL MEASUREMENT MODEL on page 254.

Some challenges to measure area included:

* Which circle is bigger?
* Which is bigger, an array of six squares or six rectangles?
* How many blocks will fit on the bench top?
* How big is the book cover?
* Use blocks to find which is bigger, the table top or the bench top.
* Which is bigger, the red rug or the green rug?

Challenges to measure capacity included:

* Which holds more meal, the box or the jar?
* Which hold more meal, 5 cans or 4 milk cartons?
* How many cans does the pitcher hold?
* Select a unit to find how much the pail holds.
* Use a can to find which holds more, the pitcher or the jar.
* Select a unit to find which holds more, the bowl or the carton.

Challenges to measure mass included:

Use the balance to find --

* Which is heavier, the block or the truck.
* Which is heavier, 9 links or 12 dominoes.

* How many dominoes does the ball weigh?
* Select a unit to find how much the pail weighs.
* Use a can to find which holds more, the pitcher or the jar.
* Select a unit and find which is heavier, the tape dispense or the block.

As Mrs. Winkie continued to write challenges, she became ever more aware that the individual challenges, as well as the sets of challenges, followed a sequential order which suggested a hierarchy from simple to complex. After the first two weeks Mrs. Winkie decided it would be wise to change the order in which task card sets were sequenced. She decided to teach **direct comparison** with area, capacity, and mass before introducing **non-standard units** in length. This variation of sequence seemed to work out quite well. Mrs. Winkie shared a comment with Miss Heine,

"Sequencing activities is a frustrating task. You never know how it will turn out until after you try it. Even now, I think some further revision might improve the sequence ... Maybe I should have the children do all equalities activities before I assign any inequality activities. I think I will go down the columns rather than across. I think my sequence for each column will be: length, area, capacity, mass."

Early in the year Mrs. Winkie decided to give each set of challenges a title and write a sentence describing its purpose. She was pleased to discover that she was doing what her professors had taught in college -- writing objectives. The objectives for the six sets of challenges related to measuring length read as follows:

1. *Children will directly compare two lengths and state which is longer, shorter, taller, thicker, thinner.*
2. *Children will count to directly compare two unequal lengths, using non-standard units.*
3. *Children will use a specified non-standard unit and count to measure a given length.*
4. *Children will select a unit appropriate to measure a given length.*
5. *Children will use a specified non-standard unit and count to compare between two or more unequal lengths.*
6. *Children will select an appropriate unit to compare between two or more unequal lengths.*

It soon became obvious that some form a management system would be necessary. Mrs. Winkie decided to create two record forms. One would be used by the children for day-to-day record keeping; the other would be a teacher kept class record.

As stated earlier, the response book, **My Measurement Book,** was used by the children as their record of the answers. Space for the first ten record book responses is shown on page 261. Mrs. Winkie found that after some guidance she was able to direct students to record their own responses.

Mrs. Winkie generally assumed that children who completed a **My Measurement Book** set of challenges correctly had mastered the objective. When she was uncertain, she would construct a **Review-Challenge** as an overall evaluation. One **Review-Challenge** used for the first set, Non-Number -- Direct Comparison was:

> Examine these three ribbons. Which one is longest? Which one is shortest?

The second form, **The Mathematics -- Class Record Form,** pages 262-263 was used to keep a record of class performance. Each of the sets of challenges was listed using objectives Mrs. Winkie had written. Mrs. Winkie observed that sometimes a child could not successfully perform the **Review-Challenge** even though the child had worked each of the learning center tasks related to the topic.   When this happened she followed one of several options:

* Work individually with the child,
* Direct the child to repeat certain challenges,
* Write new challenges for the child,
* Ask another student to act as tutor, or
* Solicit help from the parents.

Mrs. Winkie found there was no certain solution to this problem, Sometimes several strategies were necessary to help a child successfully master the objective.

It didn't take long before those students who were assigned to the regular textbook expressed a desire to use the interest center also. Mrs. Winkie arranged a schedule so they might also participate. Some children, after a while, lost interest, claiming the tasks were too easy. At this point Mrs. Winkie muttered,

Draw a (circle) around the correct answer

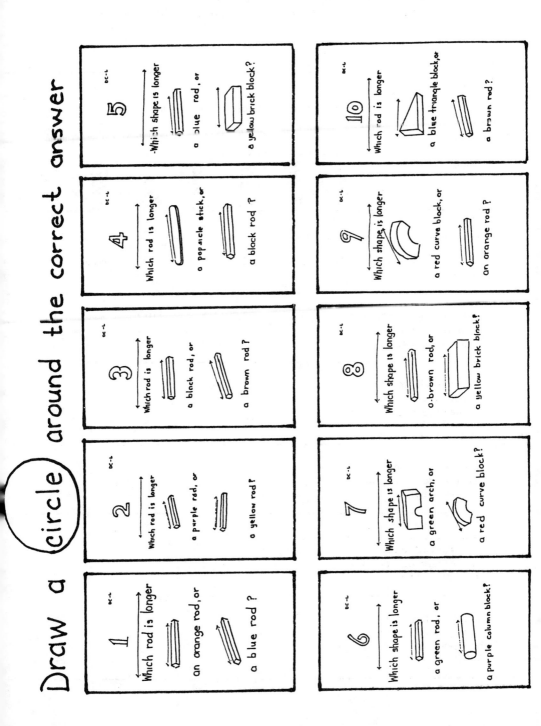

1
BC-1
Which rod is longer

an orange rod, or

a blue rod?

2
BC-1
Which rod is longer

a purple rod, or

a yellow rod?

3
BC-1
Which rod is longer

a black rod, or

a brown rod?

4
BC-1
Which rod is longer

a popsicle stick, or

a black rod?

5
BC-1
Which shape is longer

a blue rod, or

a yellow brick block?

6
BC-1
Which shape is longer

a green rod, or

a purple column block?

7
BC-1
Which shape is longer

a green arch, or

a red curve block?

8
BC-1
Which shape is longer

a brown rod, or

a yellow brick block?

9
BC-1
Which shape is longer

a red curve block, or

an orange rod?

10
BC-1
Which rod is longer

a blue triangle block, or

a brown rod?

"Is there no end? Must I write task cards for the brighter ones, too? Oh well, no one ever said teaching was going to be easy!"

Mathematics -- Class Record Form

Grade *one*   Date *September* 15

Student Name	Objective	Del	Helen	Arnold	Frida	Nora	Walter	June
A.	Direct comparison of length	9/20	9/20	9/21	9/19	9/20	9/19	9/21
B.	Counting nonstandard units to directly compare lengths	9/27	9/25	9/30	X 10/3	10/1	9/29	10/2
C.	Using specified non-standard units to measure a given length							
D.	Selecting the unit appropriate to measure a given length							
E.	Using specified non-standard units to compare between two+ unequal lengths							
F.	Selecting the unit appropriate to compare between two+ unto unequal lengths							

G.	Direct comparison of area	10/4	10/6	10/7	10/10	10/5	10/8	10/12
H.	Counting non-standard units to directly compare area	10/11	10/12		X	10/10		

.
.
.
.
.

U.	Using specified non-standard units to measure a given mass
V.	Selecting the unit appropriate to measure a given mass
W.	Using specified non-standard units to compare between two+ unequal masses
X.	Selecting the unit appropriate to compare between two+ unequal masses

Individualized Learning Modules

A unit construction design for individualizing instruction of students may employ auto-tutorial packages of learning materials called Learning Activity Packages (LAP) or Unipacs. Affective, as well as cognitive concerns are a primary motivation for encouraging use of these individualized learning models. Pat Jackson suggests five effective implications of the LAP. (Jackson:1-2)

1. Students are offered levels of learning so that every student can master the concepts or process being presented. SELF-ESTEEM is developed.

2. Students are offered the opportunity to become responsible for their own learning. SELF-DISCIPLINE is encouraged.

3. Students are offered the opportunity for interaction with their fellow students. INTERPERSONAL COMMUNICATION is enhanced.

4. Students are offered the opportunity to choose their own paths and pace for learning. DECISION- MAKING AND LIVING WITH THE CONSEQUENCES OF THOSE DECISIONS is afforded.

5. Students get immediate feedback and then choose what to do next. SELF-DIAGNOSIS is fostered.

Individualized learning modules provide a systematic plan to guide student learning. They direct students to work independent of immediate teacher direction. Many individualized learning modules include a variety of multi-media, multi-modal, and multi-level learning opportunities from which the learner selects.

Multi-media options allow selection from the printed page, visual materials, audio sources, and more. Multi-modal selection refers to variations in instructional settings. Options include individual study and small and large group arrangements. Pedagogical techniques vary from lecture, inquiry, question-answer, to intergroup discussion and one-to-one conferences. Consideration for intellectual level differences among students is resolved by providing variation in difficulty and sophistication of the learning task.

Most learning activity modules begin with a pre-test, offer a variety of learning opportunities, provide self-assessment instruments, and end with a post-test. Testing is necessary to assure that content is appropriate for students to study and is learned by students after study. The package is designed to be used by students with little or no coaching from the teacher. After the pre-test is corrected and prescriptions for study are determined, students follow directions and regulations provided in the LAP.

Volkmor, Langstaff, and Higgins suggest that a simple learning activity can be devised by following six steps (Volkmor, p.148).

1. Decide on and list the necessary skills and concepts to be learned on a given topic or subject (scope and sequence).
2. Write a rationale that explains why the student needs to learn the content.
3. Specify measurable student objectives based on the skills and concepts.
4. Develop a short pre-test with items related to each stated objective.
5. List at least three specific and different available activities, media, and/or materials through which the student can obtain the information necessary to meet each objective.
6. Translate all that has been written in steps two through five into language that the student can read and understand using pictures and drawings when appropriate.

Jackson suggests that a LAP will have section related to each of the following titles:

* Pre-test
* Rationale
* Measurable Objectives
* Required Activities
* Optional Activities
* Self-assessment
* Post-test

Each of the seven titles is discussed below as part of a LAP entitled, *Respiratory System*.

RESPIRATORY SYSTEM

Respiratory System, as part of a study of human anatomy, focuses interest on the human body and gas exchange. The student begins work on the unit by taking a pre-test. All testing is based on measurable student objectives. Three or four test items are usually written to assess each objective. If the student can successfully answer responses on the pre-test, there is probably no need to complete the LAP. Since specific test items relate directly to specific objectives, and these objectives in turn relate to specific required student activities, it follows that if certain test items are missed, certain objectives remain to be mastered, and their respective REQUIRED ACTIVITIES will become the approved study program.

Pretest

An example of one part of a pretest used by a high school teacher for the unit, Respiratory System, is shown below.

RESPIRATORY SYSTEM   PRETEST

...

* The vibrating structures within the larynx that are the voice box

  are known as the_____.

* The trachea divides into two large branches

  called_____,

  which in turn subdivide into smaller and smaller branches called

  _____.

* The lungs are enclosed within the thoracic cavity in the

  _____.

...

Rationale

A rationale should be written to and for students. Below is a LAP rationale for the unit, Respiratory System.
RATIONALE

You should have completed the LAP, Nutrition, which discussed what happens when food is taken into your body, before beginning this unit.

Respiratory System examines what happens when you breathe. You will learn the names and function of the parts of the respiratory system and what happens when air is taken into your body ... .

The LAP that follows Respiratory System will examine the circulatory system.

Measurable Objectives

Objectives are to be read by the students and therefore should be written in a language and style understandable by them. Objectives should clearly identify the specific learning students are expected to master. Each objective will be tested in both the pretest and posttest.

Each objective will have one or more student activities designed to teach the competency stated in that objective. Therefore, it is imperative that careful thought be given to a matching of objectives with student activities and test items. Below is an example of terminal objectives for the LAP, Respiratory System, written in a non-formal style.

WHAT YOU SHOULD KNOW WHEN YOU FINISH THIS LAP

You should be able to supply the correct name from the list below when it is defined, diagrammed, or its function described.

Part One: The Breathing System

capillaries   alveolus bronchi lungs   ...

Part Three: The Control of Breathing

phrenic medulla oblongata CO_2...

Part Four: General Pattern

...

Required Activities

The measurable objectives direct selection of learning activities for students. Consideration should be given to multi-media, multi-modal, and multi-level options. Each objective must have a required learning experience which teaches toward its mastery. Below is an example of a required activity designed to teach toward mastery of objectives for PART ONE: THE BREATHING SYSTEM.

PART ONE: THE BREATHING SYSTEM

Overview:

Several organs form the air channels of the breathing apparatus: nose and nasal passages, pharynx, larynx, trachea, and lungs. Air passing through the narrow spaces of the nose area is warmed and moistened ... .

The trachea divides into two bronchi, each of which subdivides ... . The alveoli are held together by connective tissue that carry nerves and a dense network of blood capillaries. ...

To Get Information:

Read from one of the following books --

a. How the Body Works, pages 26-27
b. Your Health, pages 69-72
c. Basic Physiology, pages 178-183

View one of these filmstrips --

a. What Happens When You Breath?
b. Your Lungs

View the video --

a. How the Respiratory System Works

Assignment:

Write a short report in which you describe how air passes into and out of the lungs. Describe what happens to the air in the lungs. Be sure to use the following words in your report: nose, nasal passage, trachea, pharynx, lungs, bronchi, alveolus, alveoli, bronchiole, ciliated cells, larynx, capillaries, diaphragm, oxygen, carbon dioxide.

Sharing:

Share your report with one or more students. Discuss and clarify any areas of uncertainty. Place the report in your LAP notebook.

Self-test:

Complete the self assessment included in the package.

Diagnosis:

How are you doing: Meet with your teacher if you need assistance.

Optional Activities

Some LAP plans include in-depth opportunities or remedial exercises as student electives or as prerequisites to REQUIRED ACTIVITIES. In-depth investigations or quests provide horizontal enrichment. Suggestions might include additional readings, audio-visual material examination, experiments, and more. Quest options should not be limited to advanced students. When advantageous, a student may be given the option to contract with the teacher for an opportunity to investigate an area of interest to the student that is not included as part of the LAP.

Students who possess deficiencies in content or skills that are prerequisite to successful entry into the next area of study will be directed to remedial activities. For instance, a particular investigation might require measurement using metric units. If there is reason to believe that some students might not understand metric units, a pre-test which measures understanding of metric units would be taken before beginning the REQUIRED ACTIVITY. Students found deficient would be directed to a skill exercise on metric measure. Following the remedial study students would repeat the test to assure mastery of that skill before beginning the REQUIRED ACTIVITY.

Self-Assessment

One or more self-assessments may be interspersed throughout the LAP. Usually these self-tests are taken after completion of a sub-topic. For instance, a self-test would be appropriate after completion of PART ONE: THE BREATHING SYSTEM. These self-assessments provide the student with an opportunity to examine areas of deficiency and strength before moving on to the next section. Following each self-test the student should be encouraged to diagnose personal strengths and weaknesses and self-prescribe remedial work; or consult with the teacher for direction to improve deficient areas.

Posttest

The final LAP task is taking the posttest. It is given at the completion of the unit to assure mastery of each objective. This test may be the same as the pretest. However, if there is reason to believe the student may remember pretest items, a second form of the pretest should be written and used as the posttest. The pretest and posttest should be kept by the teacher and administered under staff supervision. The tests, together with written copy and oral feedback by the student, provide the major input for student evaluation.

An Individualized Learning Module -- Mathematics

Individual learning modules are mini-units designed to provide students with learning activities appropriate to their specific competency level. The unit **Math Fun - Learning About Shapes and Sizes** is shown in its entirety to provide one complete example of what a creative teacher can construct.

Math

Fun

Learning About

Shapes and Sizes

HAVING FUN WHILE LEARNING MATHEMATICS

As you complete the activities in this booklet you will learn:

+ the names used when describing shape

polygon	quadrilateral
triangle	parallelogram
right	square
obtuse	rectangle
acute	trapezoid

length	base	perimeter
width	altitude	area
height	diagonal	

+ how to measure distance around the outside of shapes (perimeter)

+ how to measure space inside shapes (area)

+ how to make rules for finding the space inside (area of shapes)

Each of the names you will learn are spelled phonetically (fO net i kul li) in the *challenges*. When the vowel is capitalized (A E I O U) it receives the long sound (bAse, Eat, Idea, cOat, Unit). The underlined syllables receive the accent (um brel a).

Learning about shapes and sizes can be fun as well as challenging when drawing on a dotted paper or when stretching rubber bands around pegs on a geoboard.

Dotted Paper

Geometrically dotted paper is paper on which dots are placed in a pattern. The most common pattern is called a checker board pattern.

You draw designs on the paper by connecting the dots with lines.

This drawing is a
square (skwair).

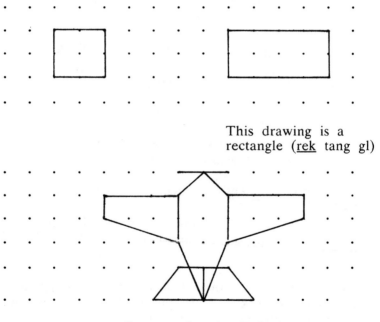

This drawing is a
rectangle (<u>rek</u> tang gl)

I can make an airplane.

The Geoboard

Ask your teacher to give you a geoboard,

or

You can build a geoboard. You will need a wooden board and some small nails. Set the nails in a checkerboard pattern so each nail is the same distance from its neighbor both vertically and horizontally. Your geoboard will look like the drawing below.

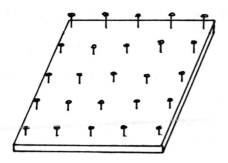

Shapes are made by stretching rubber bands around the nails.

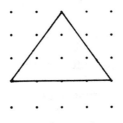

The rubber band makes a triangle (<u>tr</u>I an gl).

Experimenting with Shapes

1. Make any shape.

2. Make a shape that looks like a house.

3. Make a shape that looks like a table.

4. Make a shape that has four sides; three sides; five sides.

5. Make a shape that is twice as long as it is wide.

6. Make a shape that looks like an 'L'; 'U'; 'X'; 'O'.

7. Make as many letters of the alphabet as you can.

8. Make two shapes so one shape is two times as long as the other.

9. Make two shapes so one shape has twice as much space inside as the other.

10. Make two shapes so one is two times as far around the outside as the other.

11. Make two shapes so one shape will fit inside the other.

12. Make a six pointed star.

13. Make an eight sided shape.

14. Make a shape that looks like steps.

15. Show 1/2; 1/3; 1/4; 1/5; 1/6; 1/8.

Shapes Have Names

Challenge #1

Make a shape with several sides.
How many sides does it have?

_____

Any shape with straight line sides is called a **polygon**
(pol i gon).

```
.   .   .   .   .

.   .   .   .   .

.   .   .   .   .

.   .   .   .   .

.   .   .   .   .
```

Challenge #2

Make a shape that has three sides. Any shape with three
straight sides is called a **triangle** (trī ang l). **Tri** means three.
Each corner forms an **angle**; so **tri angle** means three angles
or three corners.

```
.   .   .   .   .

.   .   .   .   .

.   .   .   .   .

.   .   .   .   .

.   .   .   .   .
```

Challenge #3

Make a triangle with square corners.

This shape is called a **right** triangle.

```
.   .   .   .   .

.   .   .   .   .

.   .   .   .   .

.   .   .   .   .

.   .   .   .   .
```

Challenge #4

Make a triangle with one corner greater than a square corner. The corner should look like this \＿＿. This triangle is called an **obtuse** (ob t<u>Us</u>) triangle.

```
      .    .    .    .    .

      .    .    .    .    .

      .    .    .    .    .

      .    .    .    .    .

      .    .    .    .    .
```

Challenge #5

Make a triangle in which all corners are less than a square corner. This is an **acute** (a c<u>Ut</u>) triangle.

All corners will look like this ＜ ／＼ ＞.

```
      .    .    .    .    .

      .    .    .    .    .

      .    .    .    .    .

      .    .    .    .    .

      .    .    .    .    .
```

Challenge #6

Make a right triangle. Make an obtuse triangle. Make an acute triangle.

```
   .    .    .    .    .       .    .    .    .    .       .    .    .    .    .

   .    .    .    .    .       .    .    .    .    .       .    .    .    .    .

   .    .    .    .    .       .    .    .    .    .       .    .    .    .    .

   .    .    .    .    .       .    .    .    .    .       .    .    .    .    .

   .    .    .    .    .       .    .    .    .    .       .    .    .    .    .
```

Challenge #7

Make a shape that has four sides. Any shape with four straight sides is called a **quadrilateral** (kwad ri lat er 'al). **Quad** means four. **Lateral** means side; so **quadrilateral** means four sides. **Parallel** (pair a lel) lines are lines which are always the same distance apart. Railroad tracks form parallel lines. Lines on writing paper are parallel.

These lines are parallel

These lines are not parallel

Challenge #8

Make a quadrilateral in which the **opposite** sides are parallel. This shape is called a **parallelogram** (pair a lel O gram).

Some parallelograms have **square** corners

Other parallelograms have **obtuse** \⎽ and **acute** < corners.

Challenge #9

Make a parallelogram with both obtuse and acute corners. The common name for this shape is parallelogram.

Challenge #10

Make a parallelogram with square corners in which all sides are the same length. This shape is called a **square**.

```
    .   .   .   .   .
    .   .   .   .   .
    .   .   .   .   .
    .   .   .   .   .
    .   .   .   .   .
```

Challenge #11

Make a square cornered parallelogram that is longer than it is wide. This shape is called a **rectangle** (<u>rek</u> tang l).

```
    .   .   .   .   .
    .   .   .   .   .
    .   .   .   .   .
    .   .   .   .   .
    .   .   .   .   .
```

Challenge #12

Make a quadrilateral in which two sides are parallel and the other two sides are not parallel. This shape is called a **trapezoid** (<u>trap</u> u zoyd). A **slanted** side on a trapezoid is said to be **diagonal** (dI <u>ag</u> u nl).

Line B is diagonal to lines A and C.

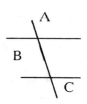

```
    .   .   .   .   .
    .   .   .   .   .
    .   .   .   .   .
    .   .   .   .   .
    .   .   .   .   .
```

Measuring Distance. Around the Outside

Let's find a way to describe how long a line is that goes around the outside of a polygon. Examine a square and two line segments below. We'll call the length of that part of the line that goes from one dot to the nearest dot either **horizontally** —— or **vertically** | one unit long. The distance around the square is **4 units.**

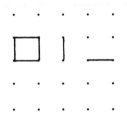

Challenge #13

Construct a square that is 2 units long on each side.

What is the perimeter of the square? _____

Challenge #14

Change the square from Challenge 13 into a rectangle by making the shape twice as long as it is wide.

What is the perimeter of the rectangle? ___

Challenge #15

Construct a shape that looks like the letter 'L' and find the perimeter.

What is the perimeter? _____

```
.   .   .   .   .

.   .   .   .   .

.   .   .   .   .

.   .   .   .   .

.   .   .   .   .
```

Challenge #16

Construct a shape that looks like the letter 'U' and find the perimeter.

What is the perimeter? _____

```
.   .   .   .   .

.   .   .   .   .

.   .   .   .   .

.   .   .   .   .

.   .   .   .   .
```

Challenge #17

Construct a shape that looks like steps and find the perimeter.

What is the perimeter? _____

```
.   .   .   .   .

.   .   .   .   .

.   .   .   .   .

.   .   .   .   .

.   .   .   .   .
```

If a shape has a diagonal side, its perimeter is harder to measure. This trapezoid has a perimeter that is greater than 9 but less than 10.

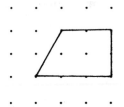

Challenge #18

Construct polygons that have at least one diagonal side. Describe the perimeter of each polygon. The first two are drawn for you.

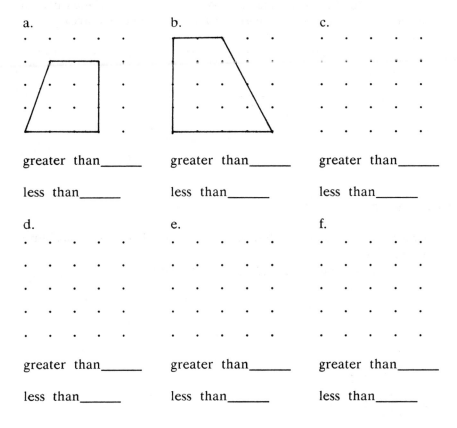

a.

greater than_____

less than_____

b.

greater than_____

less than_____

c.

greater than_____

less than_____

d.

greater than_____

less than_____

e.

greater than_____

less than_____

f.

greater than_____

less than_____

Challenge #19

Construct a square one unit long on each side. The space inside this square is **one square unit**.

. . . . .

. . . . .

. . . . .

. . . . .

. . . . .

Challenge #20

Construct a rectangle two units long and one unit wide. The space inside this rectangle is two square units. A measure of space or the size of a given surface is called its **area** (air E a).

The rectangle has an area of _____ square units.

. . . . .

. . . . .

. . . . .

. . . . .

. . . . .

Challenge #21

Construct a rectangle that is three units long and one unit wide. Find the area.

The area is _____ squares large.

. . . . .

. . . . .

. . . . .

. . . . .

. . . . .

Challenge #22

Construct the polygons described below and find the area of each.

Two by two square   An 'L' shape   A 'U' shape

a.   b.   c.

. . . .

. . . .

. . . .

. . . .

. . . .

Area =_____ squares_____ squares   _____ squares

An 'O' shape   An 'F' shape   A cross shape

d.   e.   f.

. . . .

. . . .

. . . .

. . . .

. . . .

Area =_____ squares_____ squares   _____ squares

If shape 'a' has an area of one square unit, then shape 'b' has an area of one-half square unit.

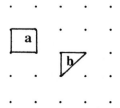

If shape 'c' has an area of two square units, then shape 'd' has an area of one square unit.

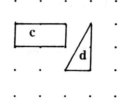

Challenge #23

If the area of rectangle 'a' is three square units, what is the area of triangle 'b'.

Area = _____ squares.

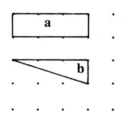

Challenge #24

If the area of rectangle 'c' is four square units, what is the area of triangle 'd'?

Area = _____ squares.

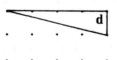

Challenge #25

If the area of square 'e' is four square units, what is the
area of triangle 'f'?

Area = _____ squares.

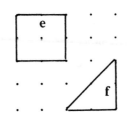

Challenge #26

If the area of rectangle 'g' is six square units, what is the area
of triangle 'h'?

Area = _____ squares.

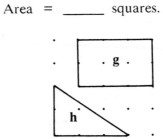

Challenge #27

Find the area of these shapes.

a.   b.   c.

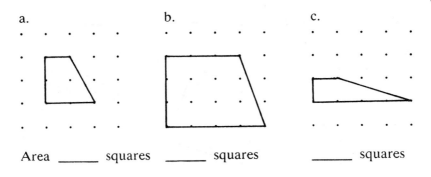

Area _____ squares   _____ squares   _____ squares

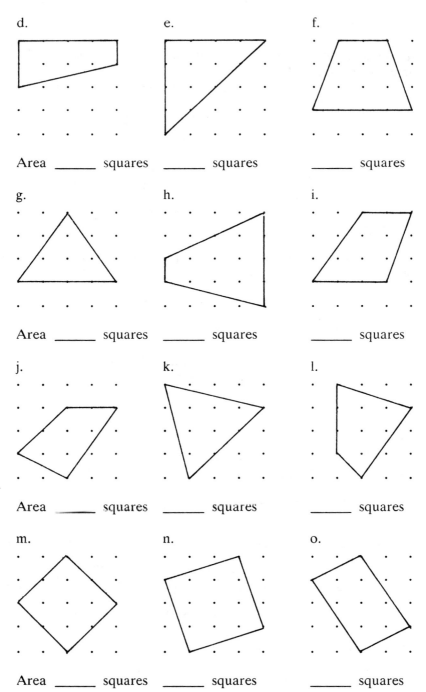

d.

Area _____ squares

e.

_____ squares

f.

_____ squares

g.

Area _____ squares

h.

_____ squares

i.

_____ squares

j.

Area _____ squares

k.

_____ squares

l.

_____ squares

m.

Area _____ squares

n.

_____ squares

o.

_____ squares

Challenge #28

Construct your own shapes and find the areas.

a.   b.   c.

. . . .

. . . .

. . . .

. . . .

. . . .

Area _____ squares   _____ squares   _____ squares

d.   e.   f.

. . . .

. . . .

. . . .

. . . .

. . . .

Area _____ squares   _____ squares   _____ squares

Making Rules

Rectangles

Challenge #29

Construct a rectangle that is 3 units long and 2 units wide. Find its area.

Area = _____ squares. 3X2 = _____.

. . . . .

. . . . .

. . . . .

. . . . .

. . . . .

Challenge #30

Construct a rectangle that is 4 units long and 3 units wide. Find its area.

Area = _____ squares. 4X3 = _____.

```
.   .   .   .   .

.   .   .   .   .

.   .   .   .   .

.   .   .   .   .

.   .   .   .   .
```

Challenge #31

Construct a rectangle that is 5 units long and 2 units wide. Find its area.

Area = _____ squares. 5X2 = _____.

```
.   .   .   .   .

.   .   .   .   .

.   .   .   .   .

.   .   .   .   .

.   .   .   .   .
```

Challenge #32

Write a rule that tells how to find the area of a rectangle when you know its length and width.

_____

_____

Parallelograms

When talking about quadrilaterals and triangles, the words **length** and **width** are often replaced with **base** and the words **height** with **altitude**. The **"bottom"** of a quadrilateral or triangle is called the **base** and the **height** is called the **altitude**. Base and altitude are always used when describing the dimensions of parallelograms that have **no** square corners.

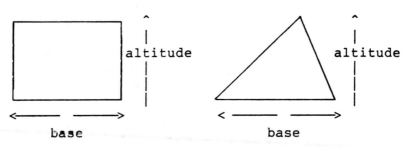

altitude

altitude

base

base

Challenge #33

Construct a parallelogram with **no** square corners that has a base of 3 and an altitude of 2.

```
.   .   .   .   .

.   .   .   .   .

.   .   .   .   .

.   .   .   .   .

.   .   .   .   .
```

You can change a parallelogram into a rectangle by "**subtracting**" a triangle from one end and "**adding**" it to the other end of the parallelogram to make a rectangle.

Make a boundary around this triangle to show it has been "**subtracted**".  Make a boundary around this triangle to show it has been "**added**".

What is the base of the rectangle? _____

What is the altitude of the rectangle? _____

What is the area of the rectangle? _____.

What is the area of the parallelogram? _____

Challenge #34

Construct a parallelogram with **no** square corners that has a base of 3 and an altitude of 3. Find the area.

Area = _____ squares.

```
.   .   .   .   .

.   .   .   .   .

.   .   .   .   .

.   .   .   .   .

.   .   .   .   .
```

Challenge #35

Construct a parallelogram with **no** square corners that has a base of 4 and an altitude of 4. Find the area.

Area = _____ squares.

```
.   .   .   .   .

.   .   .   .   .

.   .   .   .   .

.   .   .   .   .

.   .   .   .   .
```

Challenge #36

Write a rule that tells how to find the area of a parallelogram with **no** square corners when you know its base and altitude.

_____

_____

Triangles

The **"bottom"** side of a triangle is called the **base**. The distance from the base to the **"top"** of the triangle is called the **altitude**.

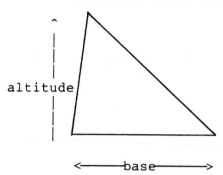

altitude

<———base———>

Challenge #36

Construct three triangles, each with a base of 3 and an altitude of 2.

right triangle   obtuse triangle   acute triangle

. . . .

. . . .

. . . .

. . . .

. . . .

Area _____ squares _____ squares   _____ squares

Challenge #37

Construct three triangles, each with a base of 2 and an altitude of 4.

right triangle   obtuse triangle   acute triangle

. . . .

. . . .

. . . .

. . . .

. . . .

Area _____ squares _____ squares   _____ squares

Challenge #38

Construct three triangles, each with a base of 3 and an altitude of 4.

right triangle   obtuse triangle   acute triangle

. . . .

. . . .

. . . .

. . . .

. . . .

Area _____ squares   _____ squares   _____ squares

Challenge #39

Write a rule that tells you how to find the area of a triangle when you know the base and the altitude _____

_____

Trapezoid

Challenge #40

Construct a trapezoid with a base of 3 and an altitude of 2. Find the area.

Area = _____ squares.

. . . . .

. . . . .

. . . . .

. . . . .

. . . . .

Challenge #41

Construct a trapezoid with a base of 4 and an altitude of 2. Find the area.

Area = _____ squares.

Trapazoids are said to have two bases. They are usually shown as b and b'.

b'

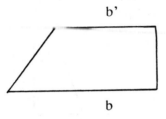

b

Challenge #42

Construct a trapezoid whose dimensions are: b = 2, b' = 1, a = 3. Now let's try to make a rule for finding the area of a trapezoid when we know b. b', and a (altitude).

One way to find the area of a trapezoid is to make **two** trapezoids side-by-side with one trapezoid up-side-down.

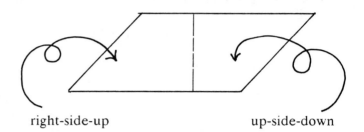

right-side-up   up-side-down

Find the area of the parallelogram. The area of each trapezoid is one-half as much.

Below is a copy of the trapezoid whose dimensions are b = 2, b' = 1, a = 3 (see challenge #42). Construct, next to the trapezoid, an up-side-down copy of this trapezoid. Its dimensions will be b = 1, b' = 2 a = 3.

The two trapezoids form a parallelogram.

The area of the parallelogram is _____ squares.
The area of each trapezoid is 1/2 the area of the parallelogram.

The area of each trapezoid is _____ squares.

Challenge #43

Construct a trapezoid whose dimensions are b = 2, b' = 1, a = 4. Construct a second trapezoid whose dimensions are b = 1, b' = 2 a = 4, so a parallelogram is formed whose dimensions are b = 3, b' = 3, a = 4. Find the area of the parallelogram. Find the area of each trapezoid.

Area of the parallelogram is _____ squares.

Area of the trapezoid is _____ squares.

```
.   .   .   .   .

.   .   .   .   .

.   .   .   .   .

.   .   .   .   .

.   .   .   .   .
```

Challenge #44

Can you make a rule to find the area of a trapezoid when you know b, b', and a? Think: (b + b') times a is the area of two trapezoids. To find the area of just one trapezoid I ... . Write a rule to find the area of a trapezoid when you know b, b', and a.

_____

_____

Challenge #45

Use the rules you wrote to find the areas of the polygons described below.

Parallelogram   **Triangle**   **Trapezoid**

a. b = 4, a = 3   d. b = 2, a = 4   g. b = 4, b' = 3, a = 5

b. b = 7, a = 4   e. b = 6, a = 3   h. b = 6, b' = 2, a = 5

c. b = 5, a = 3   f. b = 9, a = 5   i. b = 4.5, b' = 3.5, a = 7

Answers

a. _____ squares   d. _____ squares   g. _____ squares

b. _____ squares   e. _____ squares   h. _____ squares

c. _____ squares   f. _____ squares   i. _____ squares

Now you know the names of three and four sided polygons
and how to find their perimeter and area.
You are a smarty!

Bibliography

Jackson, P. (1971). <u>The writer's lap</u>. Educational Associates, Inc.

Johnson, H. & others (1978). <u>The learning center idea book</u>. Boston: Allyn and Bacon.

Volkmor, C. B., Langstaff, A. L. & Higgins, M. (1974). <u>Structuring the classroom for success</u>. Columbus, OH: Charles E. Merrill Company.

Index